My definition o
simple: if you
someo
Paul Polman, CEO, Unilever

THE TOP 50
SUSTAINABILITY BOOKS

Acknowledgements

Written by **Wayne Visser**

Research and editorial assistance by **Oliver Dudok van Heel**, Living Values

Interviews conducted by **Wayne Visser**, with organisational assistance from **Denise Hargreaves**, Cambridge Programme for Sustainability Leadership

Editorial review by **Peter Raynard**

Additional research by Helen Leech and Emma Cleave

Book design by laliabril.com

Published by Greenleaf Publishing Limited
Aizlewood's Mill
Nursery Street
Sheffield S3 8GG
UK
www.greenleaf-publishing.com

Printed and bound in the UK by Cambrian Printers Limited, Aberystwyth
Printed on Novatech Silk Matt FSC-accredited paper from well-managed forests and other controlled sources

Mixed Sources
Product group from well-managed forests and other controlled sources
www.fsc.org Cert no. TT-COC-2200
© 1996 Forest Stewardship Council

FSC

British Library Cataloguing in Publication Data:
  Visser, Wayne.
    The top 50 sustainability books.
    1. Sustainability--Bibliography. 2. Sustainable development--Bibliography.
    I. Title II. University of Cambridge. Programme for Sustainability Leadership.
    016.3'38927-dc22

ISBN-13: 9781906093327

THE TOP 50
SUSTAINABILITY BOOKS

Greenleaf
PUBLISHING

UNIVERSITY OF
CAMBRIDGE
—— PROGRAMME FOR ——
SUSTAINABILITY LEADERSHIP

Contents

Introduction

In 2008, the Cambridge Programme for Sustainability Leadership (CPSL) embarked on an ambitious project: to identify the most influential books on sustainability, to interview as many of the authors as possible and to distil their insights into an accessible digest. We knew from our work with senior executives how important the ideas of great writers had been to many of them, and how new sources of data and ways of framing the world had informed the language and practice of sustainability to the present day. This book, which follows the publication of *Landmarks for Sustainability* earlier this year,* is the result – a collection of some the world's best analyses of the global social, environmental and ethical challenges we face and the creative solutions needed to tackle them.

The Cambridge Top 50 Sustainability Books is based on a poll among senior leaders represented by CPSL's alumni of more than 3,000 people. No list could capture every dimension of sustainability thought-leadership, and many readers, of course, will miss a favourite publication that has not been included. Yet, taken together, these books reflect the evolution of the sustainability agenda over the past 50 years. We see, for example, the shift from the conservation ethic of *A Sand County Almanac* and early warning cries like *Silent Spring* and *The Limits to Growth*, to the emergence of sustainable development (*Our Common Future* and *Changing Course*) and the triple bottom line (*Cannibals with Forks*).

We see a movement from technological fixes, such as those described in *Factor Four*, to more integrated nature-inspired solutions such as *Cradle to Cradle* and *Biomimicry*. We can also notice how social activism has changed, from sector- and issue-based campaigns in the 1960s, like *Unsafe At Any Speed*, to more recent, fundamental critiques like *No Logo*, *When Corporations Rule the World* and *The Corporation*. We are also reminded that business can be a powerful force for good, in books like *Business as Unusual*, *Maverick*, *The Ecology of Commerce*, *The Fortune at the Bottom of the Pyramid* and *The Civil Corporation*.

Among the themes reflected in the Top 50 are the voice given to marginalised groups, such as women (*Staying Alive*), the poor (*Banker to the Poor*, *Human Scale Development*, *Development as Freedom* and *The End of Poverty*) and critics of sustainability movement itself (*The Skeptical Environmentalist*). Economics emerges as a common cause for concern, and we see it changing from philosophical questioning (*Small Is Beautiful*) through policy proposals (*Blueprint for a Green Economy* and *For the Common Good*) to an international reform agenda (*Globalization and its Discontents*).

---

* *Landmarks for Sustainability: Events and Initiatives That Have Changed Our World* (Wayne Visser on behalf of the University of Cambridge Programme for Sustainability Leadership; Greenleaf Publishing, 2009; www.greenleaf-publishing.com/landmarks).

This reform movement grew strong as, far from the triumph of capitalism, writers warned of a *False Dawn*, *Capitalism at the Crossroads* and *A Crisis in Global Capitalism*. We are asked 'why capitalism succeeds in the West and fails everywhere else?' (*The Mystery of Capital*) and provided with alternative visions like *Natural Capitalism* and *Capitalism as if the World Matters*.

We also see the focus on specific issues rising and falling, from an early focus on population (*The Population Bomb*) and Third World debt (*A Fate Worse Than Debt*), to rising crises like water (*When the Rivers Run Dry*) and climate (*Heat*, *An Inconvenient Truth* and *The Economics of Climate Change*). Other books reflect geopolitical shifts and their implications, such the environmental implications of the rise of China (*When Rivers Run Black*) and the challenges of Western lifestyle changes (as with *Fast Food Nation*).

Through it all, we can definitely notice a deepening in the understanding of societal, organisational and personal change, as the science of complex systems develops and is explored in *The Turning Point*, *The Chaos Point* and *Presence*. Finally, there are some books that remind us of the big picture and why we are concerned about sustainability in the first place, like *Spaceship Earth*, *Collapse*, *Gaia*, *The Dream of Earth* and *The Hungry Spirit*.

It has been an immense privilege for CPSL to interview, and in many cases to work with, so many of these thought-leaders who have helped to shape the sustainability agenda over the years. Indeed, the range and evolution of ideas captured by these 50 books reflects much of CPSL's own evolution as a provider of sustainability learning programmes and convenor of leadership groups over the past 20 years.

The Top 50 Sustainability Books shows what a rich intellectual heritage we have. It is now up to us to take responsibility for creating the low-carbon, sustainable society that so many of these great thinkers have been calling for. We trust that *The Top 50 Sustainability Books* will inform and inspire senior leaders and others to make the urgent changes needed in the next few decades to make their efforts, and those of so many others over the past 50 years, worthwhile.

Polly Courtice, *Director, University of Cambridge Programme for Sustainability Leadership*

1
A Sand County Almanac
Aldo Leopold

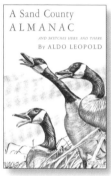

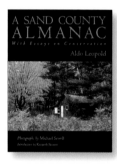

Current edn
A Sand County Almanac:
With Essays on Conservation
Oxford University Press,
2001; 194pp hbk;
978-0195146172

1st edn
A Sand County Almanac:
And Sketches Here and There
Oxford University Press,
1949; 240pp, hbk
(pbk edn, 1968;
978-0195007770)

Key ideas

▶ Land is a community of living things. This calls for the study of ecology.

▶ Land is to be loved and respected. This calls for a land or conservation ethic.

▶ Land yields a 'harvest of culture'. This calls for the integration of community and ecology.

▶ Ecosystems can be seen as a 'land pyramid' of interdependence between species.

▶ Our impact on nature is a form of violence, fuelled by a conquest ethic.

Synopsis

Written from an experiential perspective, with a style that is often poetic, the main message of *A Sand County Almanac* is that the land is not there to serve us, but that we need to live in community with the land. Community without land is empty, so by threatening the land we are threatening community. The land, the people and the other species are all part of a circular system, which humans have disconnected from since industrialisation. If we fail to reconnect with nature, nature will suffer and humanity will suffer.

Leopold's philosophy of respect for nature is called the 'land ethic', which includes the following fundamental tenets:

1. Land is a system of interdependent parts, best regarded as a community, not a commodity;

2. Humanity is a member, not the master, of the land community;

3. We can understand and appreciate our place in nature only by understanding nature as a whole; and

4. Our duty is to preserve the integrity, stability and beauty of the biotic community.

'A land ethic,' he says, 'reflects the existence of an ecological conscience, and this in turn reflects a conviction of individual responsibility for the health of the land. Health is the capacity of the land for self-renewal. Conservation is our effort to understand and preserve this capacity.' Importantly, he extends the concept of community to include soils, waters, plants and animals, or – collectively – the land.

Taking this further, Leopold introduces the concept of the 'Land Pyramid': 'The bottom layer is the soil. A plant layer rests on the soil, an insect layer on the plants, a bird and rodent layer on the insects, and so on up through various animal groups to the apex layer, which consists of the larger carnivores . . . Each successive layer depends on those below it for food and often for other services, and each in turn furnishes food and services to those above.'

He also assesses the impact human society has had on ecosystems, and notices that some biota are more resistant to change than others and that these differences are mainly due to the degree of violence in the changes imposed by humans. 'The less violent the man-made changes, the greater the probability of successful readjustment in the pyramid. Violence, in turn, varies with human population density; a dense population requires more violent conversion.' His solution to this violence is to adopt a land ethic which 'changes the role of homo sapiens from conqueror of the land-community to plain member and citizen of it. It implies respect for his fellow-members, and also respect for the community as such.'

Finally, Leopold expresses deep concern that our educational system is moving us away from an intense consciousness of the land, and that this is the most serious obstacle impeding the evolution of a land ethic. He argues for the supremacy of experience over learning, posing the provocative question: Is education possibly a process of trading awareness for things of lesser worth?

From the book

- Our bigger-and-better society is now like a hypochondriac, so obsessed with its own economic health as to have lost the capacity to remain healthy.

- We abuse land because we regard it as a commodity belonging to us. When we see land as a community to which we belong, we may begin to use it with love and respect.

- Acts of creation are ordinarily reserved for gods and poets, but humbler folk may circumvent this restriction if they know how. To plant a pine, for example, one need be neither god nor poet; one need only own a good shovel.

- A thing is right only when it tends to preserve the integrity, stability and beauty of the community; and the community includes the soil, water, fauna and flora, as well as the people.

- The opportunity to see geese is more important than television, and the chance to find a pasque-flower is a right as inalienable as free speech.

About the author

Considered by many as the father of wildlife management and of the US wilderness system, **Aldo Leopold** (1887–1948) was a conservationist, forester, philosopher, educator, writer and outdoor enthusiast.

Born and raised in Burlington, Iowa, Leopold developed an interest in the natural world at an early age, spending hours observing, journalling and sketching his surroundings. Graduating from the Yale Forest School in 1909, he eagerly pursued a career with the newly established US Forest Service in Arizona and New Mexico.

In 1922, he was instrumental in developing the proposal to manage the Gila National Forest as a wilderness area, which became the first such official designation in 1924. Following a transfer to Madison, Wisconsin, in 1924, Leopold continued his investigations into ecology and the philosophy of conservation, and in 1933 published the first textbook in the field of wildlife management. Later that year he accepted a new Chair in Game Management – a first for the University of Wisconsin and the nation.

A prolific writer, authoring articles for professional journals and popular magazines, Leopold wrote A Sand County Almanac as a book geared for general audiences examining humanity's relationship to the natural world. With over two million copies sold, it is one of the most respected books about the environment ever published. Although he never lived to see it in print, dying of a heart attack in 1948, Leopold has come to be regarded by many as the most influential conservation thinker of the 20th century.

OTHER BOOKS

Game Management (Charles Scribner's Sons, 1961)

Round River: From the Journals of Aldo Leopold (edited by Luna B. Leopold; Northwood Press, 1991)

The River of the Mother of God: And Other Essays by Aldo Leopold (edited by J. Baird Callicott and Susan L. Flader; University of Wisconsin Press, 1992)

For the Health of the Land: Previously Unpublished Essays and Other Writings (edited by J. Baird Callicott and Eric T. Freyfogle; Island Press, 2001)

MORE INFORMATION

The Aldo Leopold Foundation: www.aldoleopold.org

2
Silent Spring
Rachel Carson

1st edn
Silent Spring
Houghton Mifflin, 1962;
368pp, hbk;
978-0395075067

© Houghton Mifflin Co.

Current UK edn
Silent Spring
Penguin Classics, 2000;
336pp, pbk;
978-0141184944

© Houghton Mifflin Co.

Current US edn
Silent Spring:
40th Anniversary Edition
Mariner Books,
Houghton Mifflin Co.,
2002; 400pp, pbk;
978-0618249060

Key ideas

▶ Human beings are not in control of nature, but simply one of its parts. The survival of one part depends on the health of all in the web of life.

▶ Industrialisation in general, and the chemicals sector in particular, is having a serious and increasingly negative impact on the environment.

▶ Pesticides and herbicides do not just do harm to the environment, they also harm the human body, which is permeable and constantly exposed to toxins.

▶ Citizens should not blindly trust corporations or governments to operate in their best interests, but rather challenge both if they seem misguided.

▶ We should exercise caution and not assume that substances are benign just because they are legal, profitable or promoted as scientific progress.

Synopsis

With its mixture of deep scientific analysis and beautifully crafted prose, *Silent Spring* is a compelling warning to society of the toxic effects of chemicals in the environment and the consequent impacts on human health.

Carson is most concerned about synthetic pesticides, which employ one of the indispensable building blocks of life, namely carbon. Hence, they can be accommodated within living organisms and travel easily from, say, food crop to body or mother to offspring. For example, in Clear Lake, California, residues of the pesticide DDT accumulated initially in the plankton, then in the fish that ate the plankton, then in the water birds that ate the fish, at each stage increasing in concentration. Dead birds were eventually found with up to 1,600 parts per million (ppm) of DDD (a form of DDT), compared to the recommended safe concentration of 0.05 ppm.

Throughout the book, Carson builds her case against persistent chemicals, arguing that not only do they kill the 'good' insects as well as 'bad', but the 'pests' often adapt and mutate, becoming resistant superpests. Furthermore, the chemicals result in decimation of higher animal populations, either as a result of direct contact or ingestion of a chemical, or through induced infertility and disruption of breeding patterns.

Most controversially, Carson devotes a whole chapter to the carcinogenic characteristics of certain chemicals, sparking an acrimonious debate within the scientific and environmental communities which still rages today. She is quick to point out that dangerous chemicals are not only in use through the crop-spraying activities of the agro-industry, but also in everyday household gardening products, such as Chlordane. She is also at pains to stress that she is not against the use of pesticides and chemicals per se; rather she is against its use by people or institutions ignorant or uncaring of the consequences.

Having said that, Carson states a clear preference for the use of natural controls, such as:

- The introduction of predators in an area to mitigate the pests' or weeds' growth;

- The reduction of insect populations through the introduction of sterilised insect populations;

- The use of naturally occurring attractants (scents and sounds) to trap insect populations; and

- The use of ultrasound to kill unwanted insect populations.

Many of these practices have subsequently been adapted and adopted by the organic farming movement.

Carson was not unaware of the political implications of her claims. She comes out strongly as an advocate for greater transparency and accountability of government institutions. Quoting French biologist and moralist Jean Rostand, she says: 'The obligation to endure gives us the right to know.' She also expands her caution to include nuclear technology, bookending *Silent Spring* with the atomic tests in the Bikini Islands and the Cuban missile crisis.

Silent Spring is extremely well researched, with over 40 pages of references, including a breadth of examples that is both staggering and frightening. It rightly deserves its reputation as being the book that kick-started the modern environmental movement.

From the book

- It was a spring without voices. On the mornings that had once throbbed with the dawn chorus of robins, catbirds, doves, jays, wrens, and scores of other bird voices there was now no sound; only silence lay over the fields and woods and marsh. Even the streams were now lifeless. No witchcraft, no enemy action had silenced the rebirth of new life in this stricken world. The people had done it themselves.

- The chief public health threat has ceased to be disease; now it is a hazard we ourselves have introduced into our world.

- The 'control of nature' is a phrase conceived in arrogance, born of the Neanderthal age of biology and philosophy, when it was supposed that nature exists for the convenience of man.

- The insects are winning: We're on a pesticide treadmill. The insects adapt to the particular insecticide used, forcing us to find ever-deadlier new ones. Thus the chemical war is never won, and all life is caught in its violent crossfire.

- The earth's vegetation is part of a web of life in which there are intimate and essential relations between plants and the earth, between plants and other plants, between plants and animals. Sometimes we have no choice but to disturb the relationships, but we should do so thoughtfully – with full awareness that what we do may have consequences remote in time and place.

- Many of these substances are persistent and bio-accumulative. Health effects depend on exposure over time. Effects are delayed. But this can lull us: the danger is easily ignored. It is human nature to shrug off what may seem to us a vague threat of future disaster . . . Some of these substances have toxic effects in very small quantities. In the ecology of our bodies, minute causes produce mighty effects.

- A human being, unlike a laboratory animal living under rigidly controlled conditions, is never exposed to one chemical alone . . . we are subject to multiple exposures . . . This is a problem of ecology, of interrelationships, of interdependence.

About the author

Rachel Louise Carson (1907–1964) was an American marine biologist and nature writer whose writings are often credited with launching the global environmental movement.

Carson started her career as a biologist in the US Bureau of Fisheries, and transitioned to a full-time nature writer in the 1950s. Her widely praised 1951 bestseller

The Sea Around Us won her financial security and recognition as a gifted writer. Her next book, *The Edge of the Sea*, and the republished version of her first book, *Under the Sea-Wind*, were also bestsellers. Together, her sea trilogy explores the gamut of ocean life, from the shores to the surface to the deep sea.

In the late 1950s, Carson turned her attention to conservation and the environmental problems caused by synthetic pesticides. The result was *Silent Spring* (1962), which brought environmental concerns to an unprecedented portion of the American public. The book spurred a reversal in US pesticide policy – leading to a nationwide ban on DDT and other pesticides – and the grassroots environmental movement it inspired led to the creation of the Environmental Protection Agency.

She died of breast cancer just 18 months after the publication of *Silent Spring* in April 1964. Carson was posthumously awarded the Presidential Medal of Freedom. She was also named one of the 100 most important people of the 20th century by *Time* magazine.

Courtesy US FWS

OTHER BOOKS

Under the Sea-Wind: A Naturalist's Picture of Ocean Life (Signet Science Library, 1941)

The Sea Around Us (Oxford University Press, 1951)

The Edge of the Sea (Staples Press, 1955)

The Sense of Wonder (Perennial Library, 1984)

Lost Woods: The Discovered Writing of Rachel Carson (Beacon Press, 1999)

MORE INFORMATION

Life and Legacy of Rachel Carson:
www.rachelcarson.org

Silent Spring Institute:
www.silentspring.org

Rachel Carson Institute:
www.chatham.edu/rci

3
Unsafe At Any Speed
Ralph Nader

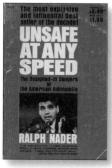

1st edn
Unsafe At Any Speed:
The Designed-In Dangers
of the American
Automobile
Grossman Publishers,
1965; 365pp, hbk

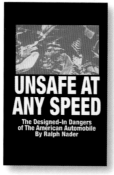

Current edn
Unsafe At Any Speed:
The Designed-In Dangers
of the American
Automobile
Knightsbridge Publishing
Co., 1991; hbk;
978-1561290505;
revised updated 25th
anniversary edition

Key ideas

► Companies, left to themselves, will tend to externalise negative impacts and internalise positive benefits.

► One of the main causes of death and injuries are automobiles, in large part due to the way they are designed.

► Automobile manufacturers have the knowledge and technical skill to make cars safe, but have failed to do so.

► It is easier to redesign automobiles to make them safe than to try to change the nature of the people who drive them.

► A safe car *can* be built, but will be built only if an informed consumer public demand it.

Synopsis

Unsafe At Any Speed, written in a political, accusative style which reflects Nader's legal background, is probably most widely known for its criticism of the safety flaws in General Motors' Chevrolet Corvair. However, Nader also attacked contemporary auto design more generally, citing a wide range of problems including brightly finished dashboards, which reflected light into the driver's eyes, poor workmanship, the failure of companies to honour warranties and the lack of standardised shift patterns on automatic cars resulting in drivers accidentally reversing into pedestrians.

All of these problems, according to Nader, were well known in the industry, but little was done to correct them. The reason often given by manufacturers was that it would take away from the styling or add excessively to the cost of the cars. But he counters that annual (and in his view unnecessary) styling changes added on average about $700 to the consumer cost of a new car, while average expenditure on crash safety improvements was only about 23¢ per car.

The book goes on to document the history of crash science, focusing on the effect on the body as it collides with the car when the car hits another object. Nader illustrates that a great deal of knowledge was available to designers by the early 1960s, but it was largely ignored by the American automotive industry.

Rather than admit manufacturers' culpability, Nader says that the traffic safety establishment deliberately blamed accidents and fatalities on the driver. The road safety mantra – the so-called '3 Es': Engineering, Enforcement and Education – was, he believes, created by the industry in the 1920s to distract attention from the real problems of vehicle safety. As late as 1965, he noted, $320 million was allocated to highway beautification, while only $500,000 was dedicated to highway safety.

The concluding chapter calls for the automotive industry to be forced by government regulation to pay greater attention to safety, in the face of mounting evidence about preventable death and injury. Safety measures, says Nader, should not require people's voluntary and repeated cooperation. And measures can be put in place to prevent injury even if we don't understand the causal chain. Moreover, there is a moral imperative to ensure that cars are built as safely as they can be. Hence, individuals within the industry need to show moral leadership.

Although the book focuses on a single industry, its real significance is as one of the catalysts of the social responsibility and civil society movement. It was the first great battle between a large multinational – General Motors, which epitomised corporate America – and an activist representing the public interest. His flagging of the automobile's impact on air pollution also made him a pioneer in the environmental movement and a prophet of the climate change challenges currently facing the auto industry.

Lessons that apply more widely are that: (1) governments do not always act in the public interest; (2) business often lags on social responsibility when action implies short-term costs; and (3) in the absence of government policy and business responsibility, consumer activism is critical.

From the book

- A major contemporary problem is how to control the power of economic interests which ignore the harmful effects of their applied science and technology. The automobile tragedy is one of the most serious of these man-made assaults on the human body.

- The accumulated power of decades of effort by the automobile industry to strengthen its control over car design is evidenced today by the difficulty we face in even beginning to bring it to justice.

- The public has never been given the information nor offered the quality of competition to enable it to make effective demands via the marketplace or through government for a safe, non-polluting and efficient automobile that can be produced economically.

- It is clear that the sales success of the automotive industry is not simply due to the willingness of customers to buy, but also to public policy that ignores needs for rapid transit and builds the highways and provides other services that make possible the growth of the automotive sub-economy.

- The regulation of the automobile must go through three stages: public awareness and demand for action; legislation; and continuing administration.

- As these attainable levels of safety rise, so do the moral imperative to use them. There are men in the automobile industry who know both the technical capability and appreciate the moral imperatives. But their timidity and conformity to the rigidities of the corporate bureaucracies have prevailed.

- When and if the automobile is designed to free millions of human beings from unnecessary mutilation, these men, like their counterparts in universities and government who knew the suppression of safer automobile development yet remained silent year after year, will look back with shame on the time when common candour was considered courage.

About the author

Ralph Nader (born 1934) is a lawyer, author and one of America's most renowned crusaders for the rights of consumers and the general public.

Born in Winsted, Connecticut, in 1955, Nader received an AB Magna Cum Laude from Princeton University, and in 1958 he received a LLB with distinction from Harvard University. His career began as a lawyer and in 1967 was named one of Ten Outstanding Young Men of Year by the US Junior Chamber of Commerce.

Photo: David Shankbone

Nader first made headlines in 1965 with *Unsafe At Any Speed* and, building on the popularity and success of this campaign against the auto industry, he created an organisation of lawyers and researchers (nicknamed 'Nader's Raiders'), which exposed industrial hazards, pollution, unsafe products and governmental neglect of consumer safety laws. He has also founded many other organisations including the Center for Study of Responsive Law, the Public Interest Research Group (PIRG) and the Project for Corporate Responsibility. This has often led to him being hailed as a founder of the consumer rights movement.

Nader played a key role in the creation of the Environmental Protection Agency, the Occupational Safety and Health Administration, the Freedom of Information Act and the Consumer Product Safety Commission. Since 1996, he has run in every US election as a presidential candidate, and, in 2000, won nearly three million votes (close to 3%) as the Green Party candidate.

OTHER BOOKS (SELECTION)

The Consumer and Corporate Accountability (Harcourt Brace Jovanovich, 1973)

Taming the Giant Corporation: How the Largest Corporations Control Our Lives (with Mark Green and Joel Seligman; Norton, 1976)

Corporate Power in America (editor, with Mark Green; Penguin, 1977)

Crashing the Party: Taking on the Corporate Government in an Age of Surrender (St Martin's Griffin, 2001)

Civic Arousal (Harper, 2004)

MORE INFORMATION

Ralph Nader's official website:
www.nader.org

An Unreasonable Man (film about Ralph Nader):
www.anunreasonableman.com

4
The Population Bomb
Paul L. Ehrlich

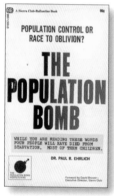

1st edn
The Population Bomb
Sierra Club/Ballantine
Books, 1968; 201pp,
pbk; 978-0345021717

Current edn
The Population Bomb
Buccaneer Books Inc.,
1995; hbk,
library binding;
978-1568495873

Key ideas

▶ Population growth is growing exponentially, which is unsustainable for human civilisation and the planet.

▶ There are only two 'solutions' to the population problem: a lower birth rate or a higher death rate.

▶ Unless we can actively manage down the birth rate, the death rate will naturally rise, through war, famine and disease.

▶ Population growth and environmental deterioration are inextricably linked.

▶ Solutions lie in population control (through various means), increasing food production and better managing the world's natural resources.

Synopsis

The Population Bomb, as its title suggests and as the tone of writing reflects, is a warning of impending crisis. It was one of the first books to discuss the inherent conflict between growing human demands and finite resources.

The most pressing concern at the time was food security. Given population and agricultural trends, it seemed likely that the world would soon be unable to feed itself. As Ehrlich famously put it: 'The battle to feed humanity is over. In the 1970s, the world will undergo famines. Hundreds of millions of people are going to starve to death in spite of any crash programs embarked upon now. Population control is the only answer.'

In addition to famine (or starvation), Ehrlich's other horses of the apocalypse were pestilence (or disease) and war. These likely harbingers of a rising death rate, all caused by overpopulation, are made extremely vivid in the book through three scenarios depicting possible futures if population growth is not curtailed. While developing countries would be worst hit by these crises, he predicted that in developed countries the impacts would be most strongly felt on the environment and the availability of resources.

Ehrlich recognised that the notion of population control was controversial, but believed it was a bitter pill we would have to swallow to survive in the long term. He allowed for the possibility that population control might come about 'through changes in our value system', but also advocated that it should be 'by compulsion if voluntary methods fail'. For example, this might include forced sterilisation (he cites India as an example) and legalisation of abortion.

Ehrlich proposes four action items to address the crisis:

1. Conscious regulation of human numbers by setting optimum population–environment goals;

2. Gargantuan efforts to increase food production;

3. Reform of the agricultural sector to minimise detrimental environmental impacts and include ecosystem restoration; and

4. Improved assessment and management of the world's non-renewable resources.

Despite many of his scenarios not coming to pass (or at least not manifesting as dramatically; after all, we *do* still see millions of children dying of starvation every year), *The Population Bomb* played a vital part in changing the way we think about living on our finite planet. And, indeed, some of his warnings still seem prophetic, like 'all of the junk we dump into the atmosphere . . . all of the carbon dioxide, have effects on the temperature balance of the Earth'.

In the final analysis, however, it is less about the details – such as whether Ehrlich's sustainable population target of one billion is exactly the right number (others, such as the Optimum Population Trust, continue to wrestle with the numbers) – and more about his general thesis, namely that unfettered population growth is a critical driver of the world's social, environmental and economic challenges. It is a warning we would still do well to heed.

From the book

- I wish I could offer you some sugar-coated solutions, but I'm afraid the time for them is long gone.

- Nothing could be more misleading to our children than our present affluent society.

- Too many cars, too many factories, too much detergent, too much pesticides, multiplying contrails, inadequate sewage treatment plants, too little water, too much carbon dioxide – all can be traced easily to too many people.

- A cancer is an uncontrolled multiplication of cells; the population explosion is an uncontrolled multiplication of people. Treating only the symptoms of cancer may make the victim more comfortable at first, but eventually he dies – often horribly. A similar fate awaits a world with a population explosion if only the symptoms are treated.

- If I'm right, we will save the world. If I'm wrong, people will still be better fed, better housed, and happier, thanks to our efforts.

About the author

Paul R. Ehrlich (born 1932) is a renowned entomologist specialising in lepidoptera (butterflies), but is more widely known for his research and writing on the subject of human overpopulation.

Ehrlich earned a BA in zoology at the University of Pennsylvania, an MA at the University of Kansas, and a PhD in 1957 at the University of Kansas. In 1959 he joined the faculty at Stanford, being promoted to full professor of biology in 1966. He was named as the Bing Professor of Population Studies in 1977, a position he still holds, as well as being president of the Center for Conservation Biology at Stanford University. He is a fellow of the American Association for the Advancement of Science, the American Academy of Arts and Sciences, and the American Philosophical Society.

In 1968, Ehrlich published *The Population Bomb*, causing extensive debate among scientists, environmentalists, agriculturalists and policy-makers. Although the Green Revolution prevented his direst scenarios about world famine from becoming reality, many of his warnings about environmental limits, climate change and overconsumption still ring true. In 1990, he updated his outlook in *The Population Explosion* (co-authored with Anne Ehrlich), continuing to warn that humanity is on a perilous path.

Ehrlich has received numerous awards, including from (among others) the Sierra Club, the World Wildlife Fund International, the

Royal Swedish Academy of Sciences and the United Nations. Ehrlich set up his own organisation called Zero Population Growth (now Population Connection) to campaign against population growth.

In his own words
(2008 interview)

Reflections on the book

The population predictions, which all come not from us but from the UN as filtered through the Population Reference Bureau, have been right on the mark; they're just exactly what was expected.

We know how to get birth rates down. It's happened in many parts of the world. If you educate women, give them job opportunities and give them the control over their reproduction, then birth rates tend to come down.

The steps that we took to avoid massive famines in the 1970s and '80s were mostly through the Green Revolution, which is a short-term and dangerous solution, but one that at least had the effect of not having the death rates escalate at the level that the agricultural experts were talking about at the time.

The sort of thing that is not made clear from demographers is that every person you add to the planet assaults our life-support systems more than the last one. So that the two or two and a half billion people that are still expected will do much more damage than the last two to two and a half billion.

It's the old IPAT equation: Impact = Population x Affluence x Technology. One of the problems with the culture of development is that people think of development as making the same mistakes the United States and the West made after the Victorian Industrial Revolution.

The role of business

Business is a social activity and has to be brought under social control. And we've seen what happens when there's no social control around the world recently.

The multinationals in particular need to be controlled very carefully by the societies in which they exist. This business that corporations have no responsibility except to make profits and stay within the law is nonsensical.

Looking to the future

The list of solutions is fairly simple to construct but very difficult to put into play:

1. Get the population going downward as soon as humanely possible.

2. Change our attitudes, to shift away from consumption to conservation, to have a worldwide discussion of what kind of consumption really helps, and what kind we can do without.

3. Look more carefully at our technologies. For example, on the thousands of novel chemicals we're putting into the environment, before we put them there, we need to have a much more careful cost–benefit analysis.

4. Spread our empathy further. We have to have greater consideration for people who are distant from us, who look different from us, who speak different languages, and who are going to live in the future. We've got to care about all of them a lot more.

5. Nation-states are very recent inventions, the last couple of hundred years. And it's crystal clear the state system doesn't work anymore. Most of our problems are utterly global and we have to find some way to deal with global problems. So we should be re-examining global governance as a species.

OTHER BOOKS (SELECTION)

The End of Affluence: A Blueprint for Your Future (with Anne H. Ehrlich; Amereon Limited, 1974)

The Population Explosion (with Anne H. Ehrlich; Simon & Schuster, 1990)

Healing the Planet: Strategies for Resolving the Environmental Crisis (with Anne H. Ehrlich; Addison-Wesley, 1991)

One with Nineveh: Politics, Consumption, and the Human Future (with Anne H. Ehrlich; Island Press, 2004)

The Dominant Animal: Human Evolution and the Environment (with Anne H. Ehrlich; Island Press, 2008)

MORE INFORMATION

The Dominant Animal:
www.dominantanimal.org

Optimum Population Trust:
www.optimumpopulation.org

Population Connection:
www.populationconnection.org

5
Operating Manual for Spaceship Earth
R. Buckminster Fuller

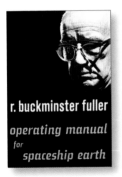

1st edn
Operating Manual for Spaceship Earth
Carbondale, Southern Illinois University Press, 1969; 151pp, hbk; 978-0809303571

Current edn
Operating Manual for Spaceship Earth
Lars Müller Publishers, 2008; 152pp, pbk; 978-3037781265

Key ideas

▶ Spaceship Earth is a metaphor for understanding the planet as a closed system (with the exception of the sun's input); hence, there is no 'away'.

▶ Specialisation has denied us our ability to see the whole system, as we fail to comprehend how different silos of knowledge interrelate.

▶ Over-specialisation eventually leads to extinction, as we lose our general adaptability to deal with change.

▶ Humanity must learn how to survive and thrive using only the sun's regenerative energy and their own intellectual abilities.

▶ Scientific discovery is key to survival; hence, scientists, planners, architects and engineers need to take the initiative.

Synopsis

Operating Manual for Spaceship Earth is a fascinating combination of Fuller's deep scientific grounding and his philosophical and metaphysical way of looking at the world. The main thesis of the book is that humanity has been too shortsighted and siloed in its thinking and, as a result, we have lost the ability to see the whole system, the big picture. He argues that this is the main cause of our impending ecological crisis.

Behind our shortsightedness and siloed thinking is intellectual specialisation. Fuller traces this back to the political and religious rulers of centuries past (he calls them the 'Great Pirates'), who surrounded themselves with the best knowledge by financing schools and universities that brought about specialisation. This allowed the rulers to have greater control, since only *they* had a comprehensive view of the world.

This trend has increased over time, so that now we are convinced of 'the theory that specialization is the key to success, not realizing that specialization precludes comprehensive thinking'. Fuller sees this as pervasive in our modern society, from science and engineering to finance and economics. Beyond its political implications, he warns that such over-specialisation is a root cause of extinction, since it results in a loss of adaptability.

The book is as remarkable for its overall message as for its elaboration of concepts that were ahead of their time. For example, he introduces terms like 'synergy' ('behaviour of wholes unpredicted by behaviour of their parts'). This and related concepts like 'topology' begin to build a theory of systems thinking for ecology. According to Fuller, 'it is obvious that the real wealth of life aboard our planet is a forwardly-operative, metabolic, and intellectual regenerating system'. And yet 'we have been misusing, abusing, and polluting this extraordinary chemical energy-interchanging system for successfully regenerating all life aboard our planetary spaceship'.

The solution, argues Fuller, is to begin decoupling from our dependence on non-renewable resources, as 'living only on our energy savings by burning up the fossil fuels which took billions of years to impound from the Sun, or living on our capital by burning up our Earth's atoms, is lethally ignorant and also utterly irresponsible to our coming generations'.

Fuller dismisses the perennial excuse that 'it costs too much'. Aside from the fact that cost never seems to prevent politicians from releasing funds for war, there is a much stronger argument, namely that the earlier we tackle problems, the cheaper it is. Pre-empting Stern by 40 years, Fuller says: 'In the end, problem solutions always cost the least if paid for adequately at the outset of the vital problem's recognition.'

Fuller concludes that 'this all brings us to a realization of the enormous educational task which must be successfully accomplished right now in order to convert man's spin-dive toward oblivion into an intellectually mastered power pullout into a safe and level flight of physical and metaphysical success, whereafter he may turn his Spaceship Earth's occupancy into a universe exploring advantage'.

From the book

- Now there is one outstandingly important fact regarding Spaceship Earth, and that is that no instruction book came with it.

- I feel that one of the reasons why we are struggling inadequately today is that we reckon our costs on too short-sighted a basis and are later overwhelmed with the unexpected costs brought about by our short-sightedness.

- Specialization is in fact only a fancy form of slavery wherein the 'expert' is fooled into accepting his slavery by making him feel that in return he is in a socially and culturally preferred, ergo, highly secure, lifelong position.

- If we do not comprehend and realize our potential ability to support all life forever we are cosmically bankrupt.

- My own picture of humanity today finds us just about to step out from amongst the pieces of our just one-second-ago broken eggshell. Our innocent, trial-and-error-sustaining nutriment is exhausted. We are faced with an entirely new relationship to the universe. We are going to have to spread our wings of intellect and fly or perish; that is, we must dare immediately to fly by the generalized principles governing the universe and not by the ground rules of yesterday's superstitious and erroneously conditioned reflexes.

About the author

R. Buckminster Fuller (1895–1983) was referred to as an architect, inventor, scientist, engineer, mathematician, educator, philosopher, poet, speaker, author, consultant, economist, futurist, transcendentalist and designer.

Born in Milton, Massachusetts, he was twice expelled from Harvard University, but received 47 honorary doctorates in the arts, science, engineering and the humanities in his lifetime. Throughout the 1940s and 1950s, Fuller gained a formidable reputation as an early researcher of renewable energy sources and innovative design. Most famously, drawing on US Navy experiences, Fuller developed tensegrity structures (minimalist structures that actually get stronger as they get larger), notably the Geodesic Dome. Famous Geodesic Domes include The EPCOT Center at Florida's Walt Disney World and the US Pavilion at the 1967 Montreal World's Fair. He also discovered the science of Synergetics, which explores holistic engineering structures in nature (long before the term 'synergy' became popular).

Fuller spent a few summers in the late '40s and early '50s teaching at the Black Mountain College. He was research professor at

Carbondale, Southern Illinois University, from 1959 to 1968. In 1968 he became a university professor and retired in 1975.

He was awarded 25 US patents; authored 28 books, including the groundbreaking *Operating Manual for Spaceship Earth* in 1969; and received dozens of major architectural and design awards. In 1981, his efforts were further recognised when he received the Presidential Medal of Freedom from Ronald Reagan.

Buckminster Fuller speaking with architectural students at the University of Detroit in 1970, during filming of *The World of Buckminster Fuller*, directed by Robert Snyder. Photograph by Jaime Snyder.

OTHER BOOKS (SELECTION)

Utopia or Oblivion: The Prospects for Humanity (Bantam, 1969)

Earth, Inc. (Doubleday, 1973)

Critical Path (St Martin's Press, 1981)

Humans in Universe (with Anwar Dil; Mouton De Gruyter, 1983)

Cosmography: A Posthumous Scenario for the Future of Humanity (with Kiyoshi Kuromiya; Macmillan, 1992)

MORE INFORMATION

Buckminster Fuller Institute:
www.bfi.org

1st edn
The Limits to Growth:
A Report for the Club of
Rome's Project on the
Predicament of Mankind
*(Donella H. Meadows, Dennis
L. Meadows, Jørgen Randers
and William W. Behrens III)*
Universe Books, 1972; 205pp;
hbk 978-0876632222;
pbk 978-0876639184

Current UK edn
Limits to Growth:
The 30-Year Update *(Donella
Meadows, Jørgen Randers
and Dennis Meadows)*
Earthscan Publications,
2004; 368pp; pbk;
978-1844071449; revised
and reappraised

Current US edn
Limits to Growth:
The 30-Year Update *(Donella
Meadows, Jørgen Randers
and Dennis Meadows)*
Chelsea Green, 2004;
368pp, pbk,
978-1931498586; revised
and reappraised

6
The Limits to Growth

Donella H. Meadows, Dennis L. Meadows, Jørgen Randers and William W. Behrens III

Key ideas

▶ Growth trends in world population, industrialisation, pollution, food production and resource depletion suggest that biophysical limits will be reached some time within the next 100 years.

▶ The most probable result will be a rather sudden and uncontrollable decline in both population and industrial capacity (so-called 'overshoot and collapse').

▶ It is possible to alter these growth trends and to establish a condition of ecological and economic stability that is sustainable far into the future.

▶ A precondition of a sustainable world is that population and capital growth need to be stabilised, to avoid reaching and exceeding the limits to growth.

▶ Allowing capital and population growth find their 'natural state' is an inadequate, irresponsible and potentially catastrophic response.

Synopsis

As a commissioned report to the Club of Rome, *The Limits to Growth* uses a computer simulation model developed at MIT to investigate five major trends of global concern: accelerating industrialisation, rapid population growth, widespread malnutrition, depletion of non-renewable resources, and a deteriorating environment.

The book is revolutionary, not only in challenging modern society's growth obsession, but also in its use of systems dynamics within a sustainability context. This approach recognises that the structure of any system is often as important in determining its behaviour as the individual components.

Based on the model, the book reports on 13 scenarios for the future. Despite variations, all of them produce a sobering conclusion, namely that 'the behaviour mode of the system is clearly that of overshoot and collapse'. The basic scenario unfolds in the following way:

'The industrial capital stock grows to a level that requires an enormous input of resources. In the very process of that growth it depletes a large fraction of the resource reserves available. As resource prices rise and mines are depleted, more and more capital must be used for obtaining resources, leaving less to be invested for future growth. Finally investment cannot keep up with depreciation, and the industrial base collapses, taking with it the service and agricultural systems, which have become dependent on industrial inputs. For a short time the situation is especially serious because population, with the delays inherent in the age structure and the process of social adjustment, keeps rising. Population finally decreases when the death rate is driven upward by lack of food and health services.'

In response to anticipated criticism that they were being too pessimistic, the authors tested more optimistic assumptions in the model. For example, they assumed a doubling of resources, effective recycling (75% of all resources), a doubling of agricultural yield per hectare, nuclear energy to meet all energy requirements, effective pollution control and perfect birth control.

Even under these assumptions, the conclusion is grim: 'The application of technology to apparent problems of resource depletion or pollution or food shortage has no impact on the essential problem, which is exponential growth in a finite and complex system. Our attempts to use even the most optimistic estimates of the benefits of technology in the model did not prevent the ultimate decline of population and industry, and in fact did not postpone the collapse beyond the year 2100.'

While the authors concede that this is 'cause for deep concern', they insist that there is 'also cause for hope' as humanity 'possesses, for a small moment in his history, the most powerful combination of knowledge, tools, and resources the world has ever known. [We have] all that is physically necessary to create a totally new form of human society – one that would be built to last for generations.'

Despite this, their subsequent updates, *Beyond the Limits* (1993) and *The 30-Year Update*, suggest that the goal of a sustainable society still eludes us.

From the book

- All the evidence available to us suggests that of the three alternatives – unrestricted growth, a self-imposed limitation to growth, or a nature-imposed limitation to growth – only the last two are actually possible.

- Faith in technology as the ultimate solution to all problems can divert our attention from the most fundamental problem – the problem of growth in a finite system – and prevent us from taking effective action to solve it.

- While technology can change rapidly, political and social institutions generally change very slowly. Furthermore, they almost never change in anticipation of social need, but only in response to one.

- We believe that the evolution of a society that favours innovation and technological development, a society based on equality and justice, is far more likely to evolve in a state of global equilibrium than it is in the state of growth we are experiencing today.

- Because of the delays in the system, if the global society waits until the constraints are unmistakably apparent, it will have waited too long.

Photo: Medora Hebert, *Valley News*

About the authors

Donella (Dana) Meadows (1941–2001) was a pioneering American environmental scientist, dynamic systems modeller, teacher and writer.

Meadows was born in Elgin, Illinois, earning a BA in chemistry from Carleton College in 1963, and a PhD in biophysics from Harvard University in 1968. She then became a research fellow at MIT, a protégé of Jay Forrester, the inventor of system dynamics as well as the principle of magnetic data storage for computers. She taught at Dartmouth College for 29 years, beginning in 1972.

Meadows founded the International Network of Resource Information Centers (INRIC) and the Sustainability Institute. She

Dennis L. Meadows

Jørgen Randers

also published eight books and wrote a weekly column called 'The Global Citizen', which commented on world events from a systems point of view; she was nominated for the Pulitzer Prize in 1991. She received numerous honours and awards in her lifetime and died unexpectedly in 2001 after a brief illness.

Dennis L. Meadows (born 1942) is an American scientist, Professor of Systems Management and Director of the Institute for Policy and Social Science Research at the University of New Hampshire.

Meadows has a PhD in Management from Massachusetts Institute of Technology, where he served on the faculty and did pioneering work on *The Limits to Growth* study. He also holds four honorary doctorates from European universities and has lectured in over 50 countries. He has been the Director of three university research institutes: at MIT, Dartmouth College and the University of New Hampshire.

Meadows co-founded the Balaton Group, a network of around 300 professionals in over 30 nations involved in systems science, public policy and sustainable development. He is also Past President of the International System Dynamics Society and the International Simulation and Games Association. He continues to lecture around the world.

Jørgen Randers (born 1945) is a Norwegian environmental scientist, dynamic systems expert and Professor of Policy Analysis at the Norwegian School of Management, where he teaches scenario analysis and corporate responsibility.

Randers also lectures internationally on the issue of sustainable development, within and outside corporations, including for the Prince of Wales's Business and the Environment Programme, run by the University of Cambridge Programme for Sustainability Leadership. He was formerly President of the Norwegian School of Management from

William W. Behrens III

1981 to 1989, and Deputy Director-General of WWF International (World Wide Fund for Nature) in Switzerland from 1994 to 1999.

He is non-executive member of a number of corporate boards, as well as the sustainability councils of British Telecom and the City of Rotterdam. He has authored a number of books and scientific papers.

William W. Behrens III (born 1949) earned a BS in Electrical Engineering, a BS in Management, and a PhD in Environmental Economics from MIT, during which time he became involved in the Club of Rome study that led to the publication of *The Limits to Growth* and several other publications.

Following one semester of teaching at Dartmouth College, Bill has pursued a lifetime personal commitment to bringing sustainable and renewable building and energy practices to New England. He now operates, with vigorous partners, ReVision Energy LLC, the leading solar contractor in Maine.

Behrens has designed and led the installation of thousands of individual solar projects including the largest photovoltaic and solar thermal systems in Maine, and has led the construction of many solar homes. He provides installation and design services to architects, engineers and contractors throughout Maine and New England.

In their own words
(2008 interview)

Dennis L. Meadows

Reflections on the book

In 1994 and 2004 we did go back and try to start understanding how we were doing. And, generally speaking, I would say that the crises are developing faster than we expected they would.

Global oil production is now generally accepted to have peaked out last year, or in the next few years. Our book didn't show resource production peaking out until another few decades from now.

It is not valid to say that the things we said haven't happened. Our concern was about the period when growth ends.

Every one of our scenarios assumed that that would be somewhere in the period between 2010 or 2020 and 2060, depending on our policies. It's just too early to tell.

I think it's useful to differentiate these problems into two categories. Universal problems affect everybody, but they can be dealt with locally. Global problems affect everybody but they can only be solved through global action.

Looking back, I think it's safe to say that there are quite a few examples of success with universal problems. When we looked at the global problems the only one we found that we felt was very relevant, was dealing with ozone depletion.

The role of technology

In our computer model analysis, we were able to convert the behaviour of overshoot and collapse – which is what you might call the default, or the central tendency of the system – into what we might loosely term 'sustainable development'.

To achieve [equilibrium in the model, or sustainability] we had to implement a number of technological changes: make resource use much more efficient; reduce the pollution generated by industrial activity; drastically alter the impact on flow fertility of agricultural production techniques, and so forth.

We showed that those [technological changes] were not sufficient. You need also some very, very important cultural and behavioural changes. The population has to stabilise [and] we need to bring people to have very different consumption goals.

There are examples of countries that have stabilised their population. I don't know of any country that has willingly stabilised its consumption.

Looking to the future

I have a kind of a Boy Scout ethic, which I will simplistically summarise as 'Leave your campsite better than you found it.' You don't have to make it perfect, but, you know, pick up a little litter and tidy things up and avoid doing real damage. And that's enough.

When I go out and talk about the future and how people should behave, I'm talking out the Boy Scout ethic. 'Don't imagine you can save the world, but you certainly at each moment have a chance to make things a little bit better than they would have been otherwise.'

I always remember, on Donella Meadows' office door was a little motto which said 'Even if I knew the world would end tomorrow I'd plant a tree today.'

Jørgen Randers

Reflections on the book

What most people believe is in the book is that it proves or tries to prove that the world is so small that if we continue growth . . . then the world would collapse around 2000. Which is not what the book really says.

The real message of the book is that, as a growing society is approaching limitations, it will not act before it is too late.

On a finite Earth with rapid physical expansion, one must be very careful in not postponing action when problems start to emerge. And that is the message: the danger of overshoot and collapse.

When you measure the ecological footprint of humanity, we are 30% above the carrying capacity of the globe. We have overshot. So those critics who said that humanity would never be so stupid as to allow activity levels to proceed beyond the sustainable level – they have been proven wrong.

On the role of technology

Over and beyond the market mechanisms, we need deliberate technology development programmes, like the Manhattan Project that created the nuclear bomb during the war.

We need some large scale upfront types of investments in carbon capture and storage, in offshore windmills – those types of technologies.

I think you won't get high enough carbon prices quickly enough for them to have the time to develop and implement the technologies, before the climate damage is too big.

Looking to the future

Either you go the optimistic route – you say, 'the problem *can* be solved and look how swell life will be if we solve the problem'. Or you go the other route and say, 'look at the disasters we will run into if we don't do anything'.

Are scare tactics better than carrots? I've moved to thinking that having a positive view has a stronger motivational force than scare tactics.

You can ask the question: is it possible to come up with sufficient carrots to make society act? And it looks as if some support from scare tactics or some of the disasters would help.

The solar power heating the surface of the Earth is of the order of 10,000 times as much as we use for the time being. So, once we have shifted society into a 100% solar society, which in my book will happen over the next 50 years, then the energy issue is solved.

It's worthwhile trying to push the climate limits sufficiently or reduce our climate footprint per unit of consumption as much as possible, so that we buy ourselves the next 50 to 100 years so that we can do the shift into a non-carbon economy.

There are of course two ways out of the overshoot: a well-organised retraction down to sustainable levels, or a nature-induced collapse to those levels.

OTHER BOOKS (SELECTION)

Elements of System Dynamics Method (Randers; Wright Allen Press, 1979)

Beyond the Limits: Confronting Global Collapse, Envisioning a Sustainable Future (Meadows, Meadows and Randers; Earthscan, 1992)

Alternatives to Growth: A Search for Sustainable Futures (edited by Dennis Meadows; Ballinger, 1992)

Limits to Growth: The 30-Year Update (Meadows, Meadows and Randers; Chelsea Green, 2004)

Thinking in Systems: A Primer (Donella Meadows, edited by Diana Wright; Chelsea Green, 2008)

MORE INFORMATION

Club of Rome:
www.clubofrome.org

7
Small Is Beautiful
E.F. Schumacher

1st edn
Small Is Beautiful:
A Study of Economics
as if People Mattered
Blond & Briggs, 1973
288pp, hbk;
978-0856340123

Current UK edn
Small Is Beautiful:
A Study of Economics
as if People Mattered
Vintage, 1993; 272pp,
pbk; 978-0099225614

Current US edn
Small Is Beautiful:
A Study of Economics
as if People Mattered
Harper Perennial, 1989;
352pp, pbk;
978-0060916305

Key ideas

▶ An economy founded on the growth paradigm and the pursuit of wealth is unsustainable, by definition.

▶ Using economics as the yardstick to measure performance will lead to inefficiencies and societal breakdown.

▶ Big is not automatically good or better, and local production leads to the best social and environmental outcomes.

▶ Labour is to be valued as it enriches the human existence and provides for our daily needs; therefore, labour avoidance will lead to inefficiencies.

▶ Human-scale technology in the service of humans is preferable to large-scale technology at the service of the economic growth.

Synopsis

Small Is Beautiful is a collection of essays outlining economist E.F. Schumacher's philosophy on modern economic, ecological and spiritual thinking. Its strength lies in Schumacher's ability to elegantly and intelligently question many assumptions of modern economics, highlighting some of the fallacies. What made his work all the more remarkable is that his starting point was indeed economics, rather than environmentalism or social activism.

Schumacher begins by pointing out that an economy is unsustainable when economic growth is seen as the measure of societal progress, most crudely in the form of 'GDP growth is good'. As a result, finite resources are treated as income rather than capital, and therefore society acts as if they are infinite. This is driven by the idea that people are separate from nature and can and should therefore control nature. However, the environment's capacity to resist or assimilate pollution is limited.

Behind this growth mentality is the Keynesian assumption of universal prosperity through enrichment, which Schumacher disputes: 'An attitude to life which seeks fulfilment in the single-minded pursuit of wealth – in short, materialism – does not fit into this world, because it contains within itself no limiting principle, while the environment in which it places itself is strictly limited.' Furthermore, such prosperity 'is attainable only by cultivating such drives of human nature as greed and envy, which destroy intelligence, happiness, serenity and thereby the peacefulness of man'.

Linked to the growth question is the seduction of large-scale technology. Schumacher argues that 'scientific or technological "solutions" which poison the environment or degrade the social structure and man himself are of no benefit, no matter how brilliantly conceived or how great their superficial attraction'. Instead, he argues for technologies that are cheap enough so that they are accessible to virtually everyone; suitable for small-scale application; and compatible with humans' need for creativity.

Part of his thinking about technology comes from Schumacher's vision of what he calls 'Buddhist economics'. Here, he is calling for a new philosophy, which values people above production and values labour above outputs. Work, he claims, should be a dignified and creative process to be encouraged, not a factor of production to be minimised or replaced through mechanisation. He also emphasises the Buddhist values of non-attachment to material goods and respect for all living things.

Finally, Schumacher tackles the issue of size, or what he calls 'the idolatry of gigantism' in modern economics. The main thrust of his argument is that 'people can be themselves only in small comprehensible groups. Therefore we must learn to think in terms of an articulated structure that can cope with the multiplicity of small-scale units. If economic thinking cannot grasp this it is useless. If it cannot go beyond its vast abstractions . . . and make contact with the human realities of poverty, frustration, alienation, despair, breakdown, crime, escapism, stress, congestion, ugliness, and spiritual death, then let us scrap economics and start afresh.'

From the book

- Economic growth, economic expansion and so forth have become the abiding interest, if not the obsession, of all modern societies. If an activity has been branded as uneconomic, its right to existence is not merely questioned but energetically denied.

- Production from local resources for local needs is the most rational way of economic life, while dependence on imports from afar and the consequent need to produce for export to unknown and distant peoples is highly uneconomic and justifiable only in exceptional cases.

- I have no doubt that a callous attitude to the land and to the animals thereon is connected with, and symptomatic of, a great many other attitudes, such as those producing a fanaticism of rapid change and a fascination with novelties – technical, organisational, chemical, biological, and so forth – which insists on their application long before their long-term consequences are even remotely understood.

- Since consumption is merely a means to human well-being, the aim should be to obtain the maximum of well-being with the minimum of consumption. Modern economics, on the other hand, considers consumption to be the sole end and purpose of all economic activity.

- Ever bigger machines, entailing ever bigger concentrations of economic power and exerting ever greater violence against the environment, do not represent progress: they are a denial of wisdom. Wisdom demands a new orientation of science and technology towards the organic, the gentle, the non-violent, the elegant and beautiful.

About the author

Ernst Friedrich 'Fritz' Schumacher (1911–1977) was an internationally influential economic thinker, with a professional background as a statistician and economist in Britain.

Schumacher was born in Germany in 1911. In the 1930s he went to England as a Rhodes Scholar and was detained there as an enemy alien during World War II. He spent the war working on a farm in the north of England, an experience of common productive labour that played an important role in the formation of his ideas. From 1950 to 1970 he was Chief Economic Advisor to the British Coal Board, one of the world's largest organisations with 800,000 employees. His farsighted planning (he predicted the rise of OPEC and the problems of nuclear power) aided Britain in its economic recovery.

In 1955, while on secondment as Economic Adviser to the Government of Burma, Schumacher first became interested in the problems of developing countries and developed his vision of 'Buddhist Economics', based on simplicity and non-violence, the importance of community, and the necessity and dignity of work.

Schumacher wrote three books, of which *Small Is Beautiful* was the flagship, as well as being a featured writer for *Resurgence* magazine. He founded the Intermediate Technology Development Group, now called Practical Action, in 1966 to demonstrate and advocate the sustainable use of technology to reduce poverty in developing countries.

Courtesy of Barbara Wood

OTHER BOOKS

A Guide for the Perplexed (Harper & Row, 1977)

Good Work (HarperCollins, 1979)

MORE INFORMATION

E.F. Schumacher Society UK:
www.schumacher.org.uk

8

Gaia
James Lovelock

1st edn
**Gaia: A New Look
at Life on Earth**
Oxford University Press,
1979; 168pp, hbk;
978-0192860309

Current edn
**Gaia: A New Look
at Life on Earth**
Oxford University Press,
2000; 176pp, pbk;
978-0192862181

Key ideas

▶ The Earth's biosphere, atmosphere, oceans and soil form a self-regulating system with the capacity to keep the planet healthy by controlling the chemical and physical environment.

▶ This self-regulating Earth system, which acts like a living organism, is nicknamed Gaia, after the Greek goddess of the Earth.

▶ Gaia is dynamic, acting like a feedback or cybernetic system which seeks an optimal set of conditions for life on this planet.

▶ The Gaia postulate is a theory or hypothesis, which provides a scientific underpinning for the interconnectedness of life on Earth.

▶ Since Gaia responds to external influences, it can be said to embody a form of intelligence.

Synopsis

Gaia, written in a style that combines scientific research with metaphysical musings, is the elaboration of a theory or hypothesis conceived by Lovelock, together with Lynn Margulis. Essentially, it postulates that the physical and chemical condition of the surface of the Earth, of the atmosphere, and of the oceans has been and is actively made fit and comfortable by the presence of life itself. This is in contrast to the conventional wisdom, which holds that life adapted to the planetary conditions as it and they evolved their separate ways.

Lovelock named his theory the Gaia Hypothesis – after the Greek Earth goddess – following a suggestion by William Golding, author of *Lord of the Flies* and a friend of Lovelock. The theory had its scientific roots in work Lovelock did for NASA trying to 'prove' whether Mars could sustain life. To help illustrate his findings, he developed 'Daisyworld', a computerised 'drastic simplification' of the Gaia Hypothesis. Daisyworld is a hypothetical planet inhabited only by light and dark daisies. The two kinds of daisies unwittingly cooperate to keep the temperature of the planet more constant than it would otherwise be.

Lovelock explains that the Earth, unlike Mars, is in a state of constant chemical flow or exchange. Despite these fluctuations, we see certain overall conditions remaining fairly constant. For example, the global surface temperature of the Earth has remained constant, despite an increase in the energy provided by the sun. Similarly, atmospheric composition remains constant, even though it should be unstable, and ocean salinity is constant. Lovelock concludes that the biosphere must actively modulate the chemical make-up, temperature, pH and other attributes of the Earth system in order to maintain conditions under which life can flourish.

Lovelock calls Gaia a physiological system because it has the unconscious goal of regulating the climate and the chemistry at a comfortable level for life. The scientific term for this phenomenon is 'homeostasis', meaning the maintenance of relatively constant conditions by active control. In terms of this system, some regulatory functions are more important than others. Or, to use the body metaphor, 'Gaia has vital organs at the core, as well as expendable ones or redundant ones on the periphery'. Hence, our impact on the planet may depend greatly not just on *what* we do, but *where* we do it.

Another key feature of the system is the way it responds to change. The strength of feedback loops and the timescale of change are important factors. For example, the regulation of oxygen has a timescale measured in thousands of years. Such slow processes give the least warning of undesirable trends. By the time it is realised that all is not well and action is undertaken, inertial drag will bring things to a worse state before an equally slow improvement can set in.

Lovelock concludes that the Gaia Hypothesis 'is an alternative to that pessimistic view which sees nature as a primitive force to be subdued and conquered. It is also an alternative to that equally depressing picture of our planet as a demented spaceship, forever travelling, driverless and purposeless, around an inner circle of the sun.'

From the book

- Is it too much to suggest that we may recognize . . . the beauty and fittingness of an environment created by an assembly of creatures?

- If Gaia exists, the relationship between her and man, a dominant animal species in the complex living system, and the possibly shifting balance of power between them, are questions of obvious importance.

- The entire range of living matter on Earth, from whales to viruses, and from oaks to algae, could be regarded as constituting a single living entity, capable of manipulating the Earth's atmosphere to suit its overall needs and endowed with faculties and powers far beyond those of its constituent parts.

- As things are, our ignorance of the possible consequences of our actions is so great that useful predictions of the future are almost ruled out.

- According to the Gaia Hypothesis, we are parts of a greater whole. Our destiny is not dependent merely on what we do for ourselves but also on what we do for Gaia as a whole. If we endanger her, she will dispense with us in the interests of a higher value – life itself (from a speech by Vaclav Havel, former president of the Czech Republic, upon accepting the Liberty Medal in the US in July 1994).

About the author

James Lovelock (born 1919) is an independent scientist, environmentalist, author and researcher and an influential figure in the history of the environmental movement.

Lovelock was born on 26 July 1919 in Letchworth Garden City in the UK. He graduated as a chemist from Manchester University in 1941 and in 1948 received a PhD in medicine from the London School of Hygiene and Tropical Medicine. In 1959 he received a DSc degree in biophysics from London University. In the United States he has taught at Yale, the Baylor University College of Medicine, and at Harvard University. He also holds honorary doctorates from several universities throughout the world.

Among Lovelock's early scientific work was for the Jet Propulsion Laboratory on Lunar and Planetary Research. Since 1964 he has conducted an independent practice in science, although continuing honorary academic associations as a visiting professor, first at the University of Houston and then at the University of Reading in the UK. Since 1982 he has been associated with the Marine Biological Association at Plymouth, first as a council member, and from 1986 to 1990 as its president.

Most famously, Lovelock is the originator of the Gaia Hypothesis (now Gaia Theory) and has written five books on the subject. He is at present an Honorary Visiting Fellow of

Green College, Oxford University, and was awarded a CBE (Commander of the Order of the British Empire) in 1990.

In his own words
(2008 interview)

Reflections on the book

The models I've made and the Earth's history suggest strongly that Gaia should be regarded as a living system. I know biologists hate this, and so do Earth scientists, but it's a good metaphor to use about the Earth.

[The Earth is] a system which always hones in on habitability or, if you like, sustainability.

The Gaia theory has now had over ten tests and they all either come out positive or there's no falsification.

The role of business

I think ever since Karl Marx . . . we've had this idea that we can blame industry for all of our problems.

One tends to forget it's not the oil companies that drive our cars; we drive them and burn the fuel. We don't have to do it, and to entirely blame industry for making a profit from selling us petrol is quite naive. The whole of society is in the game together and to single out industry for attack is quite wrong.

Looking to the future

Living things, when threatened or stressed, at first resist and the [Earth] system has been doing that for quite a while now. From about the time we started emitting gas into the air and clearing forests and burning down the ecosystems, the temperature didn't change; the atmosphere didn't change – it was all under control by the system. But somewhere around about 1900 we began to go beyond the limit. So now the system is doing the other thing that living things do and fleeing to a safe place that it knows, And the safe place which it's been at many times before is the hot regime where the global temperature is 5 or 6 degrees planet-wide hotter than now. It's a planet that's very hot and dry. There still will be oases . . . but it won't support anything like the current population. I'd be amazed if it can support a billion. I should think 500 million is more likely.

The only chance we've got of reversing global heating is to take on Gaia as an ally. Every year the Earth system pumps down 550 gigatonnes of carbon dioxide by photosynthesis from all the plants. That's huge compared with the emissions that we are making which are 30 gigatonnes. So how can we ask the system to help out a bit? All that you have to do is to, for example, take all agricultural waste and convert it to charcoal . . . If we could take 20% of the total photosynthate that's being used and bury it as charcoal in the land, and at the ocean bottom by doing it with algal farms, then we would be taking out something in the order of 110 gigatonnes of CO_2 per year. Now this is far more than our emissions and enough to start pumping down the greenhouse to more reasonable levels. So there is a way out. There is something we can do.

OTHER BOOKS

The Ages of Gaia: A Biography of Our Living Earth (W.W. Norton, 1988)

Gaia: The Practical Science of Planetary Medicine (Gaia Books, 2000)

Homage to Gaia: The Life of an Independent Scientist (Oxford University Press, 2000)

The Revenge of Gaia: Why the Earth is Fighting Back – and How We Can Still Save Humanity (Basic Books, 2006)

MORE INFORMATION

James Lovelock website:
www.ecolo.org/lovelock

9

The Turning Point
Fritjof Capra

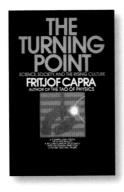

1st edn
**The Turning Point:
Science, Society, and the
Rising Culture**
Simon & Schuster, 1982;
hbk; 978- 0671244231

Current US edn
**The Turning Point:
Science, Society, and the
Rising Culture**
Bantam Books, 1984;
464pp, pbk;
978-0553345728

Current UK edn
The Turning Point
Flamingo, 1983; 540pp,
pbk; 978-0006540175

Key ideas

▶ Our modern thinking has been shaped by the mechanistic traditions of Descartes and Newton and this approach is inadequate to solve today's major world problems.

▶ We need a more holistic, systemic, balanced (Yin/Yang) way of looking at the world, a way that takes into account the interconnectedness of the different disciplines.

▶ The current crisis is a potential opportunity, as history has shown that many great civilisations have arisen from a response to a threat or challenge to the established order.

▶ This will require a paradigm shift in our way of thinking, similar to the transformation that physics went through in the 20th century with the developments in quantum physics.

▶ We are already seeing this new systems-based approach emerging in various disciplines, including medicine, psychology, economics, political science and ecology.

Synopsis

The Turning Point, drawing on diverse disciplines but written in a very accessible style, begins by considering the scale and urgency of social, ecological and economic crises faced by the world. While these are very diverse challenges, the underlying dynamics are the same. This is because the problems are systemic, and any silo-based approach will only shift the problem around within the web of interrelationships. A solution can be found only if the structure of the web itself is changed.

Capra, therefore, calls for systems thinking, which he describes as follows: 'Systems theory looks at the world in terms of the interrelatedness and interdependence of all phenomena, and in this framework an integrated whole whose properties cannot be reduced to those of its parts is called a system. Living organisms, societies, and ecosystems are all systems.'

This is in stark contrast to the increasingly unhelpful mechanistic Cartesian–Newtonian world-view that we have inherited from centuries past. For example, Descartes' emphasis on the rational mind, and the division between mind and matter has created a sense of separation between mind and body and between people and their environment. This has resulted in the exploitation of nature and of women who have historically always been associated with nature.

The book then sets out to synthesise the emergence of systems thinking in various fields and disciplines. The legacy of the '60s and '70s is a wide variety of social movements that all seem to go in the same direction but are to date unconnected. For example, we see a move from the biomedical model to wholeness and health, from Newtonian psychology to an 'ecology of the mind' and from destructive growth economics to a more human-scale and environmentally sensitive form of development.

Taken together, Capra believes we are witnessing three major social transitions:

1. The decline of patriarchy;

2. The decline of the fossil-fuel age; and

3. A paradigm shift away from the beliefs and values that have influenced Western society over the last centuries.

The Western beliefs and values referred to include: the belief in the scientific method as the only valid approach to knowledge; the view of the universe as a mechanical system composed of elementary material building blocks; the view of life in society as a competitive struggle for existence; and the belief in unlimited material progress to be achieved through economic and technological growth.

According to Capra, we need 'a deep re-examination of the main premises and values of our culture, a rejection of those conceptual models that have outlived their usefulness, and a new recognition of some of the values discarded in previous periods of our cultural history'. He contrasts this with Marxism, which believes the roots of social evolution lie in economic and technological developments, not in changes in values and beliefs. Rather, we need 'a profound modification of most social relationships and forms of social organization – by changes that will go far beyond the superficial measures of economic and political readjustment being considered by today's political leaders'.

From the book

- The major problems of our time are all different facets of one and the same crisis, which is essentially a crisis of perception. Like the crisis in physics in the 1920s, it derives from the fact that we are trying to apply the concepts of an outdated world view – the mechanistic world view of Cartesian–Newtonian science – to a reality that can no longer be understood in terms of these concepts.

- These problems are systemic problems, which means that they are closely interconnected and interdependent. A resolution can be found only if the structure of the web itself is changed, and this will involve profound transformations of our social institutions, values, and ideas.

- The current crisis, therefore, is not just a crisis of individuals, governments, or social institutions; it is a transition of planetary dimensions. As individuals, as a society, as a civilization, and as a planetary ecosystem, we are reaching the turning point.

- One of the most difficult things for people in our culture to understand is the fact that if you do something that is good, then more of the same will not necessarily be better. This, to me, is the essence of ecological thinking.

- Ecological awareness will arise only when we combine our rational knowledge with an intuition for the nonlinear nature of our environment.

About the author

Fritjof Capra (born 1939) is a physicist, systems theorist and author who has been at the forefront of 'new paradigm' thinking in society for several decades.

After receiving his PhD in theoretical physics from the University of Vienna in 1966, Capra did research in particle physics at the University of Paris (1966–68), the University of California at Santa Cruz (1968–70), the Stanford Linear Accelerator Center (1970), Imperial College, University of London (1971–74), and the Lawrence Berkeley Laboratory at the University of California

(1975–88). He also taught at UC Santa Cruz, UC Berkeley, and San Francisco State University.

In addition to his research in physics and systems theory, Capra has been engaged in a systematic examination of the philosophical and social implications of contemporary science for the past 30 years. His books and films on this subject – most famously, the million-selling *Tao of Physics* and film *Mindwalk* – have been acclaimed internationally, and he has lectured widely to lay and professional audiences in Europe, Asia, and North and South America.

Capra has been the focus of over 50 television interviews, documentaries and talk shows in Europe, the United States, Brazil, Argentina and Japan, and has been featured in major newspapers and magazines internationally. Capra is also founding director of the Center for Ecoliteracy in Berkeley, California, which promotes ecology and systems thinking in primary and secondary education; he is on the faculty of Schumacher College, an international centre for ecological studies in England.

Photo: Karl Grossman

In his own words
(2008 interview)

Reflections on the book

Since I published *The Turning Point* it has been a rocky ride, and the vision I expressed in the book was not realised. And I think I can see now why. At the end of the 1980s, I believed that we were really on the cusp of this change. Public awareness was really going towards ecology and sustainability, and I thought that by the beginning of the '90s things would really change dramatically. Well they didn't, because what happened in the 1990s was the information technology revolution. And I believe now that this technology and this new economy introduced a new materialism and sidelined the awareness. It was not lost but it got eclipsed by the fascination with this technology. And now we are coming back, so it has taken us more than ten years to make this detour.

The role of business

What we really have is an electronic global casino where people bet all the time. The rules that facilitate this free flow of money are the so-called free trade rules, and underlying them is a principle which is the quintessential principle of capitalism, namely that making money should always be more important than any other human value. So when there is a choice to be made between making more money or protecting human rights, the natural environment, democracy, health and so on, the choice automatically goes towards making money.

At present, to be an exemplary company working toward sustainability takes a lot of ingenuity and takes a lot of courage. It is not easy, because sustainability is always a property of a community within a larger context. And so if you don't live in a sustainable environment it's very hard to be sustainable yourself.

The dramatic change will come once we change our economic system, and especially our tax system, to further sustainability. Then it will be easy to strive for sustainability; now it's difficult.

I think there are two kinds of leadership. One is a traditional leader, like Mandela, who has the vision, who has charisma, who can articulate the vision, who can embody it with his own personal behaviour. The other kind of leader, which is very interesting from the systemic point of view, is a person who can facilitate change, who does not lead with ideas, but who provides an environment in which this change can happen, in which this spontaneous emergence can occur.

Looking to the future

I think now we are, in terms of public awareness and values and also awareness in business, about where we were at the end of the 1980s; but there are several differences: we know that the environmental pressure is extremely strong, we know that things have to change dramatically, and we also have the means. In the meantime we have had the growth of civil society; [and] the awareness in politics I think is stronger than it was. So things have changed quite a bit.

OTHER BOOKS (SELECTION)

The Tao of Physics (Shambhala, 1976)

Uncommon Wisdom: Conversations with Remarkable People (Simon & Schuster, 1988)

The Web of Life: A New Scientific Understanding of Living Systems (Anchor Books, 1996)

The Hidden Connections: Science for Sustainable Living (HarperCollins, 2002)

The Science of Leonardo: Inside the Mind of the Great Genius of the Renaissance (Doubleday, 2008)

MORE INFORMATION

Fritjof Capra website:
www.fritjofcapra.net

10
Our Common Future
('The Brundtland Report')
World Commission on Environment and Development

1st and current edn
Our Common Future
Oxford Paperbacks,
1987; 400pp, pbk;
978-0192820808

Key ideas

► Present trends are unsustainable and must be reversed if we are to 'secure the resources to sustain this and coming generations'.

► In particular, unmanaged and unlimited economic growth is not possible on an ecologically stressed planet.

► Despite the challenges, people can build a future that is more prosperous, more just and more secure.

► The goal is sustainable development, which is 'development that meets the needs of the present without compromising the ability of future generations to meet their own needs'.

► In order to achieve sustainable development, we need strong political will and international commitment to common goals for the future.

Synopsis

Our Common Future (also known as 'The Brundtland Report') is the report of the UN World Commission on Environment and Development, chaired by former Prime Minister of Norway, Gro Harlem Brundtland. It focuses on meeting human needs, by securing global equity for current and future generations through the redistribution of resources towards poorer nations and environmental conservation.

The report was one of the first comprehensive assessments of both the social, environmental and economic problems facing the world and of policy solutions that may help to address these challenges. Despite the severity and urgency of the problems, the report is fairly upbeat in its tone, suggesting that social equity, economic growth and environmental maintenance are simultaneously possible. Hence, each nation is capable of achieving its full economic potential, while at the same time enhancing its resource base. Achieving this equity and sustainable growth, however, will require technological and social change.

Apart from the now ubiquitous definition of sustainable development, *Our Common Future* also introduces the three fundamental components of sustainability – environment, economy and society – and highlights what is needed in each area to achieve sustainable development:

- *Environmental conservation*: we should conserve and enhance our resource base, by gradually changing the ways in which we develop and use techno.ogies;
- *Social equity*: developing nations must be allowed to meet the basic needs of employment, food, energy, water and sanitation; and
- *Economic growth*: economic growth should be revived and developing nations should be allowed a growth of equal quality to the developed nations.

The report makes it clear that we cannot achieve success in one of these three areas at the expense of the others. And, while it acknowledges a number of clear developmental successes, it also points to the growing number of failures driven by the developmental 'trends that the planet and its people cannot long bear'. It also lists the 'environmental trends that threaten to radically alter the planet, that threaten the lives of many species upon it, including the human species'.

The report recommends urgent action on eight key issues: population and human resources; industry; food security; species and ecosystems; urbanisation; managing the commons; energy; and conflict and environmental degradation. The primary target audience is global and national political institutions. Solving the sustainability challenges requires cross-silo thinking, which goes against the way most political institutions operate, both at a national and international level. The Commission calls this the 'Institutional Gap'.

In terms of the role of industry, the report states that growth must be coupled with higher productivity, increased efficiency and decreased pollution, as a five- to ten-fold output in manufacturing output will be needed to meet the needs of the growing population. Furthermore, in all international economic exchanges, the sustainability of ecosystems must be guaranteed and the economic partners must be satisfied that the basis of exchange is equitable.

The UN Conference on Environment and Development held in Rio De Janeiro in 1992 (and nicknamed the 'Earth Summit') was a direct outcome of the Brundtland Report.

From the book

- The Earth is one but the world is not. We all depend on one biosphere for sustaining our lives. Yet each community, each country, strives for survival and prosperity with little regard for its impact on others.

- We came to see development not in its restricted context of economic growth in developing countries. We came to see that a new development path was required, one that sustained human progress not just in a few places for a few years, but for the entire planet into the distant future.

- The concept of sustainable development does imply limits – not absolute limits but limitations imposed by the present state of technology and social organization on environmental resources and by the ability of the biosphere to absorb the effects of human activities.

- We do not pretend that the process is easy or straightforward. Painful choices have to be made. Thus, in the final analysis, sustainable development must rest on political will.

- The arms race – in all parts of the world – pre-empts resources that might be used more productively to diminish the security threats created by environmental conflict and the resentments that are fuelled by widespread poverty.

About the author

Building on the work and recommendations of the 1972 United Nations Conference on the Human Environment (the Stockholm Conference), which had introduced environmental concerns to the formal political development sphere, the **World Commission on Environment and Development** was established in 1984, with members from 21 countries and chaired by Gro Harlem Brundtland. The Commission worked for 900 days to publish its report, *Our Common Future*. The process included public hearings and over 500 written submissions.

The Commission had three objectives:

1. To re-examine the critical environmental and development issues and to formulate realistic proposals for dealing with them;

2. To propose new forms of international cooperation on these issues which will influence policies and events in the direction of needed changes; and

3. To raise the levels of understanding and commitment to action of individuals, voluntary organisations, businesses, institutes and governments.

Gro Harlem Brundtland (born 1939) is a Norwegian politician, diplomat, and physician, and an international leader in sustainable development and public health.

Born in Oslo, Brundtland was educated as a Medical Doctor at the University of Oslo in 1963, and Master of Public Health at Harvard University in 1965. From 1966 to 1969, she worked as a physician at the Directorate of Health in Norway, and from 1969 she worked as a doctor in Oslo's public school health service. She was Norwegian Minister for Environmental Affairs from 1974 to 1979, and became Norway's first – and to date only – female Prime Minister. She served for three terms as Prime Minister in 1981, 1986–89 and 1990–96.

In 1983, Brundtland was invited by then United Nations Secretary-General Javier Pérez de Cuéllar to establish and chair the World Commission on Environment and Development (WCED), which produced its groundbreaking report *Our Common Future* in 1987. She also served as the Director General of the World Health Organization (1998–2003) and in 2006 was a member of the Panel of Eminent Persons who reviewed the work of UNCTAD (United Nations Conference on Trade and Development).

Brundtland now serves as a Special Envoy on Climate Change for the United Nations Secretary-General Ban Ki-moon. She also sits on the Health & Wellness Advisory Board of Pepsico and is a member of the Council of Women World Leaders.

MORE INFORMATION

Our Common Future (The Brundtland Report):
www.un-documents.net/wced-ocf.htm

UN Commission on Sustainable Development:
www.un.org/esa/sustdev

11
The Dream of the Earth
Thomas Berry

1st edn
The Dream of the Earth
Sierra Club Books, 1988; 247pp, hbk; 978-0871567376

Current UK edn
The Dream of the Earth
University of California Press, 1990; 264pp, pbk; 978-0871566225

Current US edn
The Dream of the Earth
Sierra Club Books, 2006; 264pp, pbk, 2nd rev. edn; 978-1578051359

Key ideas

- ▶ Societies are shaped by their dreams and stories, i.e. the world-view and visions of progress that they have created and adopted.

- ▶ Our current Western society is based on an outdated story from the Renaissance, which emphasises control over nature.

- ▶ The result of our modern view of progress is the destruction of the Earth and the disintegration of community and all the global crises associated with these.

- ▶ We need a new vision or dream of Earth (a 'biocracy'), which emphasises our interconnectedness and interdependence with nature.

- ▶ If the new world-view is to succeed, it cannot be purely based on scientific-material change, but must incorporate a psycho-spiritual dimension.

Synopsis

The Dream of the Earth is a collection of essays which all advance a deeply spiritual and ecological interpretation of the world, its current woes and potential solutions. Berry believes we understand and interpret the world and our role within it based on our 'story of the universe', our dream or world-view. This story is the source of a society's collective psyche and not only explains the past, but also guides our future. While other animals have their behaviour embedded in their DNA, we humans need stories to find our way and understand what to do.

Berry argues that our Western story was shaped in the Renaissance by Francis Bacon, who saw a vision of a world where we exercise scientific control over nature. This vision was articulated as the doctrine of 'progress' by Bernard de Fontenelle, which was taken up both by capitalism and Marxism. The result is a distorted world-view that has led us in a destructive direction. 'The difficulty of our times,' says Berry, 'is our inability to awaken out of this cultural pathology.'

The underlying theme of the book is that our vision, or dream of progress, has brought a lot of good, but is now sowing the seeds of its own destruction. This is because we have lost our connection to the planet, a connection that has existed since ancient times and today remains only with some indigenous communities. Our story has become corrupted, or empty of deep meaning.

In response, we need to create a new historical vision 'to inspire a new creative period not only in the human community, but also in the functioning of the earth itself'.

According to Berry, such a vision does exist – it is the 'move from democracy to biocracy', whereby nature itself participates in our human decision-making processes. However, to achieve this, we must learn to listen to the planet, to resist the impulse to control and to 'quite humbly follow the guidance of the larger community on which all life depends'.

The ecological movement is an indication of the beginnings of a process to reconnect with the universe and turn away from the focus on the industrial, economic imperative. However, what is needed now is a new story or world-view, and we are currently between stories. The old story is dysfunctional, and the new story has not yet emerged. 'We need a story that will educate us, a story that will heal, guide and discipline us.'

Paradoxically, science is showing us that the purely material view of the world no longer holds true. Empirical enquiry such as quantum physics is showing that the universe carries within itself a psychic-spiritual as well as a physical-material dimension. The new story, Berry argues, will develop in places where science and spirituality can co-exist and 'a new, more integral language of value and being can emerge'.

'A new type of sensitivity is needed,' he says, 'a sensitivity that is something more than romantic attachment to some of the more brilliant manifestations of the natural world, a sensitivity that comprehends the larger patterns of nature, its severe demands as well as its delightful aspects, and is willing to see the human diminish so that other lifeforms might flourish.'

From the book

- The Universe is a communion of subjects, not a collection of objects.

- The deepest crises experienced by any society are those moments of change when the story becomes inadequate for meeting the survival demands of a present situation.

- Our secular, rational, industrial society, with its amazing scientific insight and technological skills, has established the first radically anthropocentric society and has thereby broken the primary law of the universe, the law of the integrity of the universe, the law that every component member of the universe should be integral with every other member of the universe and that the primary norm of reality and of value is the universe community itself in its various forms of expression, especially as realised on the planet earth.

- By a supreme irony this closing down of the basic life systems of the earth has resulted from a commitment to the betterment of the human condition, to 'progress'.

- Suddenly we awaken to the devastation that has resulted from the entire modern process . . . In relation to the earth, we have been autistic for centuries. Only now have we begun to listen with some attention and with a willingness to respond to the earth's demands . . .

- If the supreme disaster in the comprehensive story of the earth is our present closing down of the major life systems of the planet, then the supreme need of our times is to bring about a healing of the earth through this mutually enhancing human presence to the earth community.

- The time has come to lower our voices, to cease imposing our mechanistic patterns on the biological processes of the earth, to resist the impulse to control, to command, to force, to oppress, and to begin quite humbly to follow the guidance of the larger community on which our life depends.

About the author

Thomas Berry (1914–2009) was a Catholic priest of the Passionist order, as well as a cultural historian and eco-theologian.

Berry was born in Greensboro, North Carolina, and from his academic beginnings as a historian of world cultures and religions, he developed into a historian of the Earth and its evolutionary processes. He described himself as a 'geologian' or Earth scholar.

Berry received his PhD in European Intellectual History with a thesis on Giambattista Vico's philosophy of history. Widely read in Western history, he also spent many years studying the cultural history of Asia. He lived in China and travelled to other parts of Asia, authoring two books on Asian religions (*Buddhism* and *Religions of India*).

Among advocates of deep ecology and 'ecospirituality', he is known for proposing that a deep understanding of the history and functioning of the evolving universe is a necessary inspiration and guide for our own effective functioning as individuals and as a species. He was also considered a leader in the tradition of the French philosopher and Jesuit priest Teilhard de Chardin.

For two decades, he directed the Riverdale Center of Religious Research along the Hudson River. During this period he taught at Fordham University where he chaired the history of religions programme and directed 25 doctoral theses.

OTHER BOOKS

The Universe Story (with Brian Swimme; Harper San Francisco, 1992)

MORE INFORMATION

The Earth Community:
www.earth-community.org

12

A Fate Worse Than Debt

Susan George

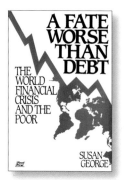

1st edn
**A Fate Worse
Than Debt:**
**The World Financial
Crisis and the Poor**
Grove Press, 1988;
292pp, hbk;
978-0802110152

Current US edn
**A Fate Worse
Than Debt:**
**The World Financial
Crisis and the Poor**
Grove Press, 1989;
300pp, pbk, rev. edn;
978-0802131218

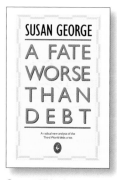

Current UK edn
**A Fate Worse
Than Debt:**
**A Radical New Analysis
of the Third World Debt
Crisis**
Penguin Books, 1994;
336pp, pbk;
978-0140135701

Key ideas

▶ The world-view of international banks and political leaders has resulted in a system of Third World debt that has had disastrous social and ecological consequences.

▶ In most cases, the wealthy elite (international banks and national political leaders) reap the benefits of Third World debt, while the poor suffer the consequences.

▶ The crisis is now such that even a healthy developing economy in Latin America or Africa can not escape its debt burden.

▶ The conditions attached to Third World debt, especially in the form of structural adjustment programmes, are resulting in increased poverty and 'ecocide'.

▶ The way out of the Third World debt problem is to link debt relief, development and democracy, as solutions to these go hand in hand.

Synopsis

A Fate Worse Than Debt is a polemic that is unapologetically confrontational, drawing heavily on personal accounts of suffering and outrage from people living in Third World countries. George describes the numerous negative consequences of the lending boom to developing countries, especially by the World Bank and IMF, that resulted from recycled 'petro-dollars' after the oil price hikes in the 1970s.

Rather than seeing the Third World debt crisis as a deliberate First World conspiracy, the book emphasises the unitary worldview of the lenders 'Consortium' – the informal financial-political club of big banks, creditor-country governments and their central banks, the World Bank and the IMF. These institutions 'don't have to conspire if they have the same worldview, aspire to similar goals and take concerted steps to attain them'.

The Consortium promotes a model of development that is geared towards growth for its own sake, placing industrialisation ahead of agriculture, and thereby creating food security problems. This model – which George calls the 'mal-development model' – ignores the interests of all but a small elite in developing states and is outward-looking, resulting in militarisation and hunger.

Not only are poor countries hooked into the trap of crippling debt repayments, the capital is often spent on badly costed, badly planned and corrupt construction projects. Or, even worse, it is sucked out of the country and invested abroad by political elites, or spent on destabilising military crusades. Meanwhile, world oil prices and interest rates remain outside the control of Third World countries and increase the burden of debt.

George is particularly critical of the loan conditions imposed by the IMF (most often under so-called 'structural adjustment programmes'), which amount to international interference with national economic policies. These conditions usually result in a cut in government services (such as health, education and environmental protection), a fall in the cost of labour, thus further 'weakening the weak' and wholesale environmental destruction or 'ecocide', as governments are forced to plunder their natural resources to keep up with export-led growth and payment requirements, while at the same time being encouraged to invest in large, damaging infrastructure projects.

George does not believe debt should be cancelled. Unconditional write-offs would reward the despotic leaders, penalising the more prudent countries and leaders. It would also give the West a perfect excuse to cut off all aid, and would drop the creditworthiness of debtor countries to zero. Rather, she proposes a 3-D (debt, development and democracy) solution: a combination of enlightened repayment policies linked to strategic investment and controlled import–export schemes with the West. Hence, debt could be used to promote democracy and real development.

The hope lies in Third World social and political creativity, through grassroots movements that can provide new impetus to debt relief, economic development and democracy efforts. George closes the book with a call to reject inertia, arguing that Third World debt is an international problem that affects us all and will impose an unacceptable burden on future generations.

From the book

- Economic policies are not neutral. Contrary to received opinion, they can even kill.

- The IMF cannot seem to understand that investing in . . . [a] healthy, well-fed, literate population . . . is the most intelligent economic choice a country can make.

- When the IMF imposes government cuts, environmental programmes are among the first to go, and all natural resources, not just forests, are cashed in to pay off the interest.

- [The IMF's] doctrine is now creating perverse effects beyond anything imaginable a few years ago. IMF rigidity may bring ruin to an entire continent, and for years to come.

- Just as war is too important to be left to generals, so the debt crisis is too serious to be left to financiers and economists.

About the author

Susan George (born 1934) is a political scientist and author of numerous books on Third World poverty, underdevelopment and debt.

George's academic degrees are in French/Government, Philosophy and Political Studies. Her current work concerns various aspects of neoliberal globalisation, particularly the World Trade Organisation (WTO), international financial institutions and North–South relations. George helped to lead the campaign in France to defeat the Multilateral Agreement on Investment (MAI) and is now engaged in the campaign to democratise the WTO, including the movement of 'GATS-Free Zones' to which over 1,500 local governments in Europe now belong.

From 1990 to 1995 she served on the board of Greenpeace International as well as that of Greenpeace France. Between 1999 and mid-2006 she served as Vice-President of ATTAC France (Association for Taxation of Financial Transaction to Aid Citizens). In January 2007 she received an honorary doctorate from Newcastle University in the UK and in early March the International Studies Association at its Congress in Chicago presented her with its first award to an Outstanding Public Scholar.

George is Chair of the Planning Board of the Transnational Institute in Amsterdam, a decentralised fellowship of scholars living throughout the world whose work is intended to contribute to social justice and who are active in civil society in their own countries.

She has acted as a consultant to various United Nations specialised agencies and is a frequent public speaker, particularly for ATTAC groups, trade unions and environment/development non-governmental organisations in many countries.

In her own words
(2008 interview)

Reflections on the book

What I was doing was bringing out the logic of the trend of managing the world under neoliberal rules. And of course these rules have led to greater ecological destruction, not only in the indebted countries but everywhere. Has it reached a peak? The answer is absolutely not. It wasn't at a peak in the '80s and maybe it isn't even at a peak now, although things are probably somewhat better in Latin America, because they have got out from under the Bank and the Fund in the past two or three years (and that's why the Fund is in crisis).

The Jubilee movement did do some good, but then it lived up to its name: it was called Jubilee 2000 and it stopped in 2000. So there's been a little bit of debt cancelled, but once the pressure was off they stopped cancelling. Sub-Saharan Africa is still paying back between 20,000 and 25,000 dollars every minute in debt service. They have never touched the principal; this is interest and it has not been cancelled. So you can see what you could do with 20,000 dollars every minute, in terms of health, education, reforestation, etc., but it doesn't get done.

The role of the multilateral institutions

The problem with the Third World is that it didn't invest. At least three-quarters of the debt was never invested; it went into armaments, it went into consumption,

Photo: Magali Delporte

purchases of oil and a lot of white-elephant projects of sub-Saharan Africa. More than that: of the loans that went to sub-Saharan Africa, 420 billion dollars since the early 1970s left Africa and was put in private accounts in tax havens. If you add the interest that could have produced, you come up with a figure that's more than 600 billion dollars that was extracted but remains on the books. And 60% of that was sent North in the same year that the loan was made.

The World Bank, between 2005 and 2008, has spent 2.6 billion dollars in projects concerning extraction, that is to say mining and the production of fossil fuels. For the same period, by itself the International Finance Corporation spent 6.6 billion dollars in fossil fuel and extractive projects. The data for the entire group of the World Bank – so-called bank for climate and clean energy – comes to 9.3 billion dollars, which includes a spectacular increase of 165% for the IFC between 2007 and 2008.

Looking to the future

The solution is to cancel the debt to the South, but on the condition that the government, through free and fair and observed elections, has a representative council of its own population that makes the decisions on where the debt savings are to go, and then follows the money using the model of the participatory budgeting system of many cities in Brazil and some regions in Brazil.

These are words to live by: 'All for ourselves, and nothing for other people, seems in every age of the world to have been the vile maxim of the masters of mankind.' That's from Adam Smith's The Wealth of Nations and I think it's true. I think there is unfortunately no level of human suffering that causes policy to change.

What must we do to make capitalism invulnerable in the 21st century? The answer is: either you have to change the system, or have far fewer people on Earth.

OTHER BOOKS (SELECTION)

How the Other Half Dies: The Real Reasons for World Hunger (Allanheld, Osmun, 1977)

The Debt Boomerang: How Third World Debt Harms Us All (University of Michigan Press, 1991)

Faith and Credit: The World Bank's Secular Empire (with Fabrizio Sabelli; Westview Press, 1994)

The Lugano Report: On Preserving Capitalism in the Twenty-first Century (Pluto Press, 2003)

Another World is Possible If . . . (Verso, 2004)

MORE INFORMATION

Transnational Institute:
www.tni.org

13
Staying Alive
Vandana Shiva

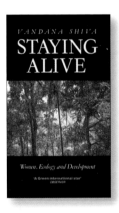

1st edn
Staying Alive:
Women, Ecology and
Development
Zed Books, 1989;
244pp, hbk;
978-0862328221

Current US edn
Staying Alive:
Women, Ecology and
Development
Zed Books, 2001;
240pp, pbk, repr. edn;
978-0862328238

Current UK edn
Staying Alive:
Women, Ecology and
Development
Zed Books, 2009;
272pp, pbk, rev. edn;
978-1848133990

Key ideas

▶ The impact of the Western mode of science, technology and politics, along with the workings of the economy itself, are inherently exploitative.

▶ The degradation of nature and the violation and marginalisation of women are linked, especially in the Third World, as both arise from Western assumptions of economic development.

▶ The dismissal by Western science of the feminine knowledge of agriculture has undermined women as experts, leading to ecological destruction and economic devastation in rural areas.

▶ The path to survival and liberation for nature, women and men is the ecological path of harmony, sustainability and diversity.

▶ The much-needed new holistic world-view is already in evidence in the grassroots environmental and women's movements in places like India.

Cross Culture - Feminine vs Masculine Societies Approach

Synopsis

Staying Alive is an unusual yet compelling mixture of Hindu mythology and scientific data. It traces the historical and conceptual roots of development as a project of gender ideology, and analyses how the particular economic assumptions of Western patriarchy, aimed exclusively at profits, have subjugated the more humane assumptions of economics as the provision of sustenance, to make for a crisis of poverty rooted in ecological devastation.

Shiva, herself a trained scientist, confronts the myth of the neutrality and universality of modern science. She traces its beginnings in the scientific revolution which, on the one hand, subjugated nature, and on the other excluded women as knowers and experts. The structure and methodology of modern science are argued to be reductionist and biased towards a patriarchal mode of knowing that is necessarily violent to nature and women.

By contrast, the survival of the world depends on the rise of ecological grassroots movements based on feminine principles. The book describes the world that Indian women inhabit, both philosophically as a world-view, and in their daily practice, in the production and renewal of life. For the women who are leading ecological struggles, the nature they protect is the living goddess, Prakriti. It is the awareness of nature as a living force, and of themselves as partners with her in the production of sustenance, that guides their ecological struggles.

Shiva goes on to trace the destruction of forests and women's expertise in forestry after the colonisation of India's forests. She shows how what is called 'scientific forestry' is actually a narrow, reductionist view of forestry that has evolved from the Western bias for maximisation of profits. Chipko, the famous movement of the peasant women of Garhwal, is showcased as an alternative, which aims at recovering the diversity of forests and sharing the wealth that they produce.

The book also analyses the food crisis in the world, suggesting that it is rooted in male-dominated agricultural science and development which have destroyed nature's capital and excluded women as experts and producers of food. The violence inherent in the Green Revolution for food crops and the White Revolution for dairying, is shown as linked to shifts in the perception of food to become a commodity, produced and exchanged for profit.

Linked to food is the water crisis, which is threatening the survival of plant, animal and human life on a cataclysmic scale. Once again, this is argued to be related to land and water use for profit, such that limited water resources are over-exploited or diverted from survival needs to the imperative of profit maximisation. The reductionist view of water and water management is contrasted with the holistic knowledge women have for conserving and using it for survival.

Finally, Shiva posits the reclaiming of the feminine principle as a non-violent, non-gendered and humanly inclusive alternative, concluding that 'recapturing the feminine principle as respect for life in nature and society appears to be the only way forward'.

From the book

- The act of living and of celebrating and conserving life in all its diversity – in people and in nature – seems to have been sacrificed to progress, and the sanctity of life been substituted by the sanctity of science and development.

- With the destruction of forests, water and land, we are losing our life-support systems. This destruction is taking place in the name of 'development' and progress, but there must be something seriously wrong with a concept of progress that threatens survival itself.

- The violence to nature, which seems intrinsic to the dominant development model, is also associated with violence to women who depend on nature for drawing sustenance for themselves, their families, their societies.

- Industrialism created a limitless appetite for resource exploitation, and modem science provided the ethical and cognitive license to make such exploitation possible, acceptable, and desirable.

- Ecological movements are political movements for a non-violent world order in which nature is conserved for conserving the options for survival. These movements are small, but they are growing. They are local, but their success lies in non-local impact. They demand only the right to survival yet with that minimal demand is associated the right to live in a peaceful and just world. With the success of these grassroots movements is linked the global issue of survival.

About the author

Vandana Shiva (born 1952) is a world-renowned thought-leader and activist in the women's, environmental and development movements. She is Director of the Research Foundation on Science, Technology, and Ecology.

Born in India, Shiva became one of India's leading physicists, holding a master's degree in the philosophy of science and a PhD in particle physics. As founder of Navdanya ('nine seeds'), a movement promoting diversity and use of native seeds, in 1993, Shiva won the Alternative Nobel Peace Prize (the Right Livelihood Award).

In 1997, Shiva set up the Research Foundation for Science, Technology, and Ecology. Its studies have validated the ecological value of traditional farming and been instrumental in fighting destructive development projects in India. In 1999, she addressed the World Trade Organisation summit in Seattle, and in 2000 the World Economic Forum in Melbourne.

Shiva is a leader in the International Forum on Globalisation, along with Ralph Nader and Jeremy Rifkin. She is also the author of many books that challenge modern conceptions and institutions of science, economics and development.

In her own words
(2008 interview)

Reflections on the book

At that time in the late '70s and early '80s, I had been deeply involved first in the Chipko movement – the movement Chamolian communities implemented to protect the forest by hugging trees. *Chipko* means 'hug'. And there are insights that come from communities and lots of insights from women that really provide the light on an issue. I wanted to tell that story.

The real trigger came in 1985, at the United Nations Women's Conference: me and Wangari Maathai were asked to do a number of speeches. And my publisher said, 'You've got to write this story of the connection between the fact that the same world-views, the same perspectives, the same processes that lead to domination over nature, lead to domination over women.' So I ended up writing *Staying Alive*.

The role of business

I am not anti-business; in fact, I am under compulsion to create a fair system, a fair economy. I am not against trade, we just want fairness in it.

I am totally against monopolies in the economy. And I think any honest businessman should be against monopolies. In fact, the very language of international trade is about competitiveness. Now, how on earth can you have competitiveness if one company is controlling the seed supply of the world, five companies are controlling the grain trade of the world, and five companies would love to control the water supply of the world? That, to me, is about another game and I have called it economic dictatorship.

I do not think corporations should be resisting regulation, if they really want to be socially responsible. A genuine authentic corporate social responsibility has to be provided by enlightened citizens and an active democratic society. They can't be voluntary programmes of the industry itself, because then it ends up very often being 'greenwash'.

Looking to the future

These millions of movements emerging on their own – I think that is so promising. But the forces that are dominating are the force of greed and the force of untrammelled, unbridled power. This is really about new global empires and they are unleashing a very, very brutal, violent backlash against democratic forces and we experience it daily in my country. That is our challenge. Our challenge is to make it through peacefully, to make it through non-violently, to make it through joyfully and not allow this closure to happen.

The biggest thing that gives me hope and inspiration is really just a very deep awareness of being part of an amazing universe. The second thing that gives me huge hope is engaging in positive action, with communities and people: every seed we save, every new farmer who goes organic, every time a new food product is brought by a local community, a good nutritious healthy ecological product – and that happens daily. It is such an experience of hope and optimism.

OTHER BOOKS

Monocultures of the Mind: Perspectives on Biodiversity and Biotechnology (Zed Books, 1993)

Stolen Harvest: The Hijacking of the Global Food Supply (South End Press, 1999)

Water Wars: Pollution, Profits, and Privatization (South End Press, 2001)

Earth Democracy: Justice, Sustainability and Peace (South End Press, 2005)

Soil Not Oil: Environmental Justice in an Age of Climate Crisis (South End Press, 2008)

MORE INFORMATION

Navdanya: Research Foundation for Science, Technology and Ecology (RFSTE): www.navdanya.org

Vandana Shiva (US website): www.vandanashiva.org

14
Blueprint for a Green Economy
David Pearce, Anil Markandya and Edward B. Barbier

1st and current edn
**Blueprint for a
Green Economy**
Earthscan Publications,
1989; pbk;
978-1853830662

Key ideas

▶ There are good economic reasons (in addition to environmental reasons) to integrate the environment into economic decision-making.

▶ There are various ways in which the environment can be economically valued and, conversely, environmental pollution and other impacts can be economically 'costed'.

▶ If environmental assets and services are not assigned an economic value, they get a value of zero by default in policy and investment decision-making.

▶ Governments can use economic instruments (such as taxation) to reduce pollution and generate revenue to clean up much of the damage.

▶ Sustainable development means valuing the environment, social equity and the future.

Synopsis

Blueprint for a Green Economy (also popularly known as *The Pearce Report*) was prepared by the London Environmental Economics Centre (LEEC) for the UK Department of the Environment. Given their mandate, the book is necessarily (and refreshingly) policy-focused, translating academic insights from the emerging discipline of environmental economics into accessible language and practical recommendations.

Blueprint seeks to answer two questions: (1) Does economics throw light on the meaning of sustainable development? (Answer: Yes, because the environment and the economy necessarily interact); and (2) Is sustainable development feasible? (Answer: Yes, but it requires a shift in the way economic progress is pursued).

If the answers to these questions are indeed positive, this has implications for the way we manage a modern economy, especially: how we record economic progress; how we appraise projects; the pricing and incentive structure; the way we weigh up gains and losses between the present and the future, including intergenerational impacts; and the policy decisions we make.

The authors offer a useful translation of sustainable development into an economics perspective, to mean 'a change in consumption patterns towards environmentally more benign products, and a change in investment patterns towards augmenting environmental capital'. However, they also suggest a broader definition, including the three elements of environment, futurity and equity:

- *Environment*: a substantially increased emphasis on the value of the natural, built and cultural environments;

- *Futurity*: a concern both with the short- to medium-term horizons (5–10 years) and with the longer-term future; and

- *Equity*: emphasis on providing for the needs of the least advantaged (intragenerational equity) and on fair treatment of future generations (intergenerational equity)

Blueprint's most pervasive theme is that, in order to integrate the environment into economic decisions, the environment needs to be assigned economic values, and these need to be taken into account in economic policy planning. The authors argue that, even though it is not possible to put an exact value on the environment, it is necessary to attempt this because it shows that environmental services are not free and it forces us to think in a rational manner about the gains and losses involved.

If we don't value the environment, we could end up trading off financial capital gains with environmental capital losses. However, this is a shortsighted approach, since many environmental functions are not substitutable once they are lost (or it is prohibitively expensive to find substitutes). Also, we may be affecting the overall resilience of the ecosystem, on which economies depend. Rather, we should be adopting a precautionary approach, which ensures 'constant natural capital'.

Translated into economic jargon, the authors define sustainable economic value as 'Total Economic Value' which takes into account actual use values, plus future (or option) values. The latter is the value of the environment as a potential benefit, as opposed to actual present value. This can result in a willingness to pay for the preservation of an environment against some probability that the individual (or society, or future generations) will make use of it later.

From the book

- Environment and economies are not distinct. Treating them as if they were is the surest recipe for unsustainable development.

- There is an interdependence, both because the way we manage the economy impacts on the environment and because environmental quality impacts on the performance of the economy.

- Prices should reflect the true social costs of production and use. Essentially, this means getting the true values of environmental services reflected in prices, rather than having them treated as 'free' goods.

- The prescription is to leave to future generations a wealth inheritance – a stock of knowledge and understanding, a stock of technology, a stock of man-made capital and a stock of environmental assets – no less than that inherited by the current generation.

- If one generation leaves the next generation with less wealth then it has made the future worse off. But sustainable development is about making people better off.

Courtesy of Sue Pearce

David W. Pearce

About the authors

David W. Pearce (1941–2005) is widely regarded as one of the pioneers of environmental economics, having published over 50 books and over 300 academic articles on the subject, including his *Blueprint for a Green Economy* series.

Pearce was born in London and graduated in Politics, Philosophy and Economics from Oxford University in 1963. He held academic posts at the Universities of Lancaster, Southampton, Leicester and Aberdeen before arriving at University College London (UCL) as Professor of Political Economy in 1983, where he later became Emeritus Professor at the Department of Economics.

During his career Pearce was the chief environmental adviser to the UK Secretaries

www.jlarrea.com

Anil Markandya

this field for over 30 years and is acknowledged as one of the leading authorities.

Markandya graduated from the London School of Economics with a Master of Science in Econometrics in 1968 and was awarded his PhD on the Economics of the Environment in 1974. He has held academic positions at the Universities of Princeton, Berkeley and Harvard in the US and at University College London and Bath University in the UK. He holds a chair of economics at the University of Bath in the UK and is a programme leader for the Fondazione Eni Enrico Mattei in International Energy Markets.

Markandya has published widely in the areas of climate change, environmental valuation, environmental policy, energy and environment, green accounting, macroeconomics and trade. He was a lead author for one of the chapters of the *3rd Assessment Report on Climate Change* (2001).

Markandya has been an advisor to many national and international organisations, including all the international development banks, UNDP, the EU and the governments of India and the UK. At the World Bank, he has worked closely with many governments in Central Europe and the Former Soviet Union on Environmental and Energy Policy.

of State between 1989 and 1992. He was a convening lead author of the Intergovernmental Panel on Climate Change and co-director of the environmental economics research centre CSERGE, from 1991 to 2001.

In 1989, Pearce was named in the Global 500 Roll of Honour for Services to the World Environment by the United Nations Environment Programme and in 2000 was awarded an OBE (Officer, Order of the British Empire). He also received a 'Lifetime Achievement Award' in December 2004 from the European Association of Environmental and Resource Economists for his contributions to the development of environmental economics in Europe.

Anil Markandya (born 1945) is an environmental economist who has worked in

Edward B. Barbier (born 1957) is an environmental and resource economist, with more than 20 years of experience, working mainly on the economics of environment and development issues.

Barbier is currently the John S. Bugas Professor of Economics in the Department of Economics and Finance, University of Wyoming. He was formerly at the Environment Department, University of York, UK, and previously served as Director of the London

Edward B. Barbier

Environmental Economics Centre of the International Institute for Environment and Development and University College London.

Barbier's applied work has focused particularly on issues of land degradation, wildlife management, trade and natural resources, coastal and wetland use, tropical deforestation, biological invasions and biodiversity loss. He has served as a consultant for a variety of national, international and non-governmental agencies, including many United Nations organisations and the World Bank.

Barbier has written or edited 15 books in the economics of environment and development field, and has been published extensively in both academic and popular journals. One of his recent books is *Natural Resources and Economic Development*. He has served on the editorial boards of several leading economics and natural science journals, and he appears in the fourth edition of *Who's Who in Economics*.

In their own words
(2008 interviews)

Anil Markandya

Reflections on the book

Immediately, it was a terrific success, because it was Chris Patten who was then the Secretary of State in the Department of the Environment who commissioned it and he took it on board. He made David Pearce an advisor. David started to have some effect on the way the thinking was going in that department. But of course politics changes.

The one thing we felt was that, to try to address these issues, it didn't help to try to predict apocalypse. But at the same time, we felt that, unless some of these environmental issues were taken seriously and were brought on board, they would not get the attention that they deserved.

One of the things we did in the book was to show that, if you value the environment, it actually may help save it, because it shows people that there are high values attached to these resources.

The role of policy

[We recommended] the use of market-based instruments to try to address environmental problems. [Today] there are hundreds of them, ranging from better water charges [to] waste charges that reflect more the composition of the waste. [In the UK] we have a landfill tax, which is a new instrument which came out particularly as a result of this book. We've had carbon levies which we've introduced. I'd also include the use of emissions trading schemes, which we pointed out were another way of addressing the same problem. [So] I think that governments are now committed to moving down this road.

There is now a very active movement called the Environmental Fiscal Reform, which takes our proposals one stage further and says we should not only tax these things, but we should then use that money to reduce the taxes on things like labour and social security.

China has accepted, and even adopted, some of the kinds of measures that we talk about in *Blueprint* where, for example, they have a water charging system which is quite sophisticated. They've experimented with some system of permits for emissions, and they are concerned that their development should have this element of sustainability.

Looking to the future

I think that, if we are going to take climate change seriously, one cannot do that without integrating climate policy into economic policy. It's just too big an issue. But if we use these instruments – a carbon tax, a permit scheme, all different kinds of incentives – then we are moving in the right direction.

I think the biggest challenge will be climate change, but also protection of our biodiversity, which we are losing at quite a rate, and in what ways can we achieve this protection. We are facing some quite significant losses in agriculture, in forestry, in the marine ecosystems, and these are not all because of climate change. We are looking at the losses from policy inaction to 2050 which run into billions and billions.

Edward B. Barbier

Reflections on the book

We wanted to tell the story of how you get from the Brundtland definition of sustainable development and this idea of natural capital as an organising principle, which is a way for economists to get in. We then wanted to deal with the practical problem of how do we make our political system and our markets reflect better the [environmental] values.

The main point we made was that, unless we start making the progress in this area [of environmental valuation], people are by default going to assume that the environmental costs are zero and we're never going to get out of this unsustainability trap.

There was a lot of interest in the UK. Because of *Blueprint*, David [Pearce] was appointed as Economic Advisor on the Environment to [the government]. And we all thought at that point we're going to see Britain in the forefront of sustainability. But this didn't happen. It became clear that the magnitude of the changes was more than what Maggie Thatcher's government really wanted. [I think they were] a little bit worried that what were green policies might actually be socialist policies dressed up.

The role of policy

I think increasingly we've realised that, if you pick any environmental problem that we want to tackle, there is a role for some kind of policy change and/or improved information through markets as a way of trying to get better behaviour.

There has been a lot of progress. What we considered at the time to be a very difficult [economic instrument] mechanism was to develop some kind of charge or tradable system for a global externality, a global pollution problem like carbon. Yet here we are – we have the EU carbon scheme going; we have voluntary schemes in the United States; and in the 1990s, we started to talk about the use of market-based instruments in the developing world to deal with problems of congestion and pollution.

Looking to the future

I think overall we've made progress. My concern has been the continuing problem of ecological scarcity. The types of problems we're facing are more complex and the type of changes that occur are huge. When we talk about ecosystems being altered and the loss of ecosystems services or benefits, they're very wide-ranging and the solutions are more difficult to implement.

I think there are three messages of hope. One is that, since *Blueprint*, economists more than ever are taking the environment seriously. Meanwhile, increasingly scientists and environmentalists are realising that there needs to be a role for economics in communicating environmental change to policy-makers. I would flag particularly the Millennium Ecosystem Report for doing that. [And, thirdly], I think now policy-makers believe there are votes in the environment.

The tools that we started to fashion in *Blueprint* are now widely recognised as the tools we need to do something about it.

OTHER BOOKS

Blueprint 2: Greening the World Economy (Pearce; Earthscan, 1991)

Blueprint 3: Measuring Sustainable Development (Pearce; Earthscan, 1993)

Blueprint 4: Capturing Global Environmental Value (Pearce; Earthscan, 1995)

Sustainable Development: Economics and Environment in the Third World (Pearce, Barbier and Markandya; Earthscan, 2000)

Blueprint for a Sustainable Economy (Pearce and Markandya; Earthscan, 2004)

MORE INFORMATION

European Association of Environmental and Resource Economists: www.eaere.org

15
For the Common Good
Herman Daly and John B. Cobb, Jr

1st edn
For the Common Good: Redirecting the Economy toward Community, the Environment, and a Sustainable Future
Beacon Press, 1989; 482pp, pbk; 978-0807047033

Courtesy of Beacon Press, Boston

Current edn
For the Common Good: Redirecting the Economy toward Community, the Environment, and a Sustainable Future
Beacon Press, 1994; 534pp, pbk, updated and expanded edn; 978-0807047057

Key ideas

▶ Modern economics has a crude, mechanistic world-view of *homo economicus* (economic man) as an autonomous individual driven solely by self-interest and of society as an aggregate of such individuals.

▶ Economics must shift its limited view of human nature from an atomistic one to a contextual one, of 'persons-in-community'.

▶ The economy needs to root economic interests at the local level, and re-establish some sense of human community and self-reliance.

▶ At the national level, measures of progress such as GNP need to be reformed to take into account the costs of economic growth.

▶ Part of the transformation needed in economics is the integration of humanistic and spiritual values, rather than its current obsession with secular materialism.

Synopsis

For the Common Good is a wide-ranging critique of contemporary economic policies, covering international trade, population, land use, agriculture, industry, labour, taxation and national security. Although it sets out to challenge conventional economics, it is written in an accessible style and largely avoids speaking in economic jargon and theoretical abstraction.

Indeed, this is one of the authors' first criticisms of mainstream economics, which they call 'the fallacy of misplaced concreteness', whereby it abstracts the market, measuring economic success, and the economic conception of land from their community context. They also challenge the two assumptions that support the economic theory of human nature (*homo economicus*): that human wants are insatiable; and the law-like status of the principle of diminishing marginal utility.

This view of humans tends to equate gains in society as a whole with the increases in goods and services acquired by its individual members, but it says nothing about the changes in the quality of the relationships that constitute that society. The authors therefore propose a shift from economics conceived as *crematistics* (maximisation of short-term monetary gain) to the sort of economics Aristotle called *oikonomia* (management of a household aimed at increasing its use value over the long run for the community).

In 'economics for community', the authors' term for the latter alternative, there is no aim for unlimited accumulation or 'growth-mania'. Instead, 'true wealth is limited by the satisfaction of the concrete need'. Such a conversion entails a departure from to-day's 'radical individualism' to the notion of a 'person-in-community', as well as a fundamental shift away from cosmopolitanism to 'communities of communities'.

The main argument throughout is the need to realign government and social structures toward smaller social and economic units. In their discussion of free trade and the international marketplace, for instance, they argue that it becomes difficult, if not impossible, for governments to perform their essential non-market functions when economic power is centralised at the global level, while political power is decentralised to national and local levels. Hence, society needs to both strengthen its global governance capacity and decentralise the economy and make economic actors more accountable at the national and subnational levels.

In order to achieve their proposed 'person-in-community' economics, the authors suggest five activities that could lead to an overall policy shift: significant university reforms; local community-building; steps toward a relatively self-sufficient national economy; bringing the question of scale into public consciousness; and changing the way we measure economic success.

In support of the last point, the book also includes an appendix where they construct an Index of Sustainable Economic Welfare (ISEW), intended as an alternative to gross national product as a measure of economic well-being. They also present their ground-breaking research, showing that, for the US, while GNP has been steadily rising since the 1950s, quality of life (measured by the ISEW) plateaued in the 1970s and has even begun to decline.

From the book

- The individualistic model of economic theory leads to advocating policies that weaken existing patterns of social relationships.

- The destruction of existing societies does not count against the success of policies designed to increase aggregate goods and services.

- The dominant patterns of economic development throughout the world have been quite the reverse of community development. They have consistently and systematically destroyed existing traditional communities, especially in the rural areas where most people in the Third World still live. Urban industrial 'development' has been purchased at the expense of rural communities.

- A community's complete dependency on outsiders for its mere survival weakens it. It is often unable to develop the policies it desires for the sake of its own members, since its survival depends on terms dictated by others.

- If economics is reconceived in the service of community, it will begin with a concern for agriculture and specifically for the production of food. This is because a healthy community will be a relatively self-sufficient one.

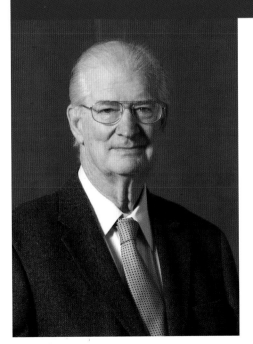

Herman Daly

About the authors

Herman Daly (born 1938) is one of the pioneers of ecological economics and a professor at the School of Public Policy of University of Maryland, College Park, in the United States.

Daly came to the Maryland School of Public Affairs from the World Bank, where he was Senior Economist in the Environment Department, helping to develop policy guidelines related to sustainable development. While there, he was engaged in environmental operations work in Latin America. Before joining the World Bank, Daly was Alumni Professor of Economics at Louisiana State University. He is a co-founder and associate editor of the journal *Ecological Economics*.

John B. Cobb, Jr

among his peers. Joining the army in 1944, he met intellectuals from other religions including Judaism and Catholicism, who showed him new perspectives. It was about this time that he had a religious experience which led him to become a minister.

He went to University of Chicago Divinity School in 1947. Cobb received his MA in 1949 and PhD in 1952 from the University of Chicago. After graduating he taught at Candler School of Theology of Emory University until 1958 when he moved to Claremont School of Theology, where he stayed until his retirement in 1990. He collaborated with Lewis S. Ford in 1971 to start a journal called *Process Studies*. In 1973 he worked with David Ray Griffin in founding the Center for Process Studies.

His interest in economic development, population, resources and environment has resulted in over a hundred articles as well as numerous books. *For the Common Good* received the Grawemeyer Award for ideas for improving World Order. He is also the recipient of the Honorary Right Livelihood Award (Sweden's alternative to the Nobel Prize), the Heineken Prize for Environmental Science from the Royal Netherlands Academy of Arts and Sciences and the Sophie Prize (Norway).

John B. Cobb, Jr (born 1925) is an American United Methodist theologian who played a crucial role in the development of process theology. He integrated Alfred North Whitehead's metaphysics into Christianity, and applied it to issues of social justice.

Cobb was born in Japan to parents who were Methodist missionaries. In 1940, he moved to Georgia to go to high school. After graduation he attended a junior college, Emory College (now Oxford College of Emory University) at Oxford, Georgia. He was deeply devout and held strong moral convictions, fighting racism and prejudice

In their own words
(2008 interview)

Herman Daly

Reflections on the book

In *For the Common Good*, we tried to look in terms of three economic problems. First, the problem of scale, the optimal or sustainable scale of the economy relative to the ecosystem. Secondly, the question of distribution, of justice. And, thirdly, the question of optimal allocation, efficiency.

It has been a disappointment to us that this challenge to standard economics of the Index of Sustainable Economic Welfare has not really been taken up very seriously by standard economists. They still go right along with GDP and don't take on board the critique that we and other people have levelled against it.

The role of policy

The World Bank and the IMF and the WTO have adopted an integrationist, globalist view which works very much to the advantage of transnational capital, and very much to the disadvantage of labouring people in different countries.

What we really want to do is to recognise the possibility – and, in some cases in wealthy countries, perhaps even now the reality – of what I've later taken to calling 'uneconomic growth'. There comes a point where the benefits, which are real, of expansion of the economy may be outweighed by the cost inflicted on the rest of the system of the expanded economy. And we see all kinds of examples. The biggest one right now of course is climate change – the costs are resulting from economic expansion and consuming more fossil fuels. And then the mobility of labour, too, uprooting communities, moving people around – these are costs. [So] growth can become uneconomic and make us poorer rather than richer, and at that point we have to back off from growth.

Looking to the future

I think we will have absolutely zero influence on the Chinese until *we* do something, until we practise what we're preaching. [However], I think China may well recognise, independently of what we do, that their costs of economic growth are hurting them. And so they may well modify their growth.

Looking at the Scandinavian countries, plus the Netherlands, in terms of their environmental economic policies, those look rather hopeful to me. I think Kerala in India offers some hope for showing that welfare can increase greatly without economic growth. And there are areas of Brazil – Curitaba and some of the southern parts – that have shown there's a lot of community there.

You can't be too impatient for change. I think maybe some of the secularist, relativist, downplaying of basic values may be reaching its end. I've been sometimes rather despondent about the degree to which there's a backing-away from any notion of values. Everything is just totally materialistic – scientific materialism kind of rules the roost as a metaphysic. But I'm beginning to see that break down a bit. I'm beginning to see a reaction to that, and I think that may have an effect on policy.

16
Human Scale Development
Manfred Max-Neef

1st edn;
Human Scale Development:
Conception, Application and Further Reflections
The Apex Press, 1989;
114pp, pbk;
978-0945257356

Key ideas

▶ The world faces a crisis of human development by failing to meet fundamental human needs, both in the industrialised and developing world.

▶ Human Scale Development addresses this crisis by focusing on generating self-reliance and satisfaction of fundamental human needs.

▶ There are nine fundamental human needs, which are non-hierarchical and do not vary by culture or over time.

▶ Satisfiers, by contrast, vary considerably from culture to culture and even from individual to individual.

▶ Many satisfiers in modern society are in fact pseudo-satisfiers, which either only partially meet human needs, or meet one need but violate others.

Synopsis

Human Scale Development grew out of the multitude of crises in Latin America in the '70s and '80s, which according to Max-Neef were 'not just economic, nor just social, cultural or political. On the contrary, it is the convergence of all these.' These circumstances place developing countries at a disadvantage: they were forced, with the complicity of government and the ruling classes, to demand tremendous sacrifices at great social costs in order to 'heal' their financial systems and meet their debt servicing obligations to the creditor countries of the industrialised world.

In essence, the crises led to the world becoming bogged down in ill-considered reactions and short-term programmes. Max-Neef contrasts the two 'isms' that have failed in developing Latin America – 'Developmentalism' (with its focus on internal markets and trade barriers) and 'Neoliberal Monetarism' (with its focus on exports fuelled by injections of foreign capital) – and offers an alternative: Human Scale Development.

Human Scale Development is 'focused and based on the satisfaction of fundamental human needs, on the generation of growing levels of self-reliance, and on the construction of organic articulations of people with nature and technology, of global processes with local activity, of the personal with the social, of planning with autonomy, and of civil society with the state'.

The concept of Human Scale Development is based on a new model of fundamental human needs. In contrast to Maslow, Max-Neef doesn't believe in a hierarchy of needs, but rather that simultaneity, complementarity and trade-offs are key features in the process of needs satisfaction. He classifies the fundamental human needs as: Subsistence, Protection, Affection, Understanding, Participation, Recreation (in the sense of leisure, time to reflect, or idleness), Creation, Identity and Freedom.

Needs are also defined according to the existential categories of Being, Having, Doing and Interacting. Furthermore, Max-Neef distinguishes between human needs and satisfiers. Human needs are few and constant, both across time and cultures, while satisfiers, the way these needs are satisfied, changes over time and between cultures. For instance, food is not a need, it is a satisfier of the need for subsistence. Needs can be satisfied within three contexts: with regard to oneself, the social group and the environment.

Max-Neef identifies five variations of satisfiers: (1) *violators or destroyers* don't necessarily fulfil the need they seek to satisfy, and in the process impair the satisfaction of other needs; (2) *pseudo-satisfiers* generate a false sense of satisfaction of a given need; (3) *inhibiting satisfiers* generally over-satisfy a given need, therefore, seriously curtailing the possibility of satisfying other needs; (4) *singular satisfiers* satisfy only one particular need; and (5) *synergic satisfiers* satisfy a given need and, simultaneously, stimulate and contribute to the fulfilment of other needs.

Max-Neef concludes that 'Human Scale Development does not exclude conventional goals such as economic growth, so that all persons may have access to required goods and services. However, the difference with respect to the prevailing development styles lies in considering the aims of development not only as points of arrival, but as components of the process itself.'

From the book

- We are losing our capacity to dream. We are struggling in an exhausting insomnia which impairs the lucidity so desperately needed to cope with our problems forcefully and imaginatively.

- The most pressing question, not only for a democratic state, but also for a society based on a democratic culture, is how to respect and encourage diversity rather than control it. In this regard, development must nurture local spaces, facilitate micro-organizations and support the multiplicity of cultural matrixes comprising civil society.

- Human Scale Development assumes a direct and participatory democracy.

- With the sole exception of the need of subsistence, that is, to remain alive, no hierarchies exist within the system [of fundamental human needs].

- [Poverty should be defined as] any fundamental need that is not adequately satisfied.

About the author

Manfred Max-Neef (born 1932) is a Chilean development economist and environmentalist, who has gained an international reputation for his work and writing on development alternatives.

After teaching economics at the University of California (Berkeley) in the 1960s, he served as a Visiting Professor at a number of US and Latin American universities. He worked for a time for Shell in Chile, and has also worked on development projects in Latin America for the Pan-American Union, the UN Food and Agriculture Organisation and the International Labour Office.

In 1981 he captured his experiences in *From the Outside Looking In: Experiences in Barefoot Economics*. It describes his experiences as an economist attempting to practise 'economics as if people matter' among the poor in South America.

In the same year he set up in Chile the organisation CEPAUR (Centre for Development Alternatives). CEPAUR is largely dedicated to the reorientation of development in terms of stimulating local self-reliance and satisfying fundamental human needs. More generally, it advocates a return to the human scale.

In addition to a long academic career, Max-Neef achieved an impressive minority vote when he stood as candidate in the Chilean Presidential election of 1993. He was subsequently appointed Rector of the Universidad Austral de Chile in Valdivia. In 1983 he was awarded the Right Livelihood Award, the alternative Nobel Prize.

In his own words
(2008 interview)

Reflections on the book

What I discovered is an absolutely fascinating world that exists in the midst of poverty – the forms of cooperation, of mutual aid, and all sorts of compensations that take place, which are absolutely extraordinary. I discovered that the first characteristic of poverty is an enormous creativity. You must be tremendously creative to stay alive. And that means really that you have tremendous potential. If you want to overcome poverty, build on the creativity that people already have.

Human Scale Development and the needs theory is a child that outgrew its father by far, with impacts all over the place. There were many projects that were developed strictly based on Human Scale Development. In Latin America, the most important country in that respect today is Colombia.

The role of government and business

At the level of governments, the reaction has been irrelevant. It's much more at the level now of social movements, NGOs, peasant groups. Governments are stuck in the mainstream and in the conventional.

One must understand that Human Scale Development is a micro-process and not a macro-process.

Globalisation is a neoliberal globalisation, so there could be nothing more contradictory with what we are trying to promote. One cannot be against globalisation as such. We can be against a certain type of globalisation, and this type of globalisation is a globalisation for the corporate greed. They are the great beneficiaries of this type of process.

In the olden days, we had the attitude that entrepreneurs are the bad guys of the picture, and we are the good guys. That's nonsense, absolute nonsense. We lost many years and many possibilities because of that attitude. If an entrepreneur changes, that has an immediate impact which politicians don't have. I don't trust the politicians anymore, that's pretty definite. But my hope now is that the entrepreneurs can change, and that a growing amount of them are willing and wanting to change.

Looking to the future

Consciousness develops at the human scale. It's again not something macro. And, if you see the movements, what do you have? More and more, a group here, another group there and another movement here, a social movement there. They are beginning to bring about the revolution. And that happens in climate change also: the consciousness of the people begins to come out from those groups and eventually have an impact in politics.

One of the dangerous things for me is the concept of certainty. What I've discovered is that the people who know exactly where to go are the people who never discover anything. So what is my advice today? If you are in trouble, learn to drift in alertness. Take out your antennae, drift and get all the messages you can get. You cannot be sure where you are going to arrive; you are going to arrive somewhere and that's the adventure, so be creative about that. That changes the picture completely. But what we have today is that we are full of certainties. We are living in a world full of solutions without questions, full of answers without questions.

I'm a musician – a pianist and composer – and music has been absolutely fundamental for all the conceptions. I sometimes even say (a little bit as a joke) that I have put music into economics.

OTHER BOOKS

From the Outside Looking In: Experiences in Barefoot Economics (Dag Hammarskjöld Foundation, 1982)

Real-life Economics: Understanding Wealth Creation (edited with Paul Ekins; Routledge, 1992)

MORE INFORMATION

Dag Hammarskjöld Foundation: dhf.uu.se

17
Changing Course
Stephan Schmidheiny and the Business Council for Sustainable Development (BCSD)

1st and current edn
**Changing Course:
A Global Business
Perspective on
Development and
the Environment**
MIT Press, 1992; 374pp,
hbk; 978-0262193184
(pbk 978-0262691536)

Key ideas

▶ Business, alongside government and civil society, has a key role to play in the transition towards sustainability.

▶ The strengths that business brings – innovation, markets and economic prosperity – are critical to achieving sustainable development.

▶ Open, prospering markets are a powerful force for creating equity of opportunity among nations and people.

▶ Integrating the 'polluter pays' principle into environmental and economic policy is essential for creating markets that support sustainable development.

▶ The sustainable development best practices of numerous pioneering companies can serve as inspiration to others in business.

Synopsis

Changing Course was written to provide a business response to the 1992 Earth Summit in Rio. Gathering the expertise of more than 50 leaders of multinational corporations and backed by an array of case studies showing existing best practices, it provides an extensive analysis of how the business community can adapt and contribute to the crucial goal of sustainable development – which combines the objectives of environmental protection and economic growth.

All of the book's recommendations are underscored by the belief that only by allowing market forces to operate freely and integrating the 'polluter pays' principle into environmental and economic policy can sustainable development be achieved. It endorses the Brundtland definition of sustainable development, but observes that 'development is more than growth, or quantitative change'.

Changing Course focuses first on the often adversarial relationship between business and government in chapters that discuss full-cost pricing and market signals, energy, capital markets, trade, and managing change. It shows how environmental costs, which are often invisible, can best be factored into production, investment and trade. And it calls for a rational long-term energy strategy that balances the energy needs for economic development with a policy shift toward the payment of pollution costs and energy efficiency – changes that demand new thinking and increased flexibility by policy-makers in both the public and the private sectors.

The book then explores business-to-business relationships, beginning with the sensitive topic of corporate reporting in environmental areas and discussion of how an environmentally conscious firm is managed. Chapters look at optimal products and processes, product stewardship in retail and trading companies, at new practices for such renewable resource industries as forestry and agriculture, and at the need for new long-term partnerships to boost economic development and environmental standards in the developing world.

Changing Course also emphasises technology, claiming that 'sustainability will require new technology, new approaches to trade to spread the technology and the goods necessary for survival, and new ways of meeting needs through markets. Business leadership will be required and is expected in all these areas.'

The book is uncompromising in its ideological position: the market mechanism if allowed to operate freely is the only conceivable means of achieving sustainable development. This includes 'open and competitive markets' because competition 'encourages producers to use as few resources as possible if resources are priced properly'.

Changing Course also claims that the primary agents of such a transition to a more sustainable world are multinational corporations, which would extend good management principles to encompass environmental concerns: 'Viewing environmental threats from a business perspective can guide both governments and companies towards plausible policies that offer protection from disaster while making the best of the challenges.'

By way of consolidating this central role, the book led to the formation of the Business Council for Sustainable Development (BCSD), which later became the World Business Council for Sustainable Development (WBCSD).

From the book

- No one can reasonably doubt that fundamental change is needed. This fact offers us two basic options: we can resist as long as possible, or we can join those shaping the future.

- We call for a long-term view, for far-reaching changes, and for action. But we do not base our hopes for success on radical changes in human nature or on the creation of a utopia.

- While the basic goal of business must remain economic growth, as long as world population continues to grow rapidly and mass poverty remains widespread, we are recommending a different course toward that goal. There will be changes in direction and changes in the measurements of progress to include indicators of quality as well as quantity.

- Business is a large vessel; it will require great common effort and planning to overcome the inertia of the present destructive course, and to create a new momentum toward sustainable development.

- Many of those with the power to effect the necessary changes have the least motivation to alter the status quo that gave them the power.

About the author

Stephan Schmidheiny (born 1947) is a pioneering Swiss businessman who has been at the forefront of the corporate sustainability movement over the past 20 years.

Born in St Gallen, after earning his law degree Schmidheiny began a business career and, aged 29, became CEO of his family's construction materials enterprise. In 1986, he established FUNDES to promote competitive development among small and medium enterprises in Latin America. In 1990, he was appointed chief advisor for business and industry to the Secretary-General of the United Nations Conference on Environment and Development (UNCED).

This led to the creation of a world council for business leaders (BCSD), which developed concepts such as eco-efficiency and the business case for sustainability, and produced *Changing Course* as an input to the Earth Summit. BCSD later became the World Business Council for Sustainable Development, with Schmidheiny as its Honorary Chair.

In 1994, Schmidheiny created AVINA, which brings together civil society and business leaders that work towards sustainable development in Latin America, Switzerland and other European nations. He also founded GrupoNueva, a conglomerate that adheres to the triple-bottom-line philosophy. Later, he was also appointed board member of ABB, Nestlé, Swatch and UBS.

Schmidheiny has received a great number of awards and distinctions in acknowledgement of his leadership and contribution to sustainable development: among others, the Instituto Centroamericano de Administración de Empresas (INCAE) PhD Honoris Causa degree, in 1993; the same degree from Yale University in 1996; and at Rollins College and Universidad Católica Andrés Bello (UCAB), both in 2001.

The **Business Council for Sustainable Development (BCSD)** was founded by Stephan Schmidheiny on the eve of the 1992 Rio Earth Summit to involve business in sustainability issues and give it a voice in the forum. This participation was a success and led to the publication of *Changing Course*. Following the summit, Schmidheiny and his fellow business partners concluded that, to keep up the momentum that had been created, it was necessary to keep the cooperation alive.

In 1995, the BCSD merged with the World Industry Council on the Environment, and the World Business Council for Sustainable Development (WBCSD) was born, opening its secretariat in Geneva. A second office in Washington, DC was opened in 2007.

Today, WBCSD is a CEO-led, global association of some 200 companies dealing exclusively with business and sustainable development. The Council provides a platform for companies to explore sustainable development, share knowledge, experiences and best practices, and to advocate business positions on these issues in a variety of forums, working with governments, non-governmental and intergovernmental organisations.

OTHER BOOKS (SELECTION)

Financing Change: The Financial Community, Eco-efficiency, and Sustainable Development (Stephan Schmidheiny and Federico J. Zorraquin; MIT Press, 1998)

Walking the Talk: The Business Case for Sustainable Development (Charles O. Holliday, Stephan Schmidheiny and Philip Watts; Greenleaf Publishing, 2002)

MORE INFORMATION

FUNDES: www.fundes.org

Fundación AVINA: www.avina.net

GrupoNueva: www.gruponueva.com

WBCSD: www.wbcsd.org

18
The Ecology of Commerce
Paul Hawken

1st edn
**The Ecology
of Commerce:
A Declaration of
Sustainability**
HarperBusiness, 1993;
288pp, hbk;
978-0887306556

Current edn
**The Ecology
of Commerce:
A Declaration of
Sustainability**
HarperBusiness, 1994;
272pp, pbk;
978-0887307041

Key ideas

▶ The biosphere is being destroyed, possibly irreversibly, by the demands placed on it by an industrial society flawed in its central components.

▶ The industrial system is a linear process, driven by fossil fuel energy, in which we deplete resources and create waste, rather than a cyclical, self-sustaining ecological system.

▶ The same forces that created the problem, both the market and state intervention, are capable of providing solutions if intelligence can prevail over greed.

▶ Environmental issues are often framed as a choice between the economy and the environment, but we can have both, i.e. environmental health can and should drive long-term economic health.

▶ We need to create a restorative economy, i.e. a system of commerce and production that is solar-powered and where all waste equals 'food' for another process.

Synopsis

The Ecology of Commerce, written in an easy-to-read style with plenty of facts and examples, asks the basic question: Can we create profitable, expandable companies that do not destroy, directly or indirectly, the world around them? Hawken says yes, but only if we redesign the flawed system of commerce with the following three objectives:

- Reduce absolute consumption of energy and natural resources in the North by 80% within the next half-century;

- Provide secure, stable and meaningful employment for people everywhere; and

- Be self-actuating as opposed to regulated or morally mandated, i.e. humans want to flourish and prosper, and they will reject any system of conservation (regulation) that interferes with these desires.

Hawken is a firm believer in market principles, but argues that our current system is too skewed towards private-sector interests, in terms of taxation, division of power and money and access to power and money. This creates inequality for individuals as income disparity increases, but also within the business community, where small businesses are at the mercy of the power of large businesses.

To begin to reform this distorted economy, the tax system needs to be redesigned so that 'bads' (pollution, environmental degradation and non-renewable energy) are taxed instead of 'goods' (labour and income). This is known as Pigovian tax, a tax levied to correct the negative externalities of a market activity.

Hawken believes that sustainability needs to offer an alternative to the current industrial model – one that is more rewarding than our present way of life. Hence, present-day limits need to become opportunities to participate, enjoy and create. He even calls on us to exceed sustainability by restoring degraded habitats and ecosystems to their fullest biological capacity.

Hawken offers a laundry-list definition of sustainable business. Companies should: replace nationally and internationally produced items with products created locally and regionally; take responsibility for the effects they have on the natural world; not require exotic sources of capital in order to develop and grow; engage in production processes that are human, worthy, dignified and intrinsically satisfying; create objects of durability and long-term utility whose ultimate use or disposition will not be harmful to future generations; and change consumers to customers through education.

Hawken proposes a three-step approach to sustainability that will allow us to meet our wants and needs within the capacity of the ecosystem:

1. Obey the waste-equals-food principle and entirely eliminate waste from our industrial production;

2. Change from an economy based on carbon to one based on hydrogen and sunshine; and

3. Create systems of feedback and accountability that support and strengthen restorative behaviour.

Hawken says that sustainability should be fun and engaging, and strive for an aesthetic outcome, since the urge to create beauty is an untapped power which exists in commerce as well as in society. This is also necessary in order to gain widespread support, since a sustainable society will come about only through the acts of billions of individuals.

From the book

- By nature, by law, and by tradition, corporations often place their interests above others, including those of the community, the state, and the environment.

- The ultimate purpose of business is not, or should not be, simply to make money. The promise of business is to increase well-being of humankind through service, a creative innovation and ethical philosophy.

- Despite all the good work, we must face a sobering fact. If every company on the planet were to adopt the best environmental practices of the 'leading' companies, the world would still be moving toward sure degradation and collapse. Rather than a management problem, we have a design problem, a flaw that runs through all business.

- If we are to create a commercial culture that does no harm to natural and human communities, society will have to define commercial crime more effectively, and begin to see it as something less than inevitable, and more than excusable.

- Companies must re-envision and re-imagine themselves as cyclical corporations.

- We must design a system where doing good is like falling off a log, where the natural, everyday acts of work and life accumulate into a better world as a matter of course not a matter of conscious altruism.

- Any viable economic program must turn back the resource clock and devote itself actively to restoring damaged and deteriorating systems – restoration is far more compelling than the algebra of sustainability.

- It is a teasing irony, but business may contain our blessing . . . Its power is more crucial than ever if we are to organise and efficiently meet the world's needs for sustainability.

- One of the purposes of the restorative economy is to ensure that innovative commercial options have a chance to survive in the monoculture of corporate capitalism.

About the author

Paul Hawken (born 1946) is an environmentalist, entrepreneur and author. Starting at the age of 20, he dedicated his life to sustainability and changing the relationship between business and the environment.

sold over 2 million copies. In 1998 *The Ecology of Commerce* was voted the number one college text on business and the environment by professors in 67 business schools.

Hawken has founded or co-founded software companies specialising in proprietary content management tools, as well as Smith & Hawken, the garden and catalogue retailer, and several of the first natural food companies in the US that relied solely on sustainable agricultural methods. He is presently the head of PaxIT, PaxTurbine and PaxFan, three companies associated with Pax Scientific – a research and development company focused on energy-saving technologies that apply biomimicry to fluid dynamics.

His practice has included starting and running ecological businesses, writing and teaching about the impact of commerce on living systems, and consulting with governments and corporations on economic development, industrial ecology and environmental policy.

He is author and co-author of dozens of articles, op-eds and papers, as well as six books. His books have been published in over 50 countries in 27 languages and have

Hawken heads the Natural Capital Institute, a research organisation located in Sausalito, California. The Natural Capital Institute has created a hub for global civil society called Wiser Earth. It is a collaboratively written, free-content, open-source networking platform that links NGOs, funders, business, government, social entrepreneurs, students, organisers, academics, activists, scientists and citizens.

OTHER BOOKS (SELECTION)

The Next Economy (Ballantine, 1983)

Growing a Business (Simon & Schuster, 1987)

Natural Capitalism: Creating the Next Industrial Revolution (with Amory B. Lovins and L. Hunter Lovins; Earthscan, 1999)

Blessed Unrest: How the Largest Movement in the World Came into Being, and Why No One Saw it Coming (Viking, 2007)

MORE INFORMATION

Paul Hawken's official website:
www.paulhawken.com

Natural Capital Institute:
www.naturalcapital.org

Wiser Earth:
www.WiserEarth.org

19
Maverick
Ricardo Semler

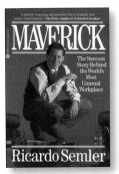

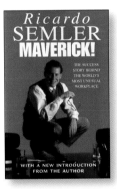

Current UK edn
Maverick!
The Success Story
Behind the World's Most
Unusual Workplace
Random House
Business Books, 2001;
332pp, pbk;
978-0712678865

Current US edn
Maverick:
The Success Story
Behind the World's Most
Unusual Workplace
Grand Central Publishing
(Hachette Book Group),
1995; 352pp, pbk;
978-0446670555

1st edn
Maverick:
The Success Story
Behind the World's Most
Unusual Workplace
Warner Books Inc.,
1993; 335pp, hbk;
978-0446516969

Key ideas

- ▶ Business is a creative exercise; therefore, any unnecessary bureaucracy should be avoided.

- ▶ Employees should be given maximum control and responsibility over their work life.

- ▶ Only a democratic work environment can tap into the potential of its people.

- ▶ Transparency of decision-making and information promotes trust and performance.

- ▶ One of the keys to employee satisfaction and innovation is to keep business units at a human scale.

Synopsis

Maverick is essentially Ricardo Semler's autobiography, about how he transformed the business of Semco, a Brazilian ship-building supplies manufacturer, into a diversified and highly innovative manufacturing and services company. Semler took over as chief executive of the company from his father at the beginning of the 1980s, when he was only just out of Harvard.

To begin with, Semler ran the company with tight disciplines and controls, but was forced to rethink his approach after being struck down by a stress-induced illness. The changes he implemented challenge much of the received wisdom on business and management. For example, Semler let his employees set their own hours, design their workplace, choose their own IT and share all information.

Other policies included the following: every six months bosses are evaluated by their subordinates and the results are posted; there is complete internal financial openness, including teaching factory workers how to read accounts and making salaries public; all employees can set their own salary; there are no receptionists, secretaries or personal assistants; each business unit is kept small and split if it grows too big; workers set their own production quotas; and profit sharing is practised right down to factory-floor level.

Semler also eliminated needless hierarchy; he inherited 11 layers; now a front-line lathe operator is only one layer away from the general manager of his division. He next set up 'factory committees' to run the plants, in an attempt to get more worker involvement. Semler then introduced far-reaching profit-sharing schemes for all the workers. The workers decide between themselves in each unit how to divide the profit-sharing bonuses.

Factories and business units were progressively spun off into self regulating units with their own profit and loss accounts. Managers are hired and fired by their own employees. The units began inventing new businesses for themselves and so Semco grew entirely due to the initiatives of its workers.

There are six principles that guide the company:

1. Forget about the top line – what matters is profitability, not sales.

2. Never stop being a start-up – keep rethinking the purpose of the business.

3. Don't be a nanny – don't treat your workers like children, or they will act like them.

4. Let talent find its place – let people choose and persuade others of their work projects.

5. Make decisions quickly and openly – bureaucracy stifles creativity.

6. Don't be too proud to ask for help – everyone is learning all the time.

Semler meanwhile redefined his own role, retiring from all executive positions at age 33 and taking on the mantle of the 'questioner', the 'challenger' and the 'catalyst'. He paraphrases his theory of management as 'Give people the freedom to do what they want and over the long haul their successes will far outnumber their failures. It seems that if you trust people to do the right thing and if it's obviously in their interest to do so, then they will do their best to make it happen.'

From the book

- Three stone cutters were asked about their jobs. The first said he was paid to cut stones. The second replied that he used special techniques to shape stones in an exceptional way, and proceeded to demonstrate his skills. The third stone cutter just smiled and said: 'I build cathedrals'.

- You can build a great company without fixed plans. You can have an efficient company without rules and controls. You can be unbuttoned and creative without sacrificing profit. All it takes is faith in people.

- On an average, maybe 2–3% of any work force will take advantage of an employer's trust. But is this a valid reason to subject 97% to a daily ritual of humiliation? It's a cost of doing business. I would rather have a few thefts once in a while than condemn everyone to a system based on mistrust.

- Rules cause employees to forget that a company needs to be creative and adaptive to survive. Rules slow it down. With few exceptions, rules and regulations only serve to divert attention from a company's objectives, provide a false sense of security for executives and create work for bean counters.

- I am not interested in . . . making sure that you (the employee) are here, that you are giving us so many hours a day. We need people who will deliver a final result.

- If we do not let people do things the way they do, we will never know what they are really capable of and they will just follow our boarding school rules.

- It's a system that puts a lot of weight on leaders because then they can no longer simply protect themselves with symbols of power like closed offices or special parking places. They have to rely exclusively on their ability to generate respect.

- Rather than force our people to expand a business beyond its natural limits, we encourage them to start new businesses.

About the author

Ricardo Semler (born 1959) is the Brazilian CEO and majority owner of Semco SA and an innovative management thinker and practitioner, best known for his radical ideas on industrial democracy and corporate re-engineering.

Semler graduated from Harvard Business School aged 20 (one of the school's youngest ever MBA recipients) and replaced his father as CEO of Semler and Company. His radical reform programme helped it to grow into a successful diversified company and

survive the economic crisis in Brazil in the early 1990s.

The publication of a series of articles in *Harvard Business Review* (1989, 1994, 2000) and the publication of his book *Maverick* led to considerable recognition. He has been named as a Global Leader of Tomorrow by the World Economic Forum, and twice as Brazil's Business Leader of the Year and Latin American Businessman of the Year by the *Wall Street Journal*'s *America Economia* magazine.

Semler founded the Lumiar School in São Paulo in 2003, where young children are taught in an unstructured environment without classrooms, homework or playtime, and learn only about what interests them. He has also been involved in building a luxury eco-tourist resort, in much the same way he has built his other companies. He is getting local community members to decide on the design, and participate not only in the decision-making process, but also in the process of building.

OTHER BOOKS

The Seven-Day Weekend: Changing the Way Work Works (Portfolio, 2004)

MORE INFORMATION

Semco:
semco.locaweb.com.br/en

Lumiar School:
www.lumiar.org.br/english/index.html

20

When Corporations Rule the World

David C. Korten

1st edn
When Corporations Rule the World
Kumarian Press Inc./
Berrett-Koehler, 1995;
374pp, hbk;
978-1887208000

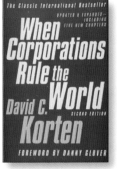

Current edn
When Corporations Rule the World
Kumarian Press Inc./
Berrett-Koehler, 2001;
385pp, pbk, expanded
2nd edn;
978-1887208048

Key ideas

▶ We have been seduced by 'corporate libertarianism', which demands that all political, economic and civic barriers to the free rein of corporate interests be removed.

▶ The result of this unhealthy power in corporate hands is ecological destruction, the loss of civil freedoms, the erosion of democracy and community disintegration.

▶ Although the current corporate globalisation represents a failure of governments, it is more fundamentally a failure of the global capitalist economic system.

▶ Instead, we should be striving for 'democratic pluralism', which requires a 'pragmatic, institutional balance between the forces of government, market, and civic society'.

▶ We are on the cusp of an Ecological Revolution, which puts people ahead of corporations, local communities ahead of global trade, and nature ahead of money.

Synopsis

When Corporations Rule the World suggests that the promises of the global economy are based on a number of myths: that growth in GNP is a valid measure of human well-being and progress; that free unregulated markets efficiently allocate a society's resources; that growth in trade benefits ordinary people; that economic globalisation is inevitable; that global corporations are benevolent institutions that, if freed from governmental interference, will provide a clean environment for all and good jobs for the poor; and that absentee investors create 'trickle-down' prosperity.

Korten believes that these myths are finally being unmasked and challenged by an Ecological Revolution that calls us 'to reclaim our political power and rediscover our spirituality to create societies that nurture our ability and desire to embrace the joyful experience of living to its fullest'. He argues that, instead of concentrating on increasing economic growth and GDP, we should concentrate on ending poverty, improving our quality of life, and achieving a sustainable balance with the Earth.

In order to achieve this goal of 'sustainable well-being for all people', Korten believes that we need a multi-level system of nested economies with the household as the basic economic unit, up through successive geographical aggregations to localities, districts, nations and regions. Each level would seek to function as an integrated, self-reliant, self-managing political, economic and ecological community.

A corporation of the future needs to show that it is 'committed to investing in the future; providing employees with secure, well-paying jobs; paying a fair share of local taxes; paying into a fully funded retirement trust fund; managing environmental resources responsibly; and otherwise managing for the long-term human interest. Such companies are a valuable community asset, and in a healthy economy, they pay their shareholders solid and reliable – but not extravagant – dividends over the long term.'

The Guiding Principles for an Ecological Revolution include environmental sustainability, economic justice, biological and cultural diversity, subsidiarity (where the economy serves human needs, not the needs of money, corporations or governments), intrinsic responsibility (internalising externalities) and common heritage (of the planet's environmental resources and the accumulated human knowledge).

The principles, Korten believes, are actively pro-business and pro-market, but they are strongly partial to locally owned businesses that provide employment to local people, pay local taxes to maintain local infrastructure and social services, meet local social and environmental standards, participate in the community and compete fairly with similar businesses in markets that have no dominant players.

Korten includes some strong reform proposals in his blueprint for an Ecological Revolution including, for example, limitations on lobbying and private ownership of the media, enforcement of anti-trust legislation, taxation of financial transactions, resource extraction and pollution, introduction of a basic citizen's income, restrictions on CEO pay to a ratio to worker pay of no more than 15 to 1, reduction of the work week, removal of corporations rights as individuals and reform of the Bretton Woods institutions (World Bank, IMF and World Trade Organisation).

From the book

- This is a crisis of governance born of a convergence of ideological, political, and technological forces behind a process of economic globalization that is shifting power away from governments responsible for the public good and toward a handful of corporations and financial institutions driven by a single imperative – the quest for short-term financial gain.

- A globalized economic system delinked from place has an inherent bias in favour of the large, the global, the competitive, the resource-extractive, the short-term, and the wants of those with money.

- We are now coming to see that economic globalization has come at a heavy price . . . The threefold crisis of deepening poverty, environmental destruction, and social disintegration manifests this dysfunction.

- The task ahead is to transform a world ruled by corporations dedicated to the love of money to a world ruled by people dedicated to the love of life.

- Millions of people around the world are awakening, as if from a deep trance, to the beauty, joy, and meaning of life . . . demanding a restoration of democracy, an end to corporate rule, and respect for the needs of all people and other living beings.

About the author

David C. Korten (born 1937) is a specialist in international development and an intellectual activist on the political and institutional consequences of economic globalisation and the expansion of corporate power at the expense of democracy, equity, and environmental health.

Trained in economics, organisation theory and business strategy with MBA and PhD degrees from the Stanford University Graduate School of Business, his early career was devoted to setting up business schools in low-income countries, in the hope that creating a new class of professional bu-siness entrepreneurs would be the key to ending global poverty. After graduation Korten completed his military service in Vietnam, before becoming a Visiting Associate Professor at Harvard University Graduate School of Business.

In the late 1970s, Korten left US academia and moved to Southeast Asia, where he lived for 15 years, serving first as a Ford Foundation project specialist, and later as Asia regional advisor on development management to the US Agency for International Development (USAID). Disillusioned by what he came to see as an inability of

USAID and other large official aid donors to strengthen community control over their natural resource base, Korten broke with the official aid system and returned to the United States in 1992 to pursue work on challenging corporate globalisation.

Korten is co-founder and board chair of Positive Futures Network, a board member of the Business Alliance for Local Living Economies, an associate of the International Forum on Globalisation and a member of the Club of Rome.

In his own words
(2008 interview)

Reflections on the book

The book grew out of some 30 years of international development work . . . It was around 1988 that I started getting increasingly aware that development as we had defined it really wasn't working. A few people were getting very rich, but most people were being pushed into ever more distressed circumstances, the environment was being trashed and the once strong and vibrant cultures were really being decimated. So this led to gradually stepping back to look at the bigger picture of what was going on.

One reason that *When Corporations Rule the World* attracted so much attention is that the timing of its release was absolutely perfect. It was just at the moment when a lot of people were beginning to ask questions about what's really going on with these trade agreements, with all this outsourcing, with these outrageous CEO packages, with corporate downsizing and so forth, and this book provided the answers that those people were looking for.

If I were to rewrite the book now, I would probably put the title *When Corporations Rule the World* with a slash through 'Corporations' and a little carrot pointing to 'Money'. It's actually *When Money Rules the World*. This has become so much more obvious, so much stronger and so much more disruptive as we've seen the rampant speculation in the financial markets. That very structure drives a predatory dynamic in the corporate system that you really can't do very much about at the level of the individual corporation. You can do a little tinkering around the edges, but those are pretty limited relative to the depth of the changes that we need to navigate.

The role of business

I'm very sceptical of corporate social responsibility initiatives because while they do some good they generally ignore the inherent limitations of what those corporations can conceivably do within the system as it's currently structured.

The corporate charter is a grant of privilege, it is not a right. It is a grant that gives some group of people a set of privileges beyond those which are granted to ordinary individuals. Now the only legitimate reason for a government to issue such a charter is to serve a public purpose. And to allow a group of people to create a monopoly for the sole purpose of enriching themselves is not a public purpose. So that is the foundation of beginning to really rethink the corporation as an institution.

It's not about companies reining themselves in; it's about the emergence of a new social force – the global resistance, which we now refer to as global civil society.

Looking to the future

What I see is getting very serious about anti-trust and breaking up the big concentrations of corporate power, eliminating public trading as we know it, moving towards systems of rooted ownership where the enterprises are owned by people that have a very direct connection with them and stake in their responsible operation, and eliminating the feature of limited liability so that the members of the corporation bear the same liabilities as anybody else in society and are not granted special privilege.

We're basically moving in the wrong direction but we see these emergent forces that are a source of hope. Change is only going to come through choice, so we need to get out there and give it everything we've got to raise awareness of the possibilities at hand and the choices that it can lead us to – a sustainable world that works not only for all people but for the whole of life.

OTHER BOOKS (SELECTION)

Community Management: Asian Experience and Perspectives (Kumarian Press, 1987)

Getting to the 21st Century: Voluntary Action and the Global Agenda (Kumarian Press, 1990)

MORE INFORMATION

Business Alliance for Local Living Economies: www.livingeconomies.org

David Korten's official website: www.davidkorten.org

21
Biomimicry
Janine M. Benyus

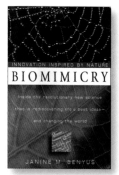

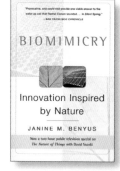

Current edn
Biomimicry:
Innovation Inspired
by Nature
Harper Perennial, 2002;
320pp, pbk;
978-0060533229

1st edn
Biomimicry:
Innovation Inspired
by Nature
William Morrow, 1997;
288p, hbk;
978-0688136918

Key ideas

▶ Biomimicry is the process of learning from and then emulating nature's genius.

▶ Nature teaches us countless lessons every day about living within our means and in harmony with nature, but we are still unwilling to listen.

▶ Change is starting to happen, and the numerous examples of biomimicry that are already applied shows that there is a different way.

▶ Business will need to play a central role in leading the biomimicry revolution, through investment in new biomimetic research and technologies.

▶ For societal change to take place, government needs to create boundary conditions that will reward industrial ecology instead of ecological destruction.

Synopsis

Biomimicry is about human society, especially business and technology, learning from nature. After 3.8 billion years, nature knows what works and what lasts here on Earth. Mimicking these designs and strategies, or 'recipes', could change the way we grow food, harvest solar energy, run our businesses, even the way we make materials. Biomimicry is innovation inspired by nature. In a society accustomed to dominating or 'improving' nature, this respectful imitation is a radically new approach, a revolution.

Biomimicry looks at nature as a model, measure and mentor. For instance, biomimicry studies nature's models and then imitates or takes inspiration from these designs and processes to solve human problems. It also uses an ecological standard to judge the 'rightness' of our innovations: what works? what is appropriate? what lasts? Biomimicry is a new way of viewing and valuing nature. It introduces an era based not on what we can extract from the natural world, but on what we can learn from it.]

There are numerous lessons from nature. For instance, nature: runs on sunlight; uses only the energy it needs; fits form to function; recycles everything; rewards cooperation; banks on diversity; demands local expertise; curbs excesses from within; and taps the power of limits. There are also growing numbers of examples of biomimicry: an ultra-tough optically clear glass that mimics the abalone's self-assembly process; manufacturing fibres without heat or toxins based on spider's web 'technology'; a glue-free, yet sticky, tape modelled on gecko feet; or computer software called genetic algorithms that mimics natural selection.

There is a central role for business in the biomimicry revolution. However, it needs to be behaving less like a ragweed (which grow as quickly as they can, while there's enough nutrition going round, before moving on to the next plot or before the changing seasons curtail their growth) and more like the redwood forests (which are highly developed ecosystems that maintain their presence in one place, make the most of what is available and endure over the long haul). Redwoods have fewer but better offspring, which have longer but more complex lives. They live in a most brilliant and artful synergy with the species around them and put a great deal of energy into optimising their relationships. Their wastes are recycled endlessly and their energy source is the sun.

To be able to engender a 'biomimetic revolution', four successive steps are required:

1. *Quieting human cleverness*: this involves the maturing of the human race, the acknowledgement that nature knows best;

2. *Listening to nature*: interviewing the flora and fauna of our own planet in an organised way;

3. *Echoing nature*: this is where we actually try to mimic what we discover, encouraging biologists and engineers to collaborate, using nature as model and measure; and

4. *Stewarding nature*: the only way to keep learning from nature is to safeguard naturalness, which is the source of those good ideas.

From the book

- Living things have done everything we want to do without guzzling fossil fuel, polluting the planet, or mortgaging their future. What better models could there be?

- Unlike the Industrial Revolution, the Biomimicry Revolution introduces an era based not on what we can extract from nature, but on what we can learn from her.

- When we stare this deeply into nature's eyes, it takes our breath away, and in a good way, it bursts our bubble. We realize that all our inventions have already appeared in nature in a more elegant form and at a lot less cost to the planet.

- I believe that we face our current dilemma not because the answers don't exist, but because we simply haven't been looking in the right places.

- Setting realistic boundary conditions would bring out sustainable behaviors in the economy. Government should draw the lines and invite industry to color within the lines in whatever way it sees fit.

About the author

Janine Benyus (born 1958) is an American natural sciences writer, innovation consultant and author, best known for her work on biomimicry.

Benyus graduated summa cum laude from Rutgers University with degrees in natural resource management and English literature/writing. She has worked as a backpacking guide and as a 'translator' of science-speak at several research labs. Now she mainly writes science books, teaches interpretive writing, lectures at the University of Montana, and works towards restoring and protecting wild lands.

In 1998, following her book *Biomimicry*, Benyus co-founded the Biomimicry Guild, which helps innovators learn from and emulate natural models in order to design sustainable products, processes and policies that create conditions conducive to life. She is also President of the Biomimicry Institute, a non-profit organisation whose mission is to promote the transfer of ideas, designs and strategies from biology to sustainable human systems design.

As a life sciences writer, Benyus has authored six books, including an animal behaviour guide and three ecosystem-first field guides. She also serves on a number of land use committees in her rural county, and is president of Living Education, a non-profit dedicated to place-based living and learning.

OTHER BOOKS (SELECTION)

The Field Guide to Wildlife Habitats of the Eastern United States (Simon & Schuster, 1989)

Northwoods Wildlife: A Watcher's Guide to Habitats (NorthWord Press, 1991)

MORE INFORMATION

Biomimicry Guild:
www.biomimicryguild.com

Biomimicry Institute:
www.biomimicryinstitute.org

22
Cannibals with Forks
John Elkington

1st edn
Cannibals with Forks:
The Triple Bottom Line of
21st Century Business
Capstone, 1997; 416pp,
hbk; 978-1900961271

Current edn
Cannibals with Forks:
The Triple Bottom Line of
21st Century Business
Capstone, 1999; 425pp,
pbk, new edn;
978-1841120843

Key ideas

▶ The sustainability agenda incorporates a triple bottom line, focusing on economic prosperity, environmental quality and social justice.

▶ Business will increasingly be driving the sustainability agenda, in most cases in response to painful experiences, but also increasingly because they see a commercial opportunity.

▶ Success in one or two of the triple bottom lines is not enough to ensure long-term sustainability; there must be a balanced approach.

▶ Stakeholder engagement is crucial to ensure that companies detect potential social, economic and environmental risks and opportunities.

Synopsis

Cannibals with Forks derives its title from the Polish poet, Stanislaw Lec, who asked: 'Is it progress if a cannibal uses a fork?' Elkington in turn asks, would it be progress if companies who 'devour competing corporations' and if industries who 'carve up and digest other industries' used the three-pronged fork of sustainability, i.e. if they embraced the triple bottom line of economic prosperity, environmental quality and social justice?

Citing companies including Nike, Wal-Mart, Levi Strauss, Volkswagen, Texaco, Intel, Volvo, Dow Chemical, Electrolux, Novo Nordisk and Shell, the book sets out seven dimensions of a sustainable future – a 7-D world – which will see paradigm shifts in markets (from compliance to competition), values (hard to soft), transparency (closed to open), life-cycle technology (product to function), partnerships (subversion to symbiosis), time (wider to longer) and governance (exclusive to inclusive).

Elkington argues that business will be operating in markets that are much more open to competition, and sustainability will become a driver in this new operating environment: 'Business will shift from using competition as an excuse not to address the triple bottom line agenda to a new approach, using the triple bottom line as part of the business case for action and investment.'

There will also be a transition from 'hard' commercial values to 'softer' triple-bottom-line values which will be central to the sustainability transition. These new value systems (which involve more questioning of authority) are coming together with new technologies to disseminate and analyse information. The resulting 'goldfish bowl' world will trigger three types of corporate response: stealth, i.e. operating under societies' radar screen; using the new information as competitive intelligence to defend entrenched interests; and integration of triple-bottom-line considerations into core business strategies.

Companies are being questioned about their activities from cradle to cradle, rather than just on the point of sale: 'Companies operating in a wide range of different industries will suddenly find themselves exposed to a new form of "x-ray environment", in which their value chains and product life-cycles will be exposed to wider scrutiny.' New forms of partnerships will develop between companies, and between companies and other organisations, including campaigning groups.

Technology and 'just-in-time' management in the 'CNN world' means that companies are being pressured to think very short-term, while the sustainability agenda is 'long-time'. This sets up a tension that is central to engaging with sustainability.

New questions are also being asked of corporate boards: What is business for? Who should have a say in how companies are run? What is the appropriate balance between shareholders and stakeholders? Elkington concludes by providing a model for business leaders and their corporations to respond to the seven sustainability revolutions. At a pragmatic level, this includes guidance on how to develop sustainability auditing frameworks for the three bottom lines.

From the book

- The sustainability agenda, long understood as an attempt to harmonize the traditional financial bottom line with emerging thinking about the environmental bottom line, is turning out to be much more complicated than some early business enthusiasts imagined.

- Increasingly, we think in terms of a 'triple bottom line', focusing on economic prosperity, environmental quality, and – the element which business has tended to overlook – social justice.

- The sustainability transition will require that we shift the emphasis from economic growth (with its focus on quantity) to sustainable development (with its focus on economic, environmental and social qualities).

- The emerging [sustainability] agenda requires us to think across decades, generations and even centuries, while business and political leaders find it difficult to think three years ahead.

- Our ability to deliver long-term sustainability will depend heavily on our ability to help switch on capitalists, financial markets, entrepreneurs, managerial classes, and consumers of the emerging economies, developing nations and less developed countries of the world.

About the author

John Elkington (born 1949) is widely regarded as a world authority on corporate responsibility and sustainable development. He is a prodigious coiner of new concepts (like 'triple bottom line'). In 2004, *Business-Week* described him as 'a dean of the corporate responsibility movement for three decades'.

Elkington is co-founder of SustainAbility (Chair from 1995 to 2005), and Founding Partner and Director of Volans Ventures. Established in 1987, SustainAbility advises clients on the risks and opportunities associated with corporate responsibility and sustainable development. Volans Ventures,

launched in April 2008, aims to find, explore, advise on and build innovative scalable solutions to the great global divides that overshadow the future. Volans is carrying forward Elkington's work with the Skoll Foundation on a $1 million, three-year field-building programme in relation to social entrepreneurship.

Over time, Elkington has authored or co-authored 17 books, including 1988's million-selling *Green Consumer Guide*. He has also written hundreds of articles for newspapers, magazines and journals; and has written or co-written some 40 published reports.

Elkington is a Faculty member of the World Economic Forum (since 2002) and a Visiting Professor at the Doughty Centre for Corporate Responsibility at the Cranfield University School of Management. He chairs the Environment Foundation and the Aflatoun Impact and Policy Analysis Steering Group. He has numerous advisory roles with, among others, the Dow Jones Sustainability Indexes, Business & Human Rights Resource Centre, WWF, Cambridge Programme for Sustainability Leadership and the United Nations Global Compact Cities Programme (UNGCCP).

In his own words
(2008 interview)

Reflections on the book

I think *Cannibals* was different; I don't think it caught a wave. But I was uneasy, because eco-efficiency took financial performance and put it alongside environmental efficiency, or energy efficiency, or resource efficiency, or whatever. And what I felt that lacked on the financial dimension was the economic impacts that companies have. And the other piece was the social agenda. So the triple bottom line, when it came together, was for corporate leaders like popping a pill where you suddenly saw the world slightly differently.

The role of business

We're in the early stages of a recession, which is profoundly different from the sort of spiky recessions that we've had in the last 15 years or so. If the pattern of the mid-seventies and early eighties repeats itself, companies will shut down or slim down what they have on the CSR and citizenship fronts, although it's harder for them to do it now.

I think we are headed towards a period where the global economy goes into a sort of thixotropic state. All of these pressures are going to mobilise a set of dynamics which are unpredictable and profoundly disruptive to incumbent companies. Most companies that we currently know will not be around in 15 to 20 years, which is almost an inconceivable statement. But periodically this happens and there's a radical bleeding of the landscape.

Looking to the future

I think key parts of our economies and societies are on a doomed path really and I think that's unavoidable. We're heading into a period of creative destruction on a scale that really we haven't seen for a very long time, and there are all sorts of factors that feed into it: the entry of the Chinese and Indians into the global market, quite apart from things like climate change and new technology.

The older I get, the more I come to realise that the really profound scientific and technological and cultural values-based transitions in our societies evolve on very protracted timescales – so 50, 60, 70 years is what we're talking about. If we think of Rachel Carson, the Santa Barbara oil spill and Earth Day 1970 as the real take-off moment of what we're talking about now, that is towards 50 years ago. So I expect, from 2020 onwards, the paradigm that we all live in will fracture, and this new one that's been emerging for quite some time will pop through.

I'm optimistic. Although it's very easy to sound like an Old Testament prophet, I think the 21st century is going to be at least as complicated, as difficult, and as bloody as the 20th, as much as it pains me to say that. The level of change that is going to be forced on our economies, our value chains, our companies and the people who work in business is going to be both profound, and profoundly exciting. There are few times in world history where I would rather have been alive.

OTHER BOOKS (SELECTION)

The Green Consumer Guide. From Shampoo to Champagne: How to Buy Goods That Don't Cost the Earth (with Julia Hailes; Gollancz, 1988)

A Year in the Greenhouse (Gollancz, 1990)

The Chrysalis Economy: How Citizen CEOs and Corporations Can Fuse Values and Value Creation (Capstone, 2001)

The Power of Unreasonable People: How Social Entrepreneurs Create Markets That Change the

MORE INFORMATION

John Elkington's official website:
www.johnelkington.com

SustainAbility:
www.sustainability.com

Volans Ventures:
www.volans.com

23
The Hungry Spirit
Charles Handy

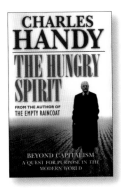

1st edn
The Hungry Spirit.
Beyond Capitalism:
The Quest for Purpose
in the Modern World
Hutchinson, 1997;
288pp, hbk;
978-0091801687

Current UK edn
The Hungry Spirit.
Beyond Capitalism: New
Thinking for a New World
Arrow Books, 1998;
288pp, pbk, rev. edn;
978-0099227724

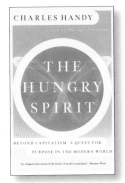

Current US edn
The Hungry Spirit.
Beyond Capitalism:
The Quest for Purpose
in the Modern World
Broadway Books, 1999;
288pp, pbk;
978-0767901888

Key ideas

▶ Individuals and organisations have an inbuilt desire to find a higher purpose beyond making money and profits (these are simply a means to an end).

▶ Rather than altruism, this requires us being 'properly selfish', i.e. accepting a responsibility for making the most of ourselves by finding a purpose beyond and bigger than ourselves.

▶ Currently, greed-driven capitalism and shareholder-driven business does not create a very conducive context for the pursuit of meaning.

▶ In order to allow purpose to flourish in the economy and workplace, we need to create citizen corporations, which treat employees and other stakeholders as part of a community.

▶ The quest for purpose in our business and personal lives implies an attempt to leave the world in a better state than we found it.

Synopsis

The Hungry Spirit, which is a philosophical treatise on business, grew out of a personal realisation by Handy that, over the course of his life, he had placed too much significance on job titles and career success. Conversely, he felt he had not paid enough attention to the importance of family, friends and becoming a more complete person, rather than simply an economic actor in the theatre of business.

As a result, Handy began searching for what he calls his 'white stone' – a symbol of the higher self that represents our true destiny, i.e. what you can become when you don't let titles and money and societal pressures get in the way. He starts by reflecting on how capitalism has not delivered on its promise, due to the multitude of unintended side-effects. In particular, free-market capitalism has five key limitations:

1. Artificial markets (such as privatising public utilities) don't work;

2. Markets can lower standards;

3. Markets have failed to globalise benefits;

4. Markets can deepen difference; and

5. Markets ignore the free, i.e. the unpriced.

As a result, American parents spend 40% less time with their children than they did 30 years ago. Per capita consumption is up 45% in 20 years, but quality of life has dropped 51%. Barely a fifth of young people believe they have a very good chance of achieving 'the good life', while salaried workers the world over are working longer and longer hours. All while we are pursuing a 'chindogu society', which focuses on selling useless things, fuelling growth but failing to provide us with purpose.

Handy urges us as individuals, companies and organisations to take responsibility for shaping our lives by finding a purpose and applying it in the world. Rather than trying to rally co-workers around a quarterly profit goal, companies should treat employees as citizens, as well as behaving as corporate citizens within the wider community. This implies diminishing the distorting influence of shareholders in the Anglo-American business model.

Capitalism itself needs to be reinterpreted to make it decent and companies need to be rethought. The current pattern of economic growth is unsustainable. Handy summarises this with a formula: $1/2 \times 2 \times 3 = P$, meaning half as many people, paid twice as much, producing three times as much work, equal productivity and profit. As a result, some people work to the exclusion of all other activities, while those who don't work face an uncertain future, and are forced to take responsibility for their lives, rather than assume employment forever.

Handy calls for corporations to take a greater role in upholding the moral structure of society and to use their power to distribute knowledge and wealth to those who need the opportunity to develop – actions that will one day benefit us all. This needs to be underscored by a reformed education system: 'We need an approach to education which fosters responsibility for oneself and others. *How* we learn then becomes as important as *what* we learn.'

From the book

- Capitalism, which was supposed to set us free, may be enslaving us in its turn, with its insistence on the dominance of the economic imperative.

- What good can it possibly do to pile up riches which you cannot conceivably use, and what is the point of the efficiency needed to create those riches if one third of the world's workers are now unemployed or under-employed?

- If 'buoyant consumer demand' means a world full of junk, it is hard to see why we should want to work so hard for it.

- As things stand, we seem to be saying that life is essentially about economics, that money is the measure of most things, and that the market is its sorting mechanism. My hunch is that most of us don't believe any of this, and that it won't work . . . but we are trapped in our own rhetoric and have, as yet, nothing else to offer, not even a different way to talk about it. There is, I believe, a hunger for something else which might be more enduring and more worthwhile.

- The real social revolution of the last thirty years, one we are still living through, is the switch from a life that is largely organised for us, once we have opted into it, to a world in which we are all forced to be in charge of our own destiny.

About the author

Charles Handy (born 1932) is from Kildare, Ireland, and was educated in England and in the United States. He graduated from Oriel College, Oxford, with first-class honours in 'Greats', a study of classics, history and philosophy.

After college, Handy worked for Shell International in South-East Asia and London and then entered the Sloan School of Management at the Massachusetts Institute of Technology. Here Handy met Warren Bennis, Chris Argyris, Ed Schein and Mason Haire, and became interested in organisations and how they work.

He returned to England in 1967 to manage the Sloan Programme at Britain's first Graduate Business School in London. In 1972, Handy became a full Professor at the School, specialising in managerial psychology. From 1977 to 1981, Handy worked at a conference and study centre in Windsor Castle which was concerned with ethics and values in society.

He was chairman of the Royal Society of Arts in London from 1987 to 1989 and holds honorary doctorates from seven British Universities. He is known to many for his 'Thoughts for Today' on the BBC Radio *To-*

day programme and his numerous books on business and society.

Handy and his wife Elizabeth, who is also his business partner, have two adult children and share their time between homes in England and Italy.

Photo: Elizabeth Handy

In his own words
(2008 interview)

Reflections on the book

The Hungry Spirit came out when the dot-com world was at its height; getting rich quick for young entrepreneurs was what it was all about and making bags of money. So what I go on about in this book

– that money isn't everything and that we have responsibilities as well as opportunities – didn't go down frightfully well. In America they said I was trying to tear down Wall Street and that would suck the juice out of the American dream. I think Wall Street needed to do a little more reflection and self-examination at that time, but they weren't ready for it.

The role of business

I've always had my doubts about shareholder capitalism, because we keep talking about the shareholders as being owners of the business, but most of them haven't a clue what business they're in. They are basically punters with no particular interest in the horse that they're backing, as long as it wins.

I want to reduce the power of shareholders. They've got too much power and too little responsibility. Everybody else says, 'Give them more responsibility. Let them exercise their power responsibly.' That's a myth. We've got to give them less power, by giving other people more power. For instance, give the people who actually create the wealth, the workers, more rights.

Corporate social responsibility starts at home; companies ought to provide a better place to work in. A recent survey in Britain said that 72% of workers really didn't like their organisation and 19% of them actually sabotaged it. That doesn't sound to me like a happy place to work in. If you want to make people proud to be in your organisation then you want to be demonstrably doing good for the world.

Looking to the future

Markets, to operate, need rules and laws and constraints and penalties, because the old paradox says good brakes make a car go faster. Governments don't lead, they follow. Therefore change actually has to come from people outside government, from the initiators of ideas, from the people who start the debate, but also then from the chief actors who are the pioneers of change, who provide living examples of what it could be.

I don't think it's easy to find your meaning in the big corporations these days. Without meaning to, they become prisons for the human soul because they force you to be somebody you are not, to work to their commands. And, because they pay you a lot, you do it, but you despise yourself for doing this thing which you don't think is necessary or particularly useful or done particularly well.

We need more emotion in our organisations. We need more stories. We need more passion. We need more love actually and care of people. In the end we'll need to make a reality of this phrase that 'people are our assets'. You should cherish your assets, not bleed them to death.

OTHER BOOKS (SELECTION)

Understanding Organisations (Penguin Books, 1976)

Gods of Management: The Changing Work of Organizations (Souvenir Press, 1986)

The Elephant and the Flea: Reflections of a Reluctant Capitalist (Arrow Books, 2001)

Myself and Other More Important Matters (Random House, 2006)

The New Philanthropists (with Elizabeth Handy; William Heinemann, 2006)

24
Banker to the Poor
Muhammad Yunus

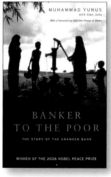

1st edn
Banker to the Poor:
The Autobiography
of Muhammad Yunus,
Founder of the
Grameen Bank
Aurum Press, 1998;
288pp, hbk;
978-1854105776

Current UK edn
Banker to the Poor:
The Story of the
Grameen Bank
Aurum Press, 2003;
338pp, pbk, new edn;
978-1854109248

Current US edn
Banker to the Poor:
Micro-lending and
the Battle against
World Poverty
Public Affairs, Perseus
Books Group, 2003;
312pp, pbk, rev. edn;
978-1586481988

Key ideas

▶ The poor are in a poverty trap because they lack access to credit. Poverty is not a natural state.

▶ Credit is a human right, as it has become indispensable in meeting basic human needs.

▶ The poor are creditworthy, contrary to popular beliefs that they are too high-risk and hence 'unbankable'.

▶ Everyone is an entrepreneur. Hence, microcredit creates a way for people to help themselves.

▶ Providing the poor with access to credit and to information technology will eliminate poverty.

Synopsis

Banker to the Poor, essentially an autobiography of Muhammad Yunus and Grameen Bank, is a fascinating mix of economic arguments, personal anecdotes and inspiring stories. What became the Grameen Bank and worldwide microcredit movement began with a simple $27 loan in 1974 by Yunus, then an economics professor, to relieve suffering when Bangladesh was struck by a severe famine. Yunus lent money to 42 women so they could purchase bamboo to make and sell stools. In a short time, the women were able to repay the loans while continuing to support themselves and their families.

With that initial success, Yunus started an experimental microcredit enterprise in 1977. After failing to gain the support of traditional banks, he decided to set up his own 'bank to the poor', the Grameen Bank, in 1983. The idea behind the Grameen Bank is simple: extend credit to poor people and they will help themselves. This concept strikes at the root of poverty by specifically targeting the poorest of the poor, providing small loans (usually less than $300) to those unable to obtain credit from traditional banks.

At Grameen, loans are administered to groups of five people, with only two receiving their money upfront. As soon as these two make a few regular payments, loans are gradually extended to the rest of the group. In this way, the programme builds a sense of community as well as individual self-reliance. Most of the Grameen Bank's loans are to women and, since its inception, there has been an astonishing loan repayment rate of over 98%.

Historically, the poor do not have access to opportunities for economic development because financing is always geared towards those who have money, not to the poor. However, Yunus argues that the only way for the poor to escape poverty is to have access to these same opportunities through the provision of credit. On the issue of creditworthiness, he says: 'Why can't the poor control any capital? Because they do not inherit any capital or credit, nor does anybody give them access to capital, because we have been made to believe that the poor are not to be trusted with credit – they are not creditworthy. But are banks people-worthy?'

The Grameen Bank is now a $2.5 billion banking enterprise in Bangladesh, while the microcredit model has spread to over 50 countries worldwide, from the US to Papua New Guinea, Norway to Nepal. It has also led to the development of other social enterprises, such as GrameenPhone, Grameen Check (loom-woven cloths), Grameen Fisheries Foundation, Grameen Cybernet and Grameen Shakti (energy).

The book is rich with Yunus's philosophy on everything from banking, economics and capitalism to education, poverty and business. His basic premise is that the current welfare state actually impedes the ability of the poor to escape poverty as it punishes poverty-freeing activities. Further, capitalism can enable the poor to escape poverty only if social impact is given a value, i.e. if it takes into account the externalities of positive social behaviour.

From the book

- The poor, once economically empowered, are the most determined fighters in the battle to solve the population problem, end illiteracy and live healthier, better lives. When policy makers finally realize that the poor are their partners, rather than bystanders or enemies, we will progress much faster than we do today.

- We should judge the quality of life of a society not by looking at the way the rich in that society live, but by the way the lowest percentile of the people live their lives.

- Greed is not the only fuel for free enterprise. Social goals can replace greed as a powerful motivational force. Social-consciousness-driven enterprises can be formidable competitors for the greed-based enterprises.

- I propose that we replace the narrow profit maximisation principle with a generalised principle – an entrepreneur who maximises a bundle consisting of two components: profit and social returns, subject to the condition that profit can not be negative.

- Economic and social empowerment which creates income-earning opportunities for poor women and brings them into organisational folds will have more impact on curbing population growth than the current system of trying to frighten people.

About the author

Muhammad Yunus (born 1940) is a Bangladeshi banker and economist, who has become the figurative and literal leader of the microcredit movement.

Born in 1940 in the seaport city of Chittagong, Yunus studied at Dhaka University in Bangladesh, then received a Fulbright scholarship to study economics at Vanderbilt University. He received his PhD in economics from Vanderbilt in 1969 and the following year became an assistant professor of economics at Middle Tennessee State University. Returning to Bangladesh, Yunus headed the economics department as a professor at Chittagong University.

Yunus established the Grameen Bank in Bangladesh in 1983, which today offers credit to seven million poor people in Bangladesh. From 1993 to 1995, Yunus was a member of the International Advisory Group for the Fourth World Conference on Women, a post to which he was appointed by the UN Secretary-General. He has served on the Global Commission of Women's Health, the Advisory Council for Sustainable Economic Development and the UN Expert Group on Women and Finance.

Yunus is the recipient of numerous international awards for his ideas and endeavours, including the 2006 Nobel Peace prize, jointly with the Grameen Bank. In early 2007 Yunus showed interest in launching a political party in Bangladesh named Nagorik Shakti (Citizen Power), but later discarded the plan. He is one of the founding members of Global Elders.

In his own words
(2008 interview)

Reflections on the book

I was teaching as an economics professor in one of the universities in Bangladesh when we were hit by a famine. So I felt totally empty. All of the economics theories sounded so hollow and useless. So I thought why don't I go out and see if I can reach out to another human being. Be next to him or her and help the person to overcome any difficulty for that particular day.

All this academic life that I had all these years gave me a bird's-eye view – I can see the whole world, I can see the terrain, but I don't see the details. Now coming to the village, I see the details in very, very clear terms. What I'm getting now is the worm's-eye view. This is an advantage. If you have the worm's-eye view, then you can find the solution right away.

The role of business

I see that now the businesses are trying to discover a new world of poor people, and they call it 'bottom of the pyramid', 'the undiscovered territory' and so on. And I feel uncomfortable with that kind of attitude. It's not getting them out of that situation. You want to make yourself rich out of the people who live there. Our primary responsibility is to lift them, rather than see it as an opportunity to make money. We should not look at the poor as consumers of our product. We should see them as potential producers, potential creative people who can take charge of their own life and transform it.

Today, I would say corporate social responsibility is a fund given to the public relations department, which they use more for promotional purposes for the company, rather than genuinely touching the life of the people. That money, which is given as corporate social responsibility, could be used to create a social business – a business that is exclusively devoted to achieving a social goal.

Looking to the future

I'm totally convinced that we can create a world where there'll be no poor person at all. People have the capacity, the unlimited potential to change their own life and contribute to this planet. But, unfortunately, they aren't given a chance. We're not asking for special chances or special policies for them. We're talking about whatever benefit – whatever chances – that others have at the top of society.

Human beings are packed with unlimited capacity; they can change their life. And poverty is an artificial imposition on human beings; it's not something that they are born with. And if you remove that artificial situation they will come out of poverty. The thing that we need to change is the economic framework. We have to include another type of business and I'm calling it social business: business totally dedicated to addressing social issues and problems. Once we bring these things together, I think we can create a world without poverty.

25
The Crisis of Global Capitalism
George Soros

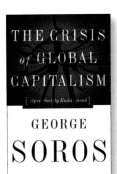

1st edn
and current US edn
The Crisis of Global Capitalism:
Open Society Endangered
Public Affairs, Perseus
Books Group, 1998;
288pp, hbk;
978-1891620270

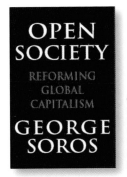

Current UK edn
Open Society:
Reforming Global Capitalism
Little, Brown, 2000;
389pp, pbk, rev. edn;
978-0316855983

Key ideas

▶ The current capitalist system is 'unsound and unsustainable', because it is based on market fundamentalism.

▶ Market fundamentalism – the belief that free markets result in the common good – is a greater threat to the well-being of society than any totalitarian ideology.

▶ Market forces, left unregulated, produce chaos and could ultimately lead to the downfall of the global capitalist system.

▶ Political institutions are equally flawed, often putting the interests of politicians or parties ahead of the common good of society.

▶ Capitalism can fulfil its promise provided it operates within an 'open society', i.e. one that properly upholds democracy and the rule of law.

Synopsis

The Crisis of Global Capitalism warns that global stability is threatened by the emergence of market fundamentalism – the belief that the common interest is best served by individual decision-making and that any attempt to maintain the common interest through government intervention distorts the market mechanism. 'It is market fundamentalism,' Soros insists, 'that has rendered the global capitalist system unsound and unsustainable.'

Soros believes that the development of a global economy has not been matched by the development of a global society. International law and international institutions, insofar as they exist, are not strong enough to prevent war or the large-scale abuse of human rights in individual countries. Ecological threats are not adequately dealt with. And global financial markets, which are inherently unstable and do not care about social and environmental needs, are largely beyond the control of national or international authorities.

Soros criticises the global capitalist system on two counts. First, market fundamentalists erroneously believe that markets tend towards equilibrium. However, financial markets are characterised by booms and busts as a result of self-reinforcing loops in the economic and trading system. Hence, the potential for disequilibrium is inherent in the financial system; it is not just the result of external shocks.

Second, we see the failures of politics and the erosion of moral values on both the national and international level. Soros distinguishes between 'making rules', which is a collective decision, and 'playing by the rules', which is an individual decision. He notes that this distinction is rarely observed, particularly with politicians who too often put personal interests above public interests. This is exacerbated by the 'promotion of self-interest to a moral principle'. The result is that markets are enjoying free rein in areas where they should not have influence, ranging from moral values and family relationships to aesthetic and intellectual achievements, with 'destructive and demoralizing effects'.

Soros believes capitalism needs democracy as a counterweight because the capitalist system by itself shows no tendency towards equilibrium. While communism has been worse than the disease it tried to cure, market fundamentalism is not the cure either: 'Communism abolished the market mechanism and imposed collective control over all economic activities. Market fundamentalism seeks to abolish collective decision making and to impose the supremacy of market values over all political and social values. Both extremes are wrong. What we need is a correct balance between politics and markets, between rule making and playing by the rules.'

The solution Soros proposes is the promotion of an 'open society', a term coined by Karl Popper and meaning a society that is, in contrast to totalitarian societies, founded on democracy and the rule of law – both elements that Soros believes market fundamentalism erodes. Within an open society, there is an acknowledgement that institutions are flawed and that errors are made. But, rather than this being a reason to abandon the institutional arrangements, it simply calls for error-correcting mechanisms to protect both markets and democracy.

From the book

- The ideology of market fundamentalism is profoundly and irredeemably flawed. Market forces, if they are given complete authority even in the purely economic and financial arenas, produce chaos and could ultimately lead to the downfall of the global capitalist system.

- We live in a global economy, but the political organization of our global society is woefully inadequate. We are bereft of the capacity to preserve peace and to counteract the excesses of the financial markets. Without these controls, the global economy is liable to break down.

- Financial markets are supposed to swing like a pendulum. Instead, as I told Congress, financial markets behave more like a wrecking ball, swinging from country to country and knocking over the weaker ones. It is difficult to escape the conclusion that the international financial system itself constituted the main ingredient in the meltdown process.

- The choice confronting us is whether we will regulate global financial markets internationally or leave it to each individual state to protect its interests as best it can. The latter course will surely lead to the breakdown of the gigantic circulatory system, which goes under the name of global capitalism.

- I do not want to abolish capitalism. In spite of its shortcomings, it is better than the alternatives. Instead, I want to prevent the global capitalist system from destroying itself.

About the author

George Soros (born 1947) is a Hungarian-born billionaire investor, philanthropist and author.

In 1947, Soros fled the Soviet Union Communist occupation of Hungary and arrived in England. He went on to study at the London School of Economics and graduated in 1952. Soros then emigrated and settled in the US in 1956.

Upon moving to America, Soros set up an investment fund that went on to create his massive fortune. It was his intention to simply support his love of writing from his Wall Street earnings, but his well-timed investment decisions saw his wealth increase dramatically each year. The Quantum Fund went on to become one of the most successful managed investment funds ever, with a more than 30% increase annually over a 30-year period.

Since 1979 he has been supporting and funding various organisations and activities worldwide. His first charitable actions helped to fund black students in the University of Cape Town in South Africa during apartheid. In 1992, Soros earned himself international fame and the nickname of 'the man who broke the Bank of England' after speculating on the Pound Sterling, believing it was overvalued and earning himself $1.1 billion in the process.

Soros is founder and chairman of the Open Society Institute, an organisation that supports activities in more than 50 countries worldwide. Soros is also the author of numerous books on the economy and politics.

OTHER BOOKS (SELECTION)

Underwriting Democracy: Encouraging Free Enterprise and Democratic Reform Among the Soviets and in Eastern Europe (Simon & Schuster, 1991)

Open Society: Reforming Global Capitalism (Public Affairs, 2000)

The Bubble of American Supremacy: Correcting the Misuse of American Power (Public Affairs, 2004)

George Soros on Globalization (Perseus Books Group, 2005)

The Age of Fallibility: The Consequences of the War on Terror (Public Affairs, 2006)

MORE INFORMATION

George Soros's website:
www.georgesoros.com

Open Society Institute and Soros Foundation:
www.soros.org

26
Factor Four
Ernst von Weizsäcker, Amory B. Lovins and L. Hunter Lovins

1st and current edn
Factor Four:
Doubling Wealth,
Halving Resource Use
Earthscan Publications,
1998; 224pp, pbk;
978-1853834066

Key ideas

- ▶ Resource productivity of our economies can and should grow fourfold, i.e. the amount of wealth extracted from one unit of natural resources can quadruple. We can live twice as well, yet use half as much.

- ▶ This would not only help us waste fewer resources, but could also offer opportunities for financial gain and contribute to meeting global needs.

- ▶ Much of the technology to achieve Factor Four already exists; it simply needs to be applied at scale.

- ▶ However, systemic barriers (in the policy and economic arena) are preventing these ideas from succeeding.

- ▶ Advanced resource productivity requires integration, not reductionism, i.e. thinking about the design challenge as a whole, not as a lot of disjointed little pieces.

Synopsis

Factor Four, a report to the Club of Rome which showcases 50 examples of best practice, argues that natural resources can be used more efficiently in all domains of daily life, either by generating more products, services and quality of life from the available resources, or by using fewer resources to maintain the same standard.

Our focus on production and productivity has had a number of negative side-effects: we are overusing the natural environment, decreasing the availability of non-renewable resources and creating enormous waste, possibly as much as $10 trillion every year globally. The alternative is Factor Four: using resources more efficiently, doing more with less, and increasing our resource productivity while using fewer resources.

While in the past such an alternative would have been expensive, advances in technology mean that 'big savings can sometimes become even cheaper than small savings'. The authors list seven compelling reasons to move towards efficiency:

1. *Live better*: resource efficiency improves quality of life.

2. *Pollute and deplete less*: efficiency reduces waste and pollution, which is simply an unutilised resource.

3. *Make money*: resource efficiency is usually undertaken at a profit.

4. *Harness markets and enlist business*: market forces combined with innovative policy structures and market mechanisms can drive resource efficiency.

5. *Multiply the use of scarce capital*: the money saved with resource efficiency practices can be reinvested to solve further efficiency problems.

6. *Increase security*: resource scarcity and competition can be the source of international conflict.

7. *Be equitable and have more employment*: resource efficiency activities can reduce the amount of unproductive resource allocation.

There are numerous barriers that actively prevent people and businesses from choosing Factor Four solutions, including: inertia that is reinforced by current education systems; vested interests of capital owners in preserving the status quo; distorted financial criteria; split incentives between those who might buy the efficiency and others who would reap its benefits; inaccurate prices that omit costs to society, the environment and to future generations; the political and financial preference for large, centralised projects, rather than small, decentralised ones; obsolete regulations that specifically discourage or outlaw efficiency; and the almost universal practice of regulating electric, gas, water and other utilities so they're rewarded for increasing usage rather than efficiency.

The authors argue that many of these incentives should be reversed: architects, utility companies and others should be paid more the more they reduce costs and resource use. The regulatory playing field should be levelled between green approaches and old-style wasteful ways of doing things. Tax systems should be changed to penalise 'bads' (pollution, inefficiency), not 'goods' (income, labour).

From the book

- We can accomplish everything we do today as well as now, or better, with only one-fourth the energy and materials we presently use. This would make it possible, for example, to double the global standard of living while cutting resource use in half.

- We are more than ten times better at wasting resources than at using them. This waste is unnecessarily expensive.

- Waste impoverishes families (especially those with lower incomes), reduces competitiveness, imperils our resource base, poisons water, air, soil, and people, and suppresses employment and economic vitality.

- The wasting disease is curable. The cure is using resources efficiently: doing more with less. It is not a question of going backward or 'returning' to prior means.

- Factor Four is the beginning of a new industrial revolution in which we shall achieve dramatic increases in the resource productivity.

Ernst Ulrich von Weizsäcker

About the authors

Ernst Ulrich von Weizsäcker (born 1939) joined the Bren School as Dean in January 2006. Previously, he served as the policy director at the United Nations Centre for Science and Technology for Development, director of the Institute for European Environmental Policy, and president of the Wuppertal Institute for Climate, Environment and Energy. He is a member of the Club of Rome, a global thinktank devoted to improving society, and he served on the World Commission on the Social Dimensions of Globalisation. Later, he became a member of the Bundestag, the federal parliament of Germany, where he was appointed chairman of the Environmental Committee. He has also served as a professor of interdisciplinary biology and was the founding president of the University of Kassel in

Amory B. Lovins

L. Hunter Lovins

Germany. Von Weizsäcker has authored several influential books on the environment.

Amory B. Lovins (born 1947) is Rocky Mountain Institute Cofounder, Chairman and Chief Scientist and a consultant experimental physicist educated at Harvard and Oxford. He has received an Oxford MA (by virtue of being a don), nine honorary doctorates, a MacArthur Fellowship, the Heinz, Lindbergh, Right Livelihood ('Alternative Nobel'), World Technology and Time Hero for the Planet awards, the Benjamin Franklin and Happold Medals, the Nissan, Shingo, Mitchell and Onassis Prizes, and honorary membership of the American Institute of Architects. He has lately led the redesign of $30 billion-worth of facilities in 29 sectors for radical energy and resource efficiency. He has briefed 19 heads of state, held several visiting academic chairs (most recently the 2007 MAP/Ming Professorship at Stanford), written 29 books and hundreds of papers, and consulted for scores of industries and governments worldwide. The *Wall Street Journal* named Mr Lovins one of 39 people worldwide 'most likely to change the course of business in the '90s'; *Newsweek* has praised him as 'one of the Western world's most influential energy thinkers'; and *Car* magazine ranked him the 22nd most powerful person in the global automotive industry.

L. Hunter Lovins (born 1950) is a leading author, consultant and lecturer on sustainable development. She is the founder and President of Natural Capitalism, Inc. and Natural Capitalism Solutions, working with businesses, governments and organisations to implement a profitable approach to developing sustainable businesses and communities. She has been at the cutting edge of environmental thinking for the past 30 years. As CEO for Strategy, she helped grow the world-renowned Rocky Mountain Institute (RMI) into a 50-person applied research centre and source of some of the most innovative environmental policy ideas of recent decades. She is co-author of nine books and dozens of papers. Lovins is also a founding professor of business at Presidio World College, which offers the first accredited MBA in Sustainable Management. For her work, she has been recognised with the Mitchell Prize, the Right Livelihood Award and the Lindbergh Award for Environment and Technology. In 2000, she was named a 'Hero for the Planet' by *Time* magazine. She is a professional speaker on natural capitalism, sustainability, governance in a globalising world, energy policy, land management, green real estate development, and community economic prosperity.

In their own words (2008 interviews)

Ernst von Weizsäcker

Reflections on the book

Factor 4 was empirics-based, using examples that were either already on the market, like the passive house which is perhaps a factor of 5 or 6 better in terms of energy use than existing buildings, or at least existing in design.

We make a distinction between energy efficiency and energy productivity. Energy efficiency is about the increase of energy efficiency of one specific instrument, like a light bulb. The old incandescent light bulbs need four times more electricity for the same light as the compact fluorescents do, so that's a factor of 4 of efficiency. However, if you then spread four times more light because now it's cheaper, the light-related energy productivity hasn't grown at all.

I would love to talk about success stories of the last 15 years or so since *Factor Four* was published, but they are nearly non-existent or at least invisible.

The role of business and policy

I believe in industry there is an increasing awareness of systems thinking, of cascades and chains. For instance, I believe, in Europe, BASF have established a system in which each waste stream is turned into a feedstock stream for the next chemical process. Similarly, General Electric with 'ecomagination' have launched a new technological and marketing idea of being efficient. And Wal-Mart is beginning to look at the entire manufacturing and supply chain for reducing their carbon footprints.

In Germany, we have seen the so-called passive house which is an almost zero-energy house becoming the architectural standard for new building and it is becoming mandatory as a standard in certain cities. And now the next wave is refurbishing existing buildings to the passive house standard. Again, a factor of 4 or so can be gained. Sweden has been the pioneer in this regard for 20 years or more and other countries are following suit.

Looking to the future

After the collapse of communism, after 1990, markets and the defenders of markets have become a bit arrogant. It may be a necessary historical development of our days to resurrect the state, the steering hand for long-termism, for social justice, for environment and other things that markets don't do.

If a country like Japan or China goes ahead with a strategy of increasing energy prices slowly and predictably, this country will have the competitive edge in future technology. It may lose some of the dinosaurs, as Japan did in the late 1970s with aluminium smelting. But at the same time the Japanese developed the fifth computer generation and that was actually very good for Japanese competitiveness.

I am very sceptical about a moralistic appeal and I'm extremely sceptical about markets providing sustainable civilisation. What we will need is a balance between state and markets and a mutually growing conviction that good signals and corresponding production and consumption patterns of sustainability have to develop. But I'm afraid this is rather a hope for the future and not a fact of today.

Amory B. Lovins

Reflections on the book

Factor Four was considered rather daring by people not really immersed in creative design, because everyone was thinking incrementally. The examples we used are still exceptional in normal practice, but they're a bit dated compared to what we're now achieving. At Rocky Mountain Institute, we've lately led the redesign of over 30 billion dollars' worth of industrial redesigns in 29 sectors. And pretty consistently we're getting 30% to 60% energy savings on retrofits paying back in two or three years, in all manner of heavy process plants. And in new facilities we save more, typically 40% to 90%.

We're talking actually not so much of technologies, as of design methods, or design mentality. Of course, the better the technologies you use the more you can achieve. But the design mentality is much more important than any technological novelty. Many of the new buildings we're designing use no, or negative amounts of, energy: that is, they create more than they use, they have very good economics. It's now perfectly normal to talk about tripled-efficiency cars, heavy lorries and airplanes.

The role of business

Wal-Mart have now demanded doubled-efficiency heavy lorries at their suppliers and they'll make billions off it, so they're highly motivated. And we're using their demand pull to drag those lorries into the market, so everybody can buy them. And Wal-Mart is quite straightforward about the fact that it likes that idea, and it's going to do the same with white goods for the household – making them very efficient at low cost, high volume.

Interface, Ray Anderson's company, has cut its greenhouse gas emissions, I think it was 82 or 83% from 1996 to 2007. So that's about 16% a year compound. United Technology has recently cut its energy intensity 45% in about five years. And DuPont has cut its greenhouse gas emissions to 80% below the 1990 level, and made three billion dollars' profit on the deal. Efficiency is cheaper than fuel. Dow made three billion; BP made two billion; and so on, just substituting efficiency for fuel. So word is getting around that efficiency matters, efficiency is cheaper than fuel, therefore planet protection is not costly, but profitable. We're seeing routinely 6–16% gains in labour productivity in efficient buildings.

Looking to the future

There are huge tectonic-plate-style movements under the surface, because I see them every day and help nudge them along. It is, of course, possible that one or more of the abrupt-change scenarios is already in train. If that's not the case, however, the problem is pretty readily and profitably soluble with existing techniques at historically observed speeds.

It's rather futile to speculate about whether we have enough time. Dana Meadows got this right. She was asked, 'Do we have enough time to solve these horrible problems?' And she said, 'Yes, we have exactly enough time, starting now.' It's like Bill McDonough's remark that negligence begins tomorrow, because now we know what to do.

L. Hunter Lovins

Reflections on the book

At the time at which we were writing *Factor Four* there was a growing recognition that no reform on sustainability can exist unless you use everything taken from the Earth and borrowed from the future dramatically more efficiently, more productively, than we are today and that this is the foundation, the cornerstone, the centre, of any movement towards sustainability. And we are still having this argument today with the energy crisis. People are saying, 'We need nuclear, we need solar, we need wind, we need some kind of supply.' No we don't: we need efficiency.

We are using resources so inefficiently that our economy digs up, puts through various resource-crunching activities and then throws away half a trillion tonnes of stuff a year. Out of all this stuff, less than 1% of it ever gets in a product and is still there six months after sale. All the rest is waste. Put another way, this is an enormous business opportunity, because squeezing out that waste is the best to way to cut your cost. It's also a great way to drive your innovation.

The role of business

STMicroelectronics announced what Jim Collins, author of *Good to Great* and *Built to Last*, calls a BHAG: a big hairy audacious goal. They said, 'We are going to be carbon-neutral, with a fortyfold increase in production by 2010.' When Pasquale Pistorio, CEO of ST, made this announcement he had no earthly idea how he was going to achieve it. But figuring it out has driven their corporate innovation, taking them from the number 12 chip maker in the world to the number 6. They are gaining market share, and winning awards. They reckon by the time they are done they will have saved about a billion dollars. This is the power of efficiency.

Why is Wal-Mart going green? Because they don't have a choice. And this is what I call 'the sustainability imperative'. Wal-Mart has made a commitment to be zero-waste, 100% renewable energy, carbon-neutral and to sell only sustainable products. You walk into Wal-Mart today, it's a long ways from it. But by setting this clear target they have signalled to their associates. And, if you go into a Wal-Mart and ask an associate what they are most excited about, it's overwhelmingly their personal sustainability project.

It's awfully easy to keep doing what it is that we have always done. It's comfortable, we know how to do it, so why change? Margaret Mead said, 'The only person who likes change is a wet baby' and I'd add that the baby squalls all the way through the process. So change is never easy. Except that humans change all the time. If we are offered something that we think is a superior product, we'll jump on it.

Looking to the future

Abba Eban said, 'People and nations behave wisely when they have exhausted all alternatives.' We are getting rather close.

OTHER BOOKS (SELECTION)

Soft Energy Paths: Toward a Durable Peace
(Amory B. Lovins; HarperBusiness, 1977)

Energy Unbound: A Fable for America's Future
(L. Hunter Lovins, Amory B. Lovins and Seth Zuckerman; Sierra Club Books, 1986)

Hypercars: Materials, Manufacturing, and Policy Implications (Amory B. Lovins; Hypercar Center and Rocky Mountain Institute, 1996)

Winning the Oil Endgame: Innovation for Profits, Jobs and Security (Amory B. Lovins; Earthscan, 2004)

Limits to Privatization: How to Avoid Too Much of a Good Thing (ed. Ernst von Weizsäcker, Oran R. Young and Matthias Finger; Earthscan, 2005)

MORE INFORMATION

Factor 10 Institute:
www.factor10-institute.org

Natural Capitalism, Inc.:
www.natcapinc.com

Rocky Mountain Institute:
www.rmi.org

Wuppertal Institute:
www.wupperinst.org

27
False Dawn
John Gray

1st edn
False Dawn:
The Delusions of Global
Capitalism
Granta Books, 1998;
400pp, hbk;
978-1862070233

Current UK edn
False Dawn:
The Delusions of Global
Capitalism
Granta Books, 2009;
272pp, pbk, 2nd rev.
edn; 978-1847081322

Current US edn
False Dawn:
The Delusions of Global
Capitalism
The New Press, 2000;
272pp, pbk;
978-1-56584-592-3

Key ideas

▶ The attempt to impose the Anglo-American-style free market on the world is a recipe for disaster, possibly on the scale of Soviet communism.

▶ Free markets aren't really free; they are the result of social engineering.

▶ A free-market economy inevitably creates instability and inequalities, which society will seek to redress by restricting the free market.

▶ The global spread of democratic capitalism to become the world political and economic system is neither inevitable nor possible.

▶ A reform of the world economy is needed that accepts a diversity of cultures, regimes and market economies as a permanent reality.

Synopsis

The underlying theme of *False Dawn* is that the US is deluded by its own 'Enlightenment thesis', believing that democratic capitalism will soon be accepted throughout the world, merging into a single universal free market. Although multinational corporations have become allies in promoting this 'unified theory' of a world civilisation, Gray believes it is destined for failure, since it is based on the same flawed assumptions as communism: 'In their cult of reason and efficiency, their ignorance of history and their contempt for the ways of life they consign to poverty or extinction, they embody the same rationalist hubris and cultural imperialism that have marked the central traditions of Enlightenment thinking throughout its history.'

Gray is not denying that the world economy can and will grow, but only under a model that is flexible and will adapt to local needs and requirements. 'The global economy that is presently under construction will not assure the free market's future. It will trigger a new competition between remaining social market economies and free markets in which social markets must reform themselves profoundly or be destroyed. Yet, paradoxically, free market economies will not be the winners in this contest. For they too are being transformed out of all recognition by global competition.'

In the past, when *laissez-faire* free markets went too far at the expense of social structures, a counterbalancing took place to ensure that social cohesion was maintained. Examples of this include Roosevelt's New Deal or European Social Democracy. However, in today's world of global markets, it is unlikely any such measures have any chance of succeeding. Gray predicts that, without this counterbalancing, 'today's regime of global *laissez-faire* will be briefer than even the *belle époque* of 1870 to 1914, which ended in the trenches of the Great War.'

Part of the reason for its pending demise, Gray believes, is that 'economic globalization actually threatens the stability of the single global market that is being constructed by American-led transnational organizations. There is nothing in today's global market that buffers it against the social strains arising from highly uneven economic development within and between the world's diverse societies. The swift waxing and waning of industries and livelihoods, the sudden shifts of production and capital, the casino of currency speculation – these conditions trigger political counter-movements that challenge the very ground rules of the global free market.'

Gray concludes that the idea that a free-market ideology could be an end-state of political and economic development is flawed: 'If "capitalism" means "the free market", then no view is more deluded than the belief that the future lies with "democratic capitalism". In the normal course of democratic political life the free market is always short-lived. Its social costs are such that it cannot for long be legitimated in any democracy.' Gray doesn't provide an 'answer', because he believes there is more than one answer: 'A reform of the world economy is needed that accepts a diversity of cultures, regimes and market economies as a permanent reality.'

From the book

- A world economy does not make a single regime – 'democratic capitalism' – universal. It propagates new types of regimes as it spawns new kinds of capitalism.

- The argument against unrestricted global freedom in trade and capital movements is not primarily an economic one. It is, rather, that the economy should serve the needs of society, not society the imperatives of the market.

- A single worldwide civilisation . . . is a Utopia that can never be realised; its pursuit has already produced social dislocation and economic and political instability on a large scale.

- The permanent revolution of the free market denies any authority to the past. It nullifies precedent, it snaps the threads of memory and scatters local knowledge. By privileging individual choice over any common good it tends to make relationships revocable and provisional.

- The Utopia of the global free market has not incurred a human cost in the way that communism did. Yet over time it may come to rival it in the suffering that it inflicts.

- At the global level, as at that of the nation-state, the free market does not promote stability or democracy. Global democratic capitalism is as unrealizable a condition as worldwide communism.

- Regulated markets . . . are the norm in every society, whereas free markets are a product of artifice, design and political coercion . . . The free market is not a gift of social evolution. It is an end-product of social engineering and unyielding political will.

- Democracy and the free market are rivals, not allies.

About the author

John N. Gray (born 1948) is a prominent British political philosopher and author.

Gray studied at Exeter College, Oxford, where he read Philosophy, Politics and Economics (PPE) and completed his BA, MPhil and DPhil. He formerly held posts as lecturer in political theory at the University of Essex, fellow and tutor in politics at Jesus College, Oxford, and lecturer and then professor of politics at the University of Oxford. He has served as a visiting professor at Harvard University, Stranahan Fellow at the Social Philosophy and Policy Center, Bowling Green State University, and has also held visiting professorships at Tulane

Photo: Nigel Stead/LSE

University's Murphy Institute, and Yale University. He was Professor of European Thought at the London School of Economics and Political Science until his retirement from academic life in early 2008.

Gray has perhaps become best known for his work, since the 1990s, on the uneasy relationship between value-pluralism and liberalism, which has ignited considerable controversy, and for his strong criticism of neoliberalism and of the global free market. More recently, he has criticised some of the central currents in Western thinking, such as humanism, and has tended towards Green thought. He has drawn from the 'Gaia theory' of James Lovelock, among others, but he is very pessimistic about human behaviour changing to prevent environmental decay.

Gray contributes regularly to the *Guardian*, *New Statesman* and *Times Literary Supplement*, and has written several influential books on political theory.

OTHER BOOKS (SELECTION)

After Social Democracy: Politics, Capitalism and the Common Life (Demos, 1996)

Two Faces of Liberalism (New Press, 2000)

Straw Dogs: Thoughts on Humans and Other Animals (Granta, 2002)

Heresies: Against Progress and Other Illusions (Granta, 2004)

Enlightenment's Wake: Politics and Culture at the Close of the Modern Age (Routledge, 2007)

28
Development as Freedom
Amartya Sen

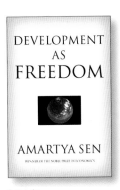

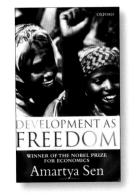

Current US edn
Development as Freedom
Anchor Books, 2000; 384pp, pbk, rev. edn; 978-0385720274

Current UK edn
Development as Freedom
Oxford University Press, 2001; 366pp, pbk, new edn; 978-0192893307

1st edn
Development as Freedom
Oxford University Press, 1999; 382pp, hbk; 978-0198297581

Key ideas

▶ Development is not just about income levels, or gross domestic product (GDP), which is simply a means to the real goal of improving the real lives of real human beings – to make those lives longer, healthier, happier, more fulfilling.

▶ Development is about expanding human freedoms, with the goal of letting people 'be subjects of their lives rather than mere objects buffeted by forces over which they have no control' and giving people the 'real capability to lead lives we have reason to value'.

▶ Poverty can be defined as 'capability deprivation'.

▶ Development requires the removal of un-freedoms: poverty, tyranny, lack of economic opportunities, systemic social deprivation, neglect of public facilities and repression.

▶ Human rights are not cultural; they are universal, especially if viewed with a lens of efficacy.

Is a freedom a right?
The abuse of freedom..

Synopsis

The recurring theme of the book is encapsulated in its title: namely, that development is about expanding human freedoms. These include but are not limited to increased GDP per capita. Hence, social and economic arrangements (education and healthcare), political and civil rights, technological progress and social modernisation are all equally important. By focusing on the end goal (freedom), one does not get trapped in a quest for part of the prize, or a focus on means to an end.

According to Sen, freedom is both the main object and the primary means of development. But this requires the removal of what he calls un-freedoms: 'Sometimes the lack of substantive freedoms relates directly to economic poverty, which robs people of the freedom to satisfy hunger, or to achieve sufficient nutrition, or to obtain remedies for treatable illnesses or the opportunity to be adequately clothed or sheltered, or to enjoy clean water or sanitary facilities. In other cases, the un-freedom links closely to the lack of public facilities and social care, such as the absence of epidemiological programs, or of organized arrangements for the health care or educational facilities, or of effective institutions for the maintenance of local peace and order. In still other cases, the violation of freedom results directly from a denial of political and civil liberties by authoritarian regimes and from imposed restrictions on the freedom to participate in the social, political and economic life of the community.'

Hence, income per head (GDP per capita) is not an accurate measure of development. There is a dissonance between income per head and the freedom of individuals to live long and live well. For instance, the citizens of South Africa or Brazil are 'richer' than the citizens of Sri Lanka or China in terms of per capita GNP, but the latter have substantially higher life expectancy. Similarly, African Americans, though much richer than people in the Third World have an absolutely lower chance of reaching maturity than do many people of Third World societies.

Women's freedom also plays a key role in development, since women's literacy and employment levels are the best predictors of both child survival and fertility rate reduction. Sen concludes that this is 'one of the more neglected areas of development studies' and that 'nothing is as important as an adequate recognition of political, economic and social participation and leadership of women'.

Sen looks in detail at five types of freedom as each of these help to advance the general capability of a person: political freedoms, economic facilities, social opportunities, transparency guarantees and protective security. In terms of political freedom, Sen argues that a democratically elected government cannot afford to let its people starve. There is also a strong role for free markets, since 'the freedom to participate in economic interchange has a basic role in social living', although 'that does not preclude the role of social support, public regulation, or statecraft when they can enrich – rather than impoverish – human lives'.

Sen does not accept that the suppression of certain rights is good for rapid economic growth. 'Indeed, the empirical evidence very strongly suggests that economic growth is more a matter of a friendlier economic climate than of a harsher political system.'

From the book

- The people have to be seen as being actively involved – given the opportunity – in shaping their own destiny, and not just as passive recipients of the fruits of cunning development programs.

- Freedoms are not only the primary ends of development, they are also among its principal means.

- In judging economic development, it is not adequate to look only at the growth of GNP or some other indicators of overall economic expansion. We have to look also at the impact of democracy and political freedoms on the lives and capabilities of the citizens.

- Development is the enhancement of freedoms that allow people to lead lives that they have reason to value.

- Development consists of the removal of various types of un-freedoms that leave people with little choice and little opportunity of exercising their reasoned agency.

- Quite often economic insecurity can relate to the lack of democratic rights and liberties.

- [Famines] never materialised in any country that is independent, that holds elections regularly, that has opposition parties to voice criticisms and that permits newspapers to report freely and question the wisdom of government policies without extensive censorship.

About the author

Amartya Kumar Sen (born 1933) is an Indian economist, philosopher and winner of the Bank of Sweden Prize in Economic Sciences (Nobel Prize for Economics) in 1998 'for his contributions to welfare economics' through his work on famine, human development theory, welfare economics, the underlying mechanisms of poverty, and political liberalism.

He received his initial education at Shan-

tiniketan and then Presidency College, Calcutta. In his early childhood he was exposed to the plight of the poor. The sight of people dying during famine shocked him – an experience that may well have influenced his choice of studying the economic mechanism underlying famines and poverty. Sen first studied in India before moving to Trinity College, Cambridge, where he earned a BA in 1956 and a PhD in 1959. He has taught economics at Calcutta, the Delhi

School of Economics (1963–71), Oxford and Harvard.

From 1998 to 2004 he was Master of Trinity College at Cambridge University, becoming the first Asian academic to head an Oxbridge college. Sen takes a keen interest in the debate about globalisation. He has given lectures to senior executives of the World Bank and is a former honorary president of Oxfam. He is currently the Lamont University Professor at Harvard University.

Sen's books have been translated into more than 30 languages. He is a trustee of the Economists for Peace and Security, and has set up the Pratichi Trust, with a part of the Nobel prize money, to take forward his work.

OTHER BOOKS (SELECTION)

Inequality Reexamined (Clarendon Press, 1992)

The Argumentative Indian: Writings on Indian History, Culture and Identity (Allen Lane, 2005)

Identity and Violence: The Illusion of Destiny (W.W. Norton & Co., 2006)

29
No Logo
Naomi Klein

1st edn
No Logo:
Taking Aim at
the Brand Bullies
Knopf Canada, 1999;
512pp, hbk;
978-0676971309

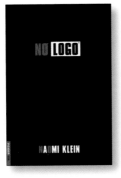

Current UK edn
No Logo:
No Space. No Choice.
No Jobs
Flamingo, 2001; 400pp,
pbk, new edn;
978-0006530404

Current US edn
No Logo:
No Space. No Choice.
No Jobs
Picador, 2002; 528pp,
pbk, rev. edn;
978-0312421434

Key ideas

▶ Multinational corporations have become so big that they have superseded governments and have become the ruling political bodies of our era.

▶ Unlike governments, multinational corporations are accountable only to their shareholders and there are no mechanisms in place to make them put people before profits.

▶ As a result of this 'corporate rule', three social pillars of our society are under threat: civil space, civil liberties and employment.

▶ As understanding of the dirty 'secrets' behind the world's biggest brands spreads, we will see the emergence of the next big political movement.

▶ The central organising principle of this movement will be targeting transnational corporations, particularly those with very high brand-name recognition.

Synopsis

No Logo is a diatribe against the trend of globalisation in general and multinational corporations in particular. Klein's main thesis is that multinationals have become too big and powerful, without any corresponding increase in accountability or responsibility. The consequence is an erosion of democratic processes, civil freedom and economic security. She foresees a global civil society backlash, which targets high-profile brands and exposes their misdemeanours.

These themes are reflected in the four sections of the book: 'No Space', 'No Choice', 'No Jobs' and 'No Logo'. 'No Space' examines the surrender of culture and education to marketing. Initially, brands were used as a means to differentiate similar products. However, in the 1980s brands became a way to associate a particular image or lifestyle with products, irrespective of their real attributes. Brands also entered the education system by signing proprietary contracts with schools and universities.

'No Choice' reports on how the promise of a vastly increased array of cultural choice was betrayed by the forces of mergers, predatory franchising, synergy and corporate censorship. Brands use their size and influence to limit competition by aggressively taking over an area or by opening proprietary stores that don't sell competitor products. Retail companies also use their power to put pressure on suppliers to sell at lower costs. In some cases, companies even try to manipulate the media to the benefit of their brands.

'No Jobs' examines the labour market trends that are decreasing employment security and social benefits. In order to cut costs and avoid legislative requirements, manufacturing jobs are being moved from Western factories to foreign countries. Often, they are relocated to Free Trade or Export Processing Zones in developing countries, which are synonymous with poor working conditions and low environmental standards. In Western countries, as manufacturing jobs are outsourced, the focus has shifted to work in the service sector, with little pay and benefits, such as a 'McJob', defined by trade unionist Dan Gallin as a 'low skill, low pay, high stress, exhausting and unstable job'. Hence, while workers are offered less and less, multinationals and their shareholders enjoy massive profits and return on investment.

The final section, 'No Logo', describes an activism that is sowing the seeds of a genuine alternative to corporate rule. Exponents of this anti-corporate movement are AdBusters, culture jamming, Reclaim the Streets and the McLibel trial. As a result of this movement, there is now an explosion of brand-based investigative activism exposing how goods are produced. These show that, while large amounts are spent on branding, advertising and marketing, very little is spent on improving labour conditions.

Klein concludes that the development of multinational branding can be linked to the growth of international sweatshops, corporate censorship and the disappearance of the steady job. She targets many famous consumer brands, including Levi Strauss, Starbucks, Pepsi, McDonald's, Wal-Mart, MTV, Tommy Hilfiger and especially Nike. Klein is not anti-globalisation per se, since global networks can also serve to better organise protests and allow for communication between grassroots movements.

From the book

- It is the assault on the three social pillars of employment, civil liberties and civic space that is giving rise to the anti-corporate activism.

- The economic trends that have so accelerated in the past decade have all been about massive redistribution and stratification of world resources: of jobs, goods, and money. Everyone except those in the very highest tier of the corporate elite is getting less.

- Despite the embrace of polyethnic imagery, market-driven globalization does not want diversity; quite the opposite. Its enemies are national habits, local brands and distinctive regional tastes.

- The lavish spending in the 1990s on marketing, mergers and brand extensions has been matched by a never-before-seen resistance to investing in production facilities and labour.

- The upshot is that entire countries are being turned into industrial slums and low-wage labour ghettos, with no end in sight.

About the author

Naomi Klein (born 1970) is a Canadian journalist, author and activist well known for her political analyses and criticism of corporate globalisation.

Klein's writing career started early with contributions to a University of Toronto student newspaper, where she served as editor-in-chief. She credits the 1989 École Polytechnique massacre of female engineering students for her wake-up call to feminism. She dropped out of the University of Toronto to become an intern at the *Toronto Globe and Mail*, followed by an editorship at *This Magazine*.

No Logo (1999), which for many became a manifesto of the anti-corporate globalisation movement, became an international bestseller, translated into over 28 languages with more than a million copies in print.

In 2004, her reporting from Iraq for *Harper's Magazine* won the James Aronson Award for Social Justice Journalism. In 2004, she released *The Take*, a feature documentary about Argentina's occupied factories, co-produced with director Avi Lewis. The film was an official selection of the Venice Biennale and won the Best Documentary Jury Prize at the American Film Institute's Film Festival in Los Angeles.

Her latest book, *The Shock Doctrine* (2007), was released with a six-minute companion film, created by Alfonso Cuaron, director of *Children of Men*, becoming an Official Selection of the 2007 Venice and Toronto International Film Festivals and downloaded over a million times.

Klein writes a regular column for *The Nation* and the *Guardian* which is syndicated internationally by the *New York Times* Syndicate. She is a former Miliband Fellow at the London School of Economics and holds an honorary Doctor of Civil Laws from the University of King's College, Nova Scotia.

Courtesy The Herald/Gordon Terris © SMG Newspapers Ltd

OTHER BOOKS (SELECTION)

Fences and Windows: Dispatches from the Front Lines of the Globalization Debate (Flamingo, 2002)

No War: America's Real Business in Iraq (with Susan Watkins, Bryan Mealer and Walter Laqueur; Gibson Square Books, 2005)

The Shock Doctrine: The Rise of Disaster Capitalism (Macmillan, 2007)

MORE INFORMATION

Naomi Klein's official website:
www.naomiklein.org

30
Natural Capitalism
Paul Hawken, Amory B. Lovins and L. Hunter Lovins

1st edn
Natural Capitalism: The Next Industrial Revolution
Earthscan Publications, 1999; 416pp, hbk; 978-1853834615

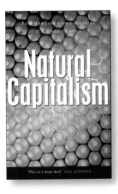

Current UK edn
Natural Capitalism: The Next Industrial Revolution
Earthscan Publications, 2010; 396pp, pbk; 978-1844071708

Current US edn
Natural Capitalism: Creating the Next Industrial Revolution
Back Bay Books, 2008; 416pp, pbk; 978-0316353007

Key ideas

- Traditional, industrial capitalism is unsustainable and is destroying the very basis on which business depends for success – the natural environment.

- There are no easy technological fixes, as many of the services nature provides are irreplaceable, or prohibitively expensive to substitute.

- We therefore need a new model, natural capitalism, which advocates four strategies: resource productivity, biomimicry, service-and-flow and natural capital reinvestment.

- There are already examples of natural capitalism being implemented; they just need to be replicated at scale.

- This approach will provide a wealth of new opportunities for business to be profitable, while accounting for the environment.

Synopsis

Natural Capitalism suggests that the world is on the verge of a new industrial revolution – one that promises to transform our fundamental notions about commerce and its role in shaping our future. The authors describe a future in which business and environmental interests increasingly overlap, and in which companies can simultaneously satisfy their customers' needs, increase profits and help solve environmental problems.

Natural capital refers to the natural resources and ecosystem services that make all economic activity possible. Yet current business practices typically fail to take into account the value of these assets, a value that is rising as they become scarcer. As a result, natural capital is being degraded and liquidated by the wasteful use of such resources as energy, materials, water, fibre and topsoil.

The book suggests a four-capital model of the economy: human capital, in the form of labour and intelligence, culture, and organisation; financial capital, consisting of cash, investments and monetary instruments; manufactured capital, including infrastructure, machines, tools and factories; and natural capital, made up of resources, living systems and ecosystem services.

Industrial capitalism neglects to assign any value to our largest stocks of capital – natural and human capital. It portrays the creation of value as a linear sequence of extraction, production and distribution, leaving out the costs of depletion and waste to the environment. And the environment is not a minor factor but 'an envelope containing, provisioning and sustaining the entire economy'.

The solution is not simply assigning monetary values to natural capital, since many living system services have no known substitutes at any price and valuing natural capital is a difficult and imprecise exercise at best. The solution has to be a different paradigm: 'natural capitalism'. The journey to natural capitalism involves four major shifts in business practices:

1. *Radically increase resource productivity*. Through fundamental changes in both production design and technology, farsighted companies are developing ways to make natural resources – energy, minerals, water, forests – stretch 5, 10, even 100 times further than they do today.

2. *Shift to biologically inspired production models and materials*. Through closed-loop production systems, modelled on nature's designs, every output is either returned harmlessly to the ecosystem as a nutrient, like compost, or becomes an input for another manufacturing process.

3. *Move to a 'service-and-flow' business model*. Value is delivered as a continuous flow of services – such as providing illumination rather than selling light bulbs – which aligns the interests of providers and customers in ways that reward them for resource productivity.

4. *Reinvest in natural capital*. Through investment in restoring, sustaining and expanding natural capital, business is creating immediate profit opportunities, as well as securing its future base for prosperity.

The authors conclude that businesses that understand natural capital will be well placed to lead the 'new industrial revolution' and become extremely successful in the process.

From the book

- Humankind has inherited a 3.8-billion-year store of natural capital. At present rates of use and degradation, there will be little left by the end of the next century. This is not only a matter of aesthetics and morality, it is of the utmost practical concern to society and all people.

- Capitalism, as practiced, is a financially profitable, non-sustainable aberration in human development.

- For all their power and vitality, markets are only tools. They make a good servant but a bad master and a worse religion.

- Natural capitalism is about choices we can make that can start to tip economic and social outcomes in positive directions. And it is already occurring – because it is necessary, possible, and practical.

- A successful business will realize that solutions lie in understanding the interconnectedness of problems, not in confronting them in isolation.

Paul Hawken

About the authors

Paul Hawken (born 1946) is an environmentalist, entrepreneur and author. Starting at the age of 20, he dedicated his life to sustainability and changing the relationship between business and the environment.

His practice has included starting and running ecological businesses, writing and teaching about the impact of commerce on living systems, and consulting with governments and corporations on economic development, industrial ecology and environmental policy.

He is author and co-author of dozens of articles, op-eds and papers, as well as six books. His books have been published in over 50 countries in 27 languages and have sold over 2 million copies. *The Ecology of*

Commerce was voted the number one college text on business and the environment by professors in 67 business schools.

Companies he has founded or co-founded include software companies specialising in proprietary content management tools; Smith & Hawken, the garden and catalogue retailer; and several of the first natural food companies in the US that relied solely on sustainable agricultural methods. He is presently the head of PaxIT, PaxTurbine and PaxFan, three companies associated with Pax Scientific, a research and development company focused on energy-saving technologies that apply biomimicry to fluid dynamics.

Hawken heads the Natural Capital Institute, a research organisation located in Sausalito, California. The Natural Capital Institute has created a hub for global civil society called Wiser Earth. It is a collaboratively written, free-content, open-source networking platform that links NGOs, funders, business, government, social entrepreneurs, students, organisers, academics, activists, scientists and citizens.

Amory B. Lovins

Amory B. Lovins (born 1947), Rocky Mountain Institute Cofounder, Chairman and Chief Scientist, is a consultant experimental physicist educated at Harvard and Oxford. He has received an Oxford MA (by virtue of being a don), nine honorary doctorates, a MacArthur Fellowship, the Heinz, Lindbergh, Right Livelihood ('Alternative Nobel'), World Technology and Time Hero for the Planet awards, the Benjamin Franklin and Happold Medals, the Nissan, Shingo, Mitchell and Onassis Prizes, and honorary membership of the American Institute of Architects. He has lately led the redesign of $30 billion dollars' worth of facilities in 29 sectors for radical energy and resource efficiency. He has briefed 19 heads of state, held several visiting academic chairs (most recently the 2007 MAP/Ming Professorship at Stanford), written 29 books and hundreds of papers, and consulted for scores of industries and governments worldwide. The *Wall Street Journal* named Mr Lovins one of 39 people worldwide 'most likely to change the course of business in the '90s'; *Newsweek* has praised him as 'one of the Western world's most influential energy thinkers'; and *Car* magazine ranked him the 22nd most powerful person in the global automotive industry.

books and dozens of papers. Lovins is also a founding professor of business at Presidio World College, which offers the first accredited MBA in Sustainable Management. For her work, she has been recognised with the Mitchell Prize, the Right Livelihood Award and the Lindbergh Award for Environment and Technology. In 2000, she was named a 'Hero for the Planet' by *Time* magazine. She is a professional speaker on natural capitalism, sustainability, governance in a globalising world, energy policy, land management, green real estate development, and community economic prosperity.

L. Hunter Lovins

In their own words
(2008 interviews)

Amory B. Lovins

Reflections on the book

L. Hunter Lovins (born 1950) is a leading author, consultant and lecturer on sustainable development. She is the founder and President of Natural Capitalism, Inc. and Natural Capitalism Solutions, working with businesses, governments and organisations to implement a profitable approach to developing sustainable businesses and communities. She has been at the cutting edge of environmental thinking for the past 30 years. As CEO for Strategy, she helped grow the world-renowned Rocky Mountain Institute (RMI) into a 50-person applied research centre and source of some of the most innovative environmental policy ideas of recent decades. She is co-author of nine

Natural Capitalism is not about internalisation of externalities; rather it is about the profoundly simple idea: that, if capitalism is the productive use of and reinvestment in capital, you have to be clear about what capital is. Industrial capitalism productively uses and reinvests in only two kinds: money and goods; that is, financial and physical capital. But it leaves out, or liquidates, two more important kinds: namely, people and nature – human and natural capital. Without nature there are no people; without people there are no economies; so this is rather a material omission. And, it turns out, if you productively use and reinvest in all four kinds of capital, if you play with the full deck, you make more money, have more fun, do more good.

The role of business

We now have quite a few biomimetic products on the market. Some are well known like the German paint that washes itself in the rain, the same way that a lotus petal rises brilliant white out of the muck. Or the tactile little round patch that Interface uses to stick together the four corners of carpet tile that uses gecko foot technology, rather than adhesives or suction cups.

It's not as straightforward as you might think to switch to a solutions economy business model. But it is starting to take off pretty well. For example, many chemicals are now provided as a service, not a bunch of molecules. I think the reinvestment in natural capital is also gaining quite good momentum. Rio Tinto and others are leading a bit of a green revolution there. I was just in Borneo watching 19 square kilometres of lush rainforest that had been recreated from scratch in six or seven years. Nobody knew you could do that.

Looking to the future

Three things give me hope for the future. One is the rapid rise of awareness and leadership in the private sector – the most powerful force we have – and the corresponding awakening of civil society empowered by the emerging global central nervous system.

Secondly, I'm encouraged by the fact that brains are evenly distributed one per person – so half of them are in the heads of women, most are in the heads of poor people who haven't taken that much part in the global conversation. But through everything, from the Internet to the honeybee network, we're now starting to get mechanisms for good ideas to bubble up and spread rapidly. And, as far as we know, there's nothing in the universe so powerful as six billion minds wrapping around a problem.

And, third, I'm very encouraged by the quality in the young people I see. They are better than we were at that age. They realise there is less time and they need to get on with it, and there's less frivolity and more focus on doing what's necessary. So I think the future is in pretty good hands.

L. Hunter Lovins

Reflections on the book

What really matters is that we buy time; that we push off the crises that are facing us by using the resources more productively. Efficiency for its own sake is largely irrelevant; it's a great way to save money, but the real point is that it buys us the time to implement more fundamental solutions. The more fundamental solutions are that we are going to get to redesign how we make and deliver everything in the economy. We are going to reinvent government, business, civil society, education, all of our institutions, because the way we do business now, the way we live our lives now, is fundamentally unsustainable.

The role of business

This is now the fault-line in the corporate world, more than just the corporate sustainability world. Corporations are under enormous pressures. The Wall Street analysts believe that corporate value derives from short-term profitability and short-term share price. Smart CEOs know that corporate value derives from good business fundamentals, and CEOs have allowed themselves to be disempowered by allowing the Wall Street analysts to tell them their business. And yet we have companies that are fundamentally solid. They are producing things that people want, they have customers, they have enduring value, and we are allowing the way in which we do accounting to drag down the economy.

We do have some fundamentally scary crises. We are probably at or near peak oil in the world. The speed with which climate change is coming on is scaring the scientists. The Arctic is melting faster than the models predicted. All of the changes are coming on faster than the models predicted. We are hitting a global climate crisis, and any CEO that is not thinking about the future of their business, and the whole planet crisis, is just doing bad business.

Looking to the future

Yes, if you look at the crises facing us, these drivers of change, the future is not possible. But I rather like the line from *Lord of the Rings* on leadership, where Gandalf says, 'The rule of no realm is mine. That all worthy things that are in peril as the world now stands, those are my care, and for my part I shall not wholly fail if anything passes through this night that can still grow fair and bear fruit and flower again in the days to come. For I too am a steward. Did you not know?'

It doesn't matter if you are a wizard or a king or the CEO of Wal-Mart, because remember in the end it was the little people, it was the two fun-loving, unassuming Hobbits who had to take on their shoulders that awesome task. And they were scared and they didn't know where they were going. But in the end all the kings and warriors and wizards could just stand by as the little people saved the world. I think real leadership is extraordinary courage by ordinary people.

OTHER BOOKS (SELECTION)

Energy Unbound: A Fable for America's Future (L. Hunter Lovins, Amory B. Lovins and Seth Zuckerman; Sierra Club Books, 1986)

The Ecology of Commerce: A Declaration of Sustainability (Paul Hawken; HarperCollins, 1993)

Winning the Oil Endgame: Innovation for Profits, Jobs and Security (Amory B. Lovins; Earthscan, 2004)

MORE INFORMATION

Natural Capital Institute:
www.naturalcapital.org

Natural Capitalism, Inc.:
www.natcapinc.com

Paul Hawken's official website:
www.paulhawken.com

Rocky Mountain Institute:
www.rmi.org

31
Business as Unusual
Anita Roddick

1st edn
Business as Unusual
Thorsons, 2000; 304pp,
hbk; 978-0722539873

Current edn
**Business as Unusual.
My Entrepreneurial
Journey: Profits with
Principles**
Anita Roddick Books,
2005; 340pp, pbk,
new edn;
978-0954395957

Key ideas

▶ It is possible to be commercially successful at a global scale and be a values-led company and business leader.

▶ The Body Shop's commitment to values gave it a voice and a market that was far more valuable than anything that could be created by advertising spend.

▶ If a values-driven business doesn't manage the tension between growth and values, it will sacrifice its purpose and culture.

▶ Big business has a responsibility to tackle the big issues facing the world, be they environmental, human rights, social or animal rights issues.

Synopsis

Business as Unusual is part autobiography, part business biography and part manifesto for how business can be an agent for positive change in the world. The book is presented in a highly visual style and is story-driven, with countless interesting anecdotes. Roddick's key message is that, by expanding the role and responsibility of the entrepreneur, as well as the definition of business ethics, the corporate world will be compelled to change. Linked to this is the power of public pressure, with waves of public consciousness steadily forcing corporations to re-evaluate their actions.

Roddick presents an alternative philosophy of business, believing that business should be about more than making money; it should be about changing things for the better. Business's role should be as incubators of the human spirit rather than factories for the production of more material goods and services. This approach relies on creating 'natural entrepreneurs' and a sense of community inside the company, in trade partnerships and among civil society. A non-hierarchical structure and open communication culture is also critical in running a 'business as unusual'.

Roddick is highly critical of the tyranny of the financial markets, which she describes as a kind of financial fascism. She is especially vocal about the inability of the financial community to judge a business on anything but its ability to make a profit, whereas The Body Shop always wanted to be judged on its actions in the larger world.

Much of the book is dedicated to how The Body Shop uses its business to make a positive difference, ranging from its cam-paigning approach and anti-advertising stance, to specific initiatives around animal testing, women's self-esteem and ethical trade ('trade not aid'). There are also in-depth analyses of their role in the campaign with the Ogoni against Shell in Nigeria ('In Nigeria it's easier to bury the protesters than the oil pipes') and The Body Shop's difficulties in becoming established in the US market ('The fact is, we just got everything wrong').

One of the most interesting sections of the book is where Roddick talks about The Body Shop's evolution as it expanded globally. The resultant tension between values and growth affected the culture of the company, which led her to reflect: 'We all knew we had made a mistake trying to fit a business with a distinct social agenda into the straitjacket of the standard disciplines of management, marketing, finance and operations.'

Roddick concludes with the following lessons learned: be quick (speed, agility and responsiveness are the key to future success); be creative about different ways of selling (e.g. Body Shop Digital and Body Shop Direct); forget identikit branding (there is no rationale in having a global brand that doesn't reflect local cultural identity); interpret the product broadly (e.g. not cosmetics, but 'skin, care and attitude'); build partnerships with communities; stay human and measure success differently; be open and transparent; make ethics part of your heritage; be different and tell stories; and remember that people aspire to more than money.

From the book

- There is no more powerful institution in society than business. It is more important than ever before for business to assume a moral leadership in society.

- Open up a typical management book and you will find it hard to avoid words like leadership, team-building, culture or customer service. But you'll be lucky if you find words like community, economic poverty, social justice, ethics, love, care or spirituality – a word that is truly kept in the closet!

- There are so many aspects of life that can't be reduced to an entry in a balance book and our survival depends on remembering this.

- One of the key problems of the business world is that greed has become so culturally acceptable that it's part of the system. Greed without legal and moral constraint can destroy everything worthwhile in life. Wealth can corrode humanity and alienate the wealthy from the human condition.

- There aren't many motivating forces more powerful than giving your staff an opportunity to exercise and express their idealism.

- We have to tell ourselves: 'If you really didn't ever want to get wrinkles, then you should have stopped smiling years ago!'

About the author

Anita Roddick (1942–2007) was an English entrepreneur, business leader, author and social and environmental activist.

Roddick was born to Italian immigrant parents in Littlehampton, UK, in 1942. A natural rebel as a child, she trained as a teacher before undertaking a working trip around the world. Having married Gordon Roddick in 1970, the couple opened a restaurant and hotel in their home town and had two baby daughters. She went on to work for the United Nations where she travelled extensively and met people from a number of different cultures. These experiences would help shape her future career.

The birth of 'The Body Shop' came about in 1976 due to a need by Roddick to create a livelihood for herself and her daughters while her husband was trekking across the Americas. The first Body Shop was basic and sold only 15 lines, embracing (for frugality, rather than environmental reasons) such concepts as refillable containers. The Body Shop today is a business with 1,980 stores serving over 77 million customers in 50 different markets and 25 different languages, with the central purpose of creating social and environmental change.

Throughout her career Roddick continued to campaign tirelessly against environmental

and social wrongs around the world. In 2003, Roddick's achievements were recognised when she was knighted by the Queen, and officially styled as Dame Anita Roddick. In 2007, Roddick revealed that she had been diagnosed with Hepatitis C and died later that year from a major brain haemorrhage.

OTHER BOOKS (SELECTION)

Body and Soul. Profits with Principles: The Amazing Success Story of Anita Roddick and The Body Shop (Crown, 1991)

Take It Personally: How to Make Conscious Choices to Change the World (Red Wheel/Weiser, 2001)

A Revolution in Kindness: Fierce, Tenacious and Visionary Views on Kindness (ed. Anita Roddick; Anita Roddick Books, 2003)

Numbers (with David Boyle; Anita Roddick Books, 2004)

Troubled Water: Saints, Sinners, Truth and Lies about the Global Water Crisis (with Brooke Shelby Biggs; Anita Roddick Books, 2004)

MORE INFORMATION

Anita Roddick's official website:
www.anitaroddick.com

I Am An Activist:
www.iamanactivist.org

The Body Shop International:
www.thebodyshop.com

32
The Mystery of Capital
Hernando de Soto

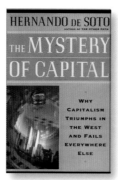

1st edn
**The Mystery
of Capital:**
**Why Capitalism Succeeds
in the West and Fails
Everywhere Else**
Basic Books, 2000;
276pp, hbk;
978-0465016143

Current US edn
**The Mystery
of Capital:**
**Why Capitalism Succeeds
in the West and Fails
Everywhere Else**
Basic Books, 2003;
288pp, pbk;
978-0465016150

Current UK edn
**The Mystery of
Capital:**
**Why Capitalism Succeeds
in the West and Fails
Everywhere Else**
Black Swan, 2001;
288pp, pbk;
978-0552999236

Key ideas

▶ Capitalism has only been successful in developed countries and has made little progress in the Third World or former communist states.

▶ The reason for capitalism's relative failure in developing countries is the lack of well-defined property rights in these countries.

▶ Well-defined (legally enshrined and enforced) property rights allow the poor to convert their assets into capital.

▶ Capital is a necessary condition in any modern economy for creating wealth, since it allows investment in asset improvement and business opportunities.

▶ There is an erosion of property rights in the West, which puts these countries at risk of regressing as capitalistic economies.

Synopsis

The Mystery of Capital argues that capital is the engine of a market economy and that property rights – namely, the ability to have secure title over land and housing – provide the mechanism. De Soto notes that, more than a decade after the fall of Marxism, the expected capitalist revolution has not occurred. Capitalism has been successful only in the developed nations and has made little progress in developing or transition economies.

The problem, according to De Soto, is that 'you cannot carry out macroeconomic reforms on sand. Capitalism requires the bedrock of the rule of law, beginning with that of property. This is because the property system is much more than ownership: it is in fact the hidden architecture that organizes the market economy in every Western nation.'

He argues that the poor in under-developed countries have assets, but that their property is often owned informally. Through this failure to achieve legal property rights and ownership, these classes are greatly restricted in acquiring capital to improve their properties or grow their business.

De Soto proposes the obvious solution: formalisation of informal property rights. He concedes that this will be politically difficult, but points out that both rich and poor will benefit economically, since it results in 'trickle-up economics'. Formal property systems should produce six effects in order to allow their citizens to generate capital:

1. *Fixing the economic potential of assets*. Capital is born by representing in writing – in a title, a security, a contract and other such records – the most economically and socially useful qualities about the asset as opposed to the visually more striking aspects of the asset.

2. *Integrating dispersed information into one system*. Most of the assets in Western nations have been integrated into one formal representational system. Where property information is standardised and universally available, what owners can do with their assets benefits from the collective imagination of a larger network of people.

3. *Making people accountable*. The integration of all property systems under one formal property law shifts the legitimacy of the rights of owners from the political context of local communities to the impersonal context of law.

4. *Making assets fungible*. One of the most important things a formal property system does is transform assets; by uncoupling the economic features of an asset from its rigid, physical state, a representation makes the asset 'fungible'.

5. *Networking people*. By making assets fungible, by attaching owners to assets, assets to addresses, and ownership to enforcement, and by making information on the history of assets and owners easily accessible, formal property systems convert citizens into a network of individually identifiable and accountable business agents.

6. *Protecting transactions*. One important reason why the Western formal property system works like a network is that all the property records (titles, deeds, securities and contracts that describe the economically significant aspects of assets) are continually tracked and protected as they travel through time and space.

From the book

- Capital is the lifeblood of the capitalist system, the foundation of progress, and the one thing that the poor countries of the world cannot seem to produce for themselves, no matter how eagerly their people engage in all the other activities that characterize a capitalist economy.

- The triumph of capitalism only in the West could be a recipe for economic and political disaster.

- The major stumbling block that keeps the rest of the world from benefiting from capitalism is its inability to produce capital.

- The enterprises of the poor are very much like corporations that cannot issue shares or bonds to obtain new investment and finance. Without representations, their assets are dead capital.

- Because the rights to these possessions are not adequately documented, these assets cannot readily be turned into capital, cannot be traded outside of narrow local circles where people know and trust each other, cannot be used as collateral for a loan, and cannot be used as a share against an investment.

- The poor have houses but not titles; crops but not deeds; businesses but not statutes of incorporation.

- The Western nations have so successfully integrated their poor into their economies that they have lost even the memory of how it was done, how the creation of capital began.

- Most of the poor already possess the assets they need to make a success of capitalism.

About the author

Hernando de Soto (born 1941) is a Peruvian economist known for his work on the informal economy and on the importance of property rights. He is the president of Peru's Institute for Liberty and Democracy (ILD).

He was educated in Switzerland, where he did postgraduate work at the Graduate Institute of International Studies in Geneva. He returned to Peru at the age of 38. De Soto was Peruvian president Alberto Fujimori's personal representative and principal advisor and has served as an economist for the General Agreement on Tariffs and Trade, as President of the Executive Committee of the Copper Exporting Countries Organisation (CIPEC), as CEO of Universal Engineering Corporation (Continental Europe's largest consulting engineering firm), as a principal of the Swiss Bank Corporation Consultant Group, and as a governor of Peru's Central Reserve Bank.

Currently, de Soto, together with his colleagues at the ILD, is focused on designing and implementing capital formation programmes to empower the poor in Africa, Asia, Latin America, the Middle East and former Soviet nations. Some 30 heads of state have invited him to carry out these ILD programmes in their countries. He also co-chairs with former US Secretary of State Madeleine Albright the Commission on Legal Empowerment for the Poor.

De Soto has been honoured with numerous awards, including the 2006 Innovation Award (Social and Economic Innovation) from *The Economist* magazine.

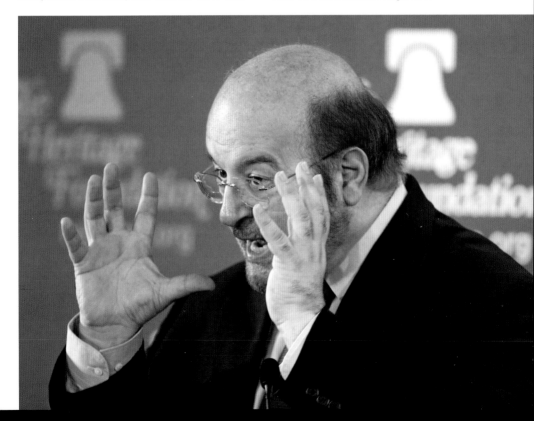

OTHER BOOKS

The Other Path: The Invisible Revolution in the Third World (Harper & Row, 1989)

MORE INFORMATION

Institute for Liberty and Democracy:
ild.org.pe

33
The Civil Corporation
Simon Zadek

1st edn
**The Civil Corporation:
The New Economy of
Corporate Citizenship**
Earthscan Publications,
2001; 257pp, hbk;
978-1853838132

Current edn
The Civil Corporation
Earthscan Publications,
2007; 302pp, pbk, rev.
edn; 978-1844074310

Key ideas

- ▶ The role of business in society is the 21st century's most important and contentious public policy issue, given its growing impact, both positive and negative.

- ▶ We can expect to see a gradual transition from today's way of operating business to a model where business will play a central role in protecting and enhancing the broader interests of society.

- ▶ This evolution reflects the three generations of corporate responsibility, from defensive through strategic to responsibly competitive.

- ▶ In order to achieve this transition, we will need the emergence of the 'civil corporation', which builds social and environmental objectives into its core business.

- ▶ Success will depend on a collaborative, stakeholder-driven approach in which new governance frameworks are designed and tested by business, government and civil society.

Synopsis

The Civil Corporation questions our traditional view of business – as 'legalized poacher responsible to financial capital' – and the state – as 'paternalistic gamekeeper accountable to the people'. This, argues Zadek, not only fails to describe the current situation, but is way off the mark in mapping what things are likely to look like in the future. Corporations will, on the one hand, have more influence on public processes by virtue of their size and international characteristics but, on the other hand, they will need to be increasingly accountable to civil society and show that they are contributing to the public good.

Corporate responsibility will be essential in ensuring that business's contributions are positive and balanced. It is 'a critical arena where both tomorrow's business models and practices, and the next generation of broader accountability innovations, will be invented, tested and contested. Success will rewrite the rules of economy and business and with it the nature of citizens' participation and the place of the State.'

The book explores three generations of corporate citizenship. Each generation frames the essential question of the role of business in society differently:

1. *First-generation corporate responsibility* is focused on fixing problems (pain alleviation, short-term reputation and localised cost–benefit) and asks: can corporations be responsible in ways that do not detract from, and may add commercial value to, their business?

2. *Second-generation corporate responsibility* is focused on evolving strategies (strategic planning, risk management and learning/innovation) and asks: are more responsible companies likely to prosper in the future?

3. *Third-generation corporate responsibility* is focused on reshaping markets (responsible competitiveness) and asks: is corporate citizenship likely to make a significant contribution to addressing the growing levels of poverty, exclusion and environmental degradation?

Zadek notes that, in the last few years, many more examples of second-generation corporate responsibility have appeared. This also reflects a shift from intensive to extensive accountability, i.e. from accountability to a narrow group of stakeholders such as shareholders, to accountability to a broader set of stakeholders. This leads to the idea of a third-generation corporation, where 'business becomes active in promoting and institutionalizing new governance frameworks that effectively secure civil market behaviour, globally'.

Hence, civil corporations will be those that go beyond getting their own house in order, and actively engage in promoting governance frameworks that enable the wider business community to address the aspirations underpinning sustainable development. This third generation, then, is about reshaping markets such that they systematically reward responsible business practices and penalise the converse.

This transition towards the next generation will occur at the intersection between business and politics: 'Envisioned is a collaborative approach to governance involving blended institutions engaged in business and matters of public concern underpinned by powerful new accountability mechanisms and processes.' In the future, Zadek also envisions a fourth generation, where the paradigm that business exists only for profit is challenged.

From the book

- If the aim for those in the vanguard over the last decade was to embed social and environmental issues into codified practices for the mainstream business community, they should be quite satisfied that this task has been well advanced.

- Failure not just to rein in business's misdemeanours, but to re-empower it with a broader set of rights and responsibilities, will leave old political systems in place, degenerating liberalism at best, or at worst a new era of authoritarian states acting in the dual cause of security and economic development.

- Stakeholder engagement is arguably the most critical ingredient in the development of the civil corporation.

- Business leaders systematically abandon prospective financial returns in favour of winning immediate beauty contests whose judges are financial analysts and fund managers focused more on their Christmas bonus than the interests of the owners of the capital that they are stewarding.

- Extended accountabilities will arise not through a collective epiphany, but through the result of a sequence of traditional business responses that will add up to far more than the sum of their parts.

- Corporate citizenship can become a significant route for overcoming global poverty, inequality and environmental insecurity. This requires that it evolves to a point where business becomes active in promoting and institutionalizing new governance frameworks that effectively secure civil market behaviour, globally.

About the author

Simon Zadek is a pioneer of the accountability movement, working on the cusp between business, government and civil society in the creation of new governance frameworks.

Zadek is CEO of AccountAbility and currently a Senior Fellow at the Center for Government and Business of Harvard University's Kennedy School, and a 'Professor Extraordinaire' at the University of South Africa's Centre for Corporate Citizenship. He sits on the International Advisory Board of Instituto Ethos, the Advisory Board of Generation Investment Management and is a Member of the Clinton-Dalberg Task Force programme, aimed at leveraging private enterprise for development. In 2003 he was named one of the World Economic Forum's 'Global Leaders for Tomorrow'.

Zadek's previous roles include Visiting Professor at the Copenhagen Business School, Development Director of the New Economics Foundation, and founding Chair of the Ethical Trading Initiative. He has served on numerous boards and advisory councils, including the State of the World's Commission for Globalisation, the ILO's World Commission on the Social Dimensions of Globalisation, the UN Commission for Social Development Expert Group on CSR, and the founding Steering Committee of the Global Reporting Initiative.

Zadek has written extensively on the role of business in society, most recently focusing on the impact of corporate responsibility on the competitiveness of nations. *The Civil Corporation* has been recognised by the Academy of Management as the Best Book Social Issues Award 2006.

In his own words
(2008 interview)

Reflections on the book

What's interesting looking back at *The Civil Corporation* are the bits that are missing, as well as the bits that are there. I was clearly interested in partnerships and collaboration, but I don't think at that point I'd really grasped just how significant that was going to become. My organising principle was still the business, and today increasingly my organising principle is collaboration. But some of the things that were there were the early DNA of accountability.

I define the civil corporation as one that is able and willing to take full advantage of the degrees of freedom in their context, to advance sustainability as part of their business strategy and performance. If there was anything right in the book it was that definition, because what we've seen is that the capacity to move externally has been incredibly limited, and that the internal culture of most large companies is apparently almost incapable of responding to that environment, except by trying to backfill in backward-looking markets.

The role of business

The companies that have been most interesting in the sustainability area are ones that have tried to create space, not only for themselves, but for other companies, to advance, whether it be responsible drinking, cheaper drugs, improved labour standards, less corruption. Although individual companies have done things about their own practices, it's in creating space within markets for other companies to perform better that the greatest innovations have taken place.

At the moment, the prisoners' dilemmas and first-mover disadvantages that are prevalent in markets are unlikely to be overcome through government regulation, or at least not at the scale that we need. Quite the reverse, in fact. And so the question is whether, through a mixture of public and private actors, we can create rule systems that help businesses and countries navigate away from first-mover disadvantages in advancing sustainability by creating micro-climates within markets that are trans-border, that offer competitiveness upsides without having to have everybody play ball.

Looking to the future

When I look at the codes and standards that we've produced in the last ten years, I feel quite optimistic about the experience of the last decade and a half. I think we've experimented in how to create norms in radically different ways in a global economy where national rules don't work in relation to global institutions, pushed by civil-society pressure that didn't exist before.

I'm very taken by the view that we don't need to imagine the future; we simply have to observe the present more carefully. We actually see the prototypes of competing futures playing themselves out. And what we have to do is identify which prototypes actually seem to prefigure the futures we're interested in.

Will our grandchildren know what a company is? It isn't just that we can blend these different organisations, NGOs and companies and governments, but it seems that the real institutional challenge is to create a new type of institution.

OTHER BOOKS (SELECTION)

An Economics of Utopia: Democratising Scarcity (Avebury, 1993)

Building Corporate Accountability: Emerging Practices in Social and Ethical Accounting, Auditing and Reporting (with Peter Pruzan and Richard Evans; Earthscan, 1997)

Mediating Sustainability: Growing Policy from the Grassroots (with Jutta Blauert; Kumarian Press, 1998)

MORE INFORMATION

AccountAbility:
www.accountability21.net

New Economics Foundation:
www.neweconomics.org

34
Fast Food Nation
Eric Schlosser

1st edn
Fast Food Nation:
The Dark Side of the
All-American Meal
Houghton Mifflin, 2001;
288pp, hbk;
978-0395977897

Current US edn
Fast Food Nation:
The Dark Side of the
All-American Meal
Harper Perennial, 2005;
416pp, pbk;
978-0060838584

Current UK edn
Fast Food Nation
Penguin Books, 2007;
400pp, pbk;
978-0141035314

Key ideas

▶ Fast-food companies have evolved as a result of industrialisation and the drive to reduce costs and increase speed.

▶ Fast food has a pervasive influence on our society, affecting not just the food we eat, but our retail landscape, employment agenda, agricultural survival and scale.

▶ Fast food has hastened the 'malling' of our landscape, widened the chasm between rich and poor, fuelled an epidemic of obesity, and propelled the juggernaut of American cultural imperialism abroad.

▶ The modern fast-food business is defined by the industrialisation of most of its parts, a factory-farming approach with significant environmental, labour and animal rights concerns.

▶ There are alternatives to both the agrochemical, factory-farming methods and the low-cost, low-wage fast-food restaurant chains providing unhealthy food.

Synopsis

Fast Food Nation shows how the evolution of fast food coincided with the advent of the automobile, transforming a nation of independent restaurants into a few uniform franchises. This shift led to a production-line kitchen prototype, standardisation, self-service, and a fundamental change in the demographics of target marketing: from teenager to family.

Schlosser provides extensive analysis of the phenomenon of child-targeted marketing, explaining how the McDonald's Corporation modelled its marketing tactics on the Walt Disney Company, which inspired the creation of advertising icons such as Ronald McDonald. Marketing executives theorised this shift to children-oriented marketing would result not only in attracting children, but their parents and grandparents as well, while instilling brand loyalty that would persist through adulthood.

Schlosser is highly critical of this marketing approach, claiming that it is an exploitation of children's naïveté and trusting nature. A related concern is that fast-food companies have also infiltrated schools through sponsorship and other means. According to his sources, 80% of the sponsored textbooks contain material that is biased in favour of the sponsors, and 30% of high schools offer fast foods in their cafeterias. Anecdotes are given suggesting that students that disregarded sponsorships could be punished.

Another theme of the book is the industrialisation of the food industry that supports fast food and its associated supply chain issues. For example, in the meat packing industry, Schlosser finds that it is now dominated by casual, easily exploited immigrant labour and that levels of injury are among the highest of any occupation in the United States. He also explains how, in meat processing, chicken manure and the remains of pigs and horses are used in cattle feed, practices that were responsible for the spread of BSE (or Mad Cow Disease), as well as introducing harmful bacteria, such as *E. coli*, into the food supply.

Other areas of critical concern raised by Schlosser are the fast-food industry's role in globalisation (which he argues is a form of 'cultural imperialism') and the crisis of obesity in the West, which is rapidly spreading to the East with the arrival of fast food. He cites the 'McLibel' case as a window into the fast-food industry. This was a 313-day trial (the longest ever in British legal history), which began after McDonald's took a UK campaigning organisation to court for publishing a six-page leaflet called 'What's Wrong with McDonald's? Everything they don't want you to know'.

Schlosser concludes with a few stories that represent an alternative to the current model of the fast-food industry, such as the Colorado Cattle rancher who doesn't use chemicals and only feeds his cattle directly from the prairie, or the story of Red Top or In-N-Out, alternative equivalents to fast-food restaurants. In later editions, Schlosser provides an additional section that answers his critics and advocates greater government intervention and industry accountability. His take-away message (if you'll excuse the pun) is that readers (or eaters) should vote with their feet (or mouths) and simply stop buying 'junk food'.

From the book

- Americans now spend more money on fast food than on higher education, personal computers, computer software, or new cars. They spend more on fast food than on movies, books, magazines, newspapers, videos, and recorded music – combined.

- The basic thinking behind fast food has become the operating system of today's retail economy, wiping out small businesses, obliterating regional differences, and spreading identical stores throughout the country like a self-replicating code.

- The centralized purchasing decisions of the large restaurant chains and their demand for standardized products have given a handful of corporations an unprecedented degree of power over the nation's food supply.

- Fast food is heavily marketed to children and prepared by people who are barely older than children. This is an industry that both feeds and feeds off the young.

- McDonald's spends more money on advertising and marketing than any other brand. As a result it has replaced Coca-Cola as the world's most famous brand. McDonald's operates more playgrounds than any other private entity in the United States. It is one of the nation's largest distributors of toys . . . The Golden Arches are now more widely recognized than the Christian cross.

- The value meals, two-for-one deals, and free refills of soda give a distorted sense of how much fast food actually costs. The real price never appears on the menu.

- The leading fast food chains still embrace a boundless faith in science – and as a result have changed not just what Americans eat, but also how their food is made . . . Much of the taste and aroma of American fast food, for example, is now manufactured at a series of large chemical plants off the New Jersey Turnpike.

- In town after town statues of Lenin have come down, and statues of Ronald McDonald have gone up.

About the author

Eric Schlosser (born 1959) is an American journalist and bestselling author and has been a correspondent for the *Atlantic Monthly* since 1996.

After graduating from Princeton with a degree in American History, Schlosser tried his hand at several professions (playwright, novelist, script writer) before finally turning

to non-fiction in his early thirties. Although his idea for an article on homosexuals in the military was turned down by the *Atlantic Monthly*, the magazine offered him another assignment: writing about the New York City bomb squad after the 1993 World Trade Center bombing. Other assignments followed, one of which was about America and its fast-food industry.

What began as a simple magazine article turned into an international bestseller. *Fast Food Nation* was on the *New York Times* bestseller list for nearly two years and also appeared on numerous other bestseller lists in America and internationally. His second *New York Times* bestseller, *Reefer Madness*, was also inspired by his earlier articles on the enforcement of marijuana laws in America and illegal immigration in California, which won a National Magazine Award for reporting. Another of his articles, 'In the Strawberry Fields', received a Sidney Hillman Foundation award.

Schlosser has appeared on various television shows, including *Sixty Minutes*, *CNN*, *CBS Evening News*, *NBC Nightly News*, *Fox News*, *The O'Reilly Factor* and *Extra!*.

OTHER BOOKS (SELECTION)

Reefer Madness: Sex, Drugs, and Cheap Labor in the American Black Market (Allen Lane, 2003)

Chew on This: Everything You Don't Want to Know about Fast Food (with Charles Wilson; Houghton Mifflin Co., 2006)

MORE INFORMATION

McSpotlight:
www.mcspotlight.org

35
The Skeptical Environmentalist
Bjørn Lomborg

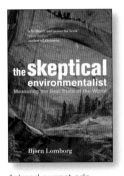

1st and current edn
The Skeptical Environmentalist: Measuring the Real State of the World
Cambridge University Press, 2001; 540pp, pbk; 978-0521010689

Key ideas

▶ Many current claims about the state of the world are overly pessimistic, based on environmental data that is analysed and presented in a distorted or misleading way.

▶ The accurate message should be that real progress has been and continues to be made in virtually every area of social and environmental well-being.

▶ The pessimistic, distorted view of the world results in the wrong policy decisions and resource allocations being made.

▶ Assessing the world's problems using a cost–benefit method produces radically different priorities for governments and business.

▶ The prevailing pessimism tends to undermine our confidence in our ability to solve the problems at hand.

Synopsis

The *Skeptical Environmentalist* is an unapologetic and highly controversial challenge to many of the prevailing views on the nature and extent of the so-called environmental crisis we face. The subtitle of the book – 'The Real State of the World' – is an implicit criticism of the Worldwatch Institute's *State of the World* series of reports, which Lomborg sees as typical of the alarmist and unjustifiably pessimistic approach of much of the environmental movement.

Far from simply presenting a philosophical objection to the conventional wisdom on environmental issues, Lomborg adopts a highly detailed, data-rich approach in which much-cited 'facts' are examined and questioned in the light of competing and, in his view, more accurate data. For example, in looking at human welfare, Lomborg points out that, despite population growth, there has never been such prosperity, including improvements in health and life expectancy, as now. Even income disparity is decreasing, if figures are seen from a Purchasing Power Parity perspective.

In response to the question 'Can human prosperity continue?' Lomborg concludes that there are sufficient future resources, including food, forests, energy, non-energy resources and water, for sustained prosperity. We will not run out of oil, he argues, because, as it becomes more scarce, investment in new technologies will make alternatives more easily available. Furthermore, 'oil will come not only from the sources we already know, but also from many sources of which we do not yet know'.

On the topic of pollution, Lomborg examines air pollution, acid rain and forest death, indoor air pollution, water pollution and waste and concludes that the pollution burden has diminished. This progress, he believes, is linked to wealth; hence, as developing economies grow, they will also have the ability to reduce their pollution. 'We often assume air pollution is a new phenomenon that has got worse and worse – in truth it is an old phenomenon, that has been getting better and better.' In looking at tomorrow's problems, including chemicals, biodiversity and global warming, Lomborg concludes that the fear of chemicals and reduction of species is exaggerated, and that the colossal sums governments are planning to deploy on reducing global warming will be money poorly spent. Lomborg does not deny that climate change is taking place. However, he feels there is too much emphasis on it in comparison with other issues and that 'the cure is worse than the ailment'.

Lomborg's critique centres on research methodology. Most data, he claims, is presented as a short-term view of current trends, and fails to make adequate comparisons. Furthermore, we place too much trust in the press with regards to environmental reporting, where only negative stories sell. He concludes that 'being presented with the real state of the world makes us realize that, given our past record, it is likely that by humanity's creativity and collected efforts we can handle and find solutions to these problems. Consequently we can approach the remaining problems with confidence and inspiration to create an even better world.'

From the book

- Children born today – in both the industrialized world and developing countries – will live longer and be healthier. They will get more food, a better education, a higher standard of living, more leisure time and far more possibilities – without the global environment being destroyed. And that is a beautiful world.

- Air pollution has been a major nuisance for most of civilisation, and the air of the western world has not been as clean as it is now for a long time.

- Our intake of coffee is about 50 times more carcinogenic than our intake of DDT before it was banned, more than 1,200 times more carcinogenic than our present DDT intake, and more than 66 times more carcinogenic than the most dangerous present-day pesticide intake.

- Global warming is not anywhere near the most important problem facing the world.

- One of the most serious consequences of the litany of the environmentally worried elite is that it undermines our confidence in our ability to solve our remaining problems. This fear is absolutely decisive because it paralyses our reasoned judgment. It is imperative that we regain our ability to prioritize the many different worthy causes.

About the author

Bjørn Lomborg (born 1965) is a Danish political and environmental scientist who is renowned for his critical views on the mainstream environmental movement.

Lomborg obtained an MA in political science in 1991 and a PhD in political science from the University of Copenhagen in 1994. He has been Director of Denmark's national Environmental Assessment Institute (2002–2004) and is currently adjunct professor at the Copenhagen Business School. He is the organiser of the Copenhagen Consensus Center, which brings together some of the world's top economists, including five Nobel laureates, to set priorities for the world.

The Skeptical Environmentalist had its genesis in 1998, when Lomborg worked as an associate professor of statistics at the Department of Political Science at the University of Aarhus in Denmark. He published four lengthy articles about the state of the environment in a leading Danish newspaper, which resulted in a firestorm debate spanning over 400 articles in major metropolitan newspapers. The articles led to the publication of The Skeptical Environmentalist in 2001, which has now been published in every major language in the world.

Time magazine named Lomborg one of the world's 100 most influential people in 2004 and the World Economic Forum named him a *Young Global Leader* in 2005. In 2008 he was named 'one of the 50 people who could save the planet' by the UK *Guardian*; and 'one of the world's 75 most influential people of the 21st century' by *Esquire*.

Photo: Emil Jupin

In his own words
(2008 interview)

Reflections on the book

I came from a background of deep concern for the environment and an understanding of the world being in peril. Then I read an interview with an American economist called Julian Simon in 1997 who said things are actually getting better in many indicators, not worse. I thought it would actually be fun to disprove him, so I set out in the fall of '97 to show that this was wrong. As it turned out, a lot of what he said was actually true. And that was really the background for the book.

I felt, if you consistently have an incorrect understanding of where the world is headed, it's unlikely that we will actually take the right measures. So my book is saying, 'Listen, in many ways the environment is getting better; things are not as bad as you think.' This does not mean that there are no problems, but it means we can stop panicking and start thinking smartly about where can we do the most good.

The role of business

In virtually all areas and certainly when you look at environmental impacts, companies have become much, much better over the last 30 to 100 years. So we are actually shaping up. This doesn't mean we couldn't do it even faster but of course what this requires us to realise is that there is a very clear trade-off with all the other things we presumably also want: namely, easier access to education, better health facilities, to be able to take care of our old, and more infrastructure.

Whether companies are going to be the ones who save the planet, I think is a very, very odd argument. Companies are in place to deal with production. It's unreasonable to expect that they are also supposed to be cutting back on CO_2 or saving people from malaria. Companies do CSR and that's all to the good, but social problems, like lack of healthcare, education, clean drinking water, and also CO_2 emissions, have to be public policy problems.

Looking to the future

If you look at the problems in general, most of the solutions that the world should be focusing on are non-environmental. Environmental concern is still very much a First World concern. Most of the world are still pretty worried about the fact that their kids can die from easily curable infectious diseases, don't get enough education, don't even have access to clean drinking water or electricity or all the other things that we take for granted.

Of course, it's also important to deal with environmental problems, but these are very, very simple issues, the most obvious environmental problem being lack of clean drinking water for most of the world's population. And of course we also need to deal with climate change, but we need to do so smartly: that is, invest in research and development which will allow us to cut dramatic amounts by mid-century by making non-carbon-emitting energy technologies much cheaper, possibly even competitive.

The evidence points very clearly to the fact that things are getting better, not worse. That does not mean we shouldn't worry, but it means we should worry about the right things; we should stop worrying about things that just look good on TV and ask how much can we do, at what cost? So, basically, ask: what is the benefit–cost ratio?

And, surprisingly, that turns out – as we've done with the Copenhagen Consensus – to fix problems in the Third World that are very basic, very simple in nature. But it also means that fixing some of the top things that are on the Western agenda, namely terrorism and climate change, we fix very poorly. Instead of fixing it poorly as we do right now we should fix them smartly. For terrorism, by investing in better cooperation between nations through Interpol, rather than putting lots of security in our airports. And for climate change, it should not be about cutting carbon emissions, which cost a lot and do very little good, but about making sure that we have better technology.

At the end of the day this really is a conversation about not just doing what's fashionable, but what's rational.

OTHER BOOKS (SELECTION)

Global Crises, Global Solutions (Cambridge University Press, 2006)

Cool It: The Skeptical Environmentalist's Guide to Global Warming (Cyan Communications, 2007)

MORE INFORMATION

Bjørn Lomborg official website: www.lomborg.com

Copenhagen Consensus Center: www.copenhagenconsensus.com

36
Cradle to Cradle
William McDonough and Michael Braungart

1st and current US edn
**Cradle to Cradle:
Remaking the Way
We Make Things**
North Point Press, 2002;
208pp, pbk;
978-0865475878

Current UK edn
**Cradle to Cradle:
Remaking the Way
We Make Things**
Vintage Books, 2009;
208pp, pbk;
978-0099535478

Key ideas

▶ Rather than design products to minimise negative impacts (as eco-efficiency does), we should design to have positive impacts (eco-effectiveness).

▶ All 'waste' must be transformed into either a biological nutrient for nature or a technical nutrient for industry.

▶ Designing for environment, equity and economy, rather than managing these impacts after the fact, constitutes a 'triple top line' approach.

▶ Much of the inspiration for good design already exists in nature.

▶ We need to design with the future in mind, rather than being locked into the mediocrity of the past.

Synopsis

Cradle to Cradle begins where eco-efficiency ends. Eco-efficiency, according to McDonough and Braungart, is just about making a bad system a little less bad. Eco-effectiveness, on the other hand, is about redesigning products and services to make them good – bigger and better in a way that replenishes, restores and nourishes the rest of the world. Hence, industry can have a positive impact on the environment, provided it is designed with that positive impact in mind.

Cradle-to-cradle goes beyond 'cradle-to-grave' thinking. Hence, rather than simply considering impacts across the life-cycle of a product and trying to minimise waste, the authors argue for closed-loop production, where waste is acceptable only if it is entirely re-used by the system. Hence, all waste becomes 'food' inputs to the cycles of nature and the cycles of industry, i.e. either as a biological nutrient or a technical nutrient.

The authors argue that cradle-to-cradle is only possible if environment, equity and economy are incorporated from the outset in the design of new products and services. As opposed to the 'triple bottom line', which they see as managing impacts after they have occurred, they see this design-led approach as a 'triple top line'.

The vision of *Cradle to Cradle* is the creation of: buildings that, like trees, produce more energy than they consume and purify their own wastewater; factories with effluents that are drinking water; products that, when their useful life is over, do not become useless waste but can be tossed onto the ground to decompose and become food for plants and animals and nutrients for soil; or, alternately, that can return to industrial cycles to supply high-quality raw materials for new products. In other words, a world of abundance, not one of limits, pollution and waste.

The authors propose five steps to eco-effectiveness:

1. *Get free of known culprits*: remove from a product any chemicals or other substances known to be harmful (e.g. heavy metals, carcinogens).

2. *Follow informed personal preferences*: develop a list of preferred, readily available materials known to be healthful or harvested with minimal impact.

3. *Create a 'passive positive' list*: conduct a more comprehensive review, examining all of the materials used in an existing product.

4. *Activate the positive list*: actively define a product's ingredients, not to limit the impact of a product or system but to conceive one with positive effects on the world.

5. *Reinvent*: ask not simply what ingredients would be nutritious but how a product might best celebrate a basic human need, revitalise an aspect of culture, or renew our engagement with the natural world.

Underlying these efforts are five guiding principles: signal your intention beyond incremental improvement; restore (think good growth, not just economic growth); be ready to innovate further; understand and prepare for the learning curve; and exert intergenerational responsibility. In essence, cradle-to-cradle is about imagining what a better world will look like in the future and designing for it now. As the authors say, negligence starts tomorrow.

From the book

- Eco-effectiveness means working on the right things – on the right products and services and systems – instead of making the wrong things less bad.

- Eliminate the concept of waste: not reduce, minimize, or avoid waste, but eliminate the very concept by design.

- Nature doesn't have a design problem. People do.

- As long as human beings are regarded as 'bad', zero is a good goal. But to be less bad is to accept things as they are, to believe that poorly designed, dishonourable, destructive systems are the best humans can do. This is the ultimate failure of the 'be less bad' approach: a failure of the imagination. From our perspective, this is a depressing vision of our species' role in the world. What about an entirely different model? What would it mean to be 100 percent good?

- Don't just reinvent the recipe, rethink the menu.

About the authors

William McDonough (born 1951) is an American architect whose career is focused on designing environmentally sustainable buildings and transforming industrial manufacturing processes.

McDonough was trained at Dartmouth College and Yale University. In 1981 he founded his own architectural practice and his first major commission was the 1984 Environmental Defense Fund Headquarters. McDonough moved his practice from New York City to Charlottesville in 1994, when he was appointed as the Dean of the School of Architecture at the University of Virginia. He relinquished this position in 1999 to focus on expanding his professional practice.

McDonough is also the co-founder and principal, with German chemist Michael Braungart, of McDonough Braungart De-

sign Chemistry (MBDC), which employs a comprehensive cradle-to-cradle design protocol for chemical benchmarking, supply-chain integration, energy and materials assessment, clean-production qualification, and sustainability issue management and optimisation.

McDonough is winner of three US presidential awards: the Presidential Award for Sustainable Development (1996), the National Design Award (2004) and the Presidential Green Chemistry Challenge Award (2003). *Time* magazine recognised him as a 'Hero for the Planet' in 1999, stating that 'his utopianism is grounded in a unified philosophy that – in demonstrable and practical ways – is changing the design of the world'.

Michael Braungart (born 1958) is a German chemist who advocates that humans can have a positive ecological footprint by redesigning systems that support life.

After completing studies in process engineering in Darmstadt, Germany, Braungart went on to investigate the chemical processes of industrial production techniques with the Chemistry Department at Konstanz, Germany. He subsequently led the formation of the Chemistry Section of Greenpeace International.

In 1987, Braungart founded the Environmental Protection Encouragement Agency (EPEA) in Hamburg. At the heart of EPEA is cradle-to-cradle design, which creates products oriented toward a life-cycle economy. He is also co-founder of MBDC (McDonough Braungart Design Chemistry) in Charlottesville, Virginia.

Since 1994, Braungart has been teaching process engineering at the University of Lüneburg in Suderburg, Germany, also serving as director of an interdisciplinary materials-flow management masters programme. Braungart also serves as Scientific Manager of the Hamburg Environmental Institute, the non-profit research centre that produces the 'Top 50 Study'. This study ranks the quality of environmentally sound production of companies within the chemical industry.

In 2003, Braungart was awarded the Presidential Green Chemistry Challenge Award for his work with EcoWorx carpeting tile. He has also accepted a visiting professorship at the Darden School of Business, lecturing on such topics as eco-efficiency and eco-effectiveness, cradle-to-cradle design and intelligent materials pooling, and he continues to teach at institutions of higher learning all over the world.

In their own words
(2008 interviews)

William McDonough

Reflections on the book

The book has created a lot of people who want to send us things to review and put into the cradle-to-cradle protocol. Now we're developing affiliates that will be able to assess products all over the world using our 19 chemical and ecological filters and then send them to us for certification based on cradle-to-cradle. When we look back 10 to 15 years from now, what we'll see as a manifestation of the book will be thousands and thousands and thousands of products that are based on the protocol.

The book is a polymer; it's plastic. And that's a part of our polemic: to put forward the idea of the technical nutrient. It's designed to be continuously recycled over the centuries. And by making it out of plastic we were trying to make that point that things can be different, and we can have fun.

The role of business

The 'triple bottom line' has been very useful for a lot of people who are used to thinking in terms of economic growth or economic steadiness as the profitability of enterprise. What we're finding is that the exciting part, the part that relates to the design and intentionality of the sustaining world, is the triple top line. This means that we're top line for environment so that things are safe and healthy, we're top line for society so that things are productive and fair and can

Looking to the future

I think the barriers are really around human creativity and the raw economic pressures of daily life for most people. People who aren't trained to stretch the limits of their ordinary decision-making find themselves locked into certain economic and design structures that replicate what happened yesterday rather than imagine what could happen tomorrow. Our job in sustainability leadership is to reach out, make mistakes, try out different ideas and get some successful examples that could be used as inspiration.

I think *de facto* as a designer I have to be optimistic because the nature of design is to make the world better. Also, when I see the energy in the people helping to solve these problems, and with the resources and the funding that is being put towards these kinds of questions, I think it's quite a different moment. And I don't think of it as a bubble; I think of it as a boom.

Michael Braungart

Reflections on the book

In 1987 I was looking at complex household products and I identified in the TV set 4,360 different chemicals; I thought, it doesn't help just to take any toxic stuff out of it. And so I took the Western way of analysing things, put it together with the Eastern way of getting things together and with the Southern way of having fun with it. And out of this I designed criteria for production and products no longer to be less bad but to be good.

It is really about the management of the biosphere and of the technosphere, as technical nutrients and biological nutrients.

Michael Braungart (left) and William McDonough

be distributed in a way that's equitable and we're deriving profit through intelligent revenue generation.

To give you a sense of what this means, in the United States there is four and a half billion pounds of carpet waste every year. Now the largest player in the industry, Shaw, takes its old carpet back and all the new carpet is designed around the cradle-to-cradle protocol. So you have this closed cycle of intelligent, safe material chipping away at a four and a half billion pound a year waste issue. That's a huge shift.

So there is no waste; it's just materials going back into the technosphere and the biosphere where they can be beneficial. This is the differentiation between efficiency and effectiveness. Nature is completely inefficient, but amazingly effective. Traditional eco-efficiency only optimises the existing stuff and makes it less bad. What happened in the last 20 years, we basically lost 20 years by optimising the wrong stuff.

The role of business

Eco-efficiency just means to sit on the *Titanic* and to bail out the water with a tablespoon instead of a teaspoon. That doesn't help us. So you really need to say first, what is the right thing to do? And then we need to optimise it and, if you call this a revolution, I'm okay with it. It's a complete reinvention of the industrial system that we have.

When people talk about green chemistry or sustainable chemistry, then basically they put themselves in a little niche. I'm just talking about good chemistry. Chemistry is not good when the chemicals accumulate in the biosphere; that's just stupid. Young scientists immediately understand that a chemical is not good when it accumulates in mothers' breast milk. It's just primitive chemistry. So we can now make far better chemistry, far better material science, far better physics.

Looking to the future

There's this joke: One planet meets another planet, and the planet says, 'Oh, you really look terrible today.' And the planet says, 'Yes, I have *homo sapiens*.' And the other planet says, 'Yeah, I had that before. Don't worry, it will disappear.'

Sustainability is boring. What would you say if I were to ask you about your relationship with your wife? How would you characterise it? As sustainable? If this is the bigger goal – sustainability – then I feel really sorry because it doesn't celebrate human creativity and human nature.

You will see the Netherlands become a complete cradle-to-cradle country. Israel is being amazingly fast to change. New Zealand is becoming cradle-to-cradle. We have similar activities now in Wales going on. And, from there, the unit is big enough to reproduce it, to transfer it to others. And it's amazing because it frees people from feeling guilty for being here, for giving them the opportunity to become native, and to celebrate human genius on this planet. That's why it's so fast.

MORE INFORMATION

McDonough Braungart Design Chemicals:
www.mbdc.com

Michael Braungart's official website:

William McDonough's official website:
www.mcdonough.com

William McDonough + Partners:
www.mcdonoughpartners.com

37
Globalization and its Discontents
Joseph E. Stiglitz

Current UK edn
Globalization and its Discontents
Penguin Books, 2002;
320pp, pbk, new edn;
978-0141010380

Current US edn
Globalization and its Discontents
W.W. Norton, 2003;
304pp, pbk;
978-0393324396

1st edn
Globalization and its Discontents
W.W. Norton, 2002;
282pp, hbk;
978-0393051247

Key ideas

▶ Globalisation, led by international institutions like the World Bank and the IMF, has not delivered on its promise of world upliftment.

▶ The World Bank and IMF's commitment to free markets as an ideology has led to many, in some cases drastic, errors at the expense of the poor.

▶ There is no such thing as perfect information in markets, and the 'invisible hand' therefore does not operate in everyone's best interests.

▶ It is not globalisation per se that is a problem, but the way in which it has been and is being promoted and managed.

▶ If we can overcome the ideological inflexibility and powerful vested interests of Western-led multilateral institutions and multinationals, globalisation can bring enormous benefits to all.

Synopsis

The underlying thesis of *Globalization and its Discontents* is that globalisation has not brought the promised economic benefits to some of the poorest nations in the world. In fact, the rich are getting richer and the poor are getting poorer. Much of this failure is due to perverse effects of multilateral institutions, especially the IMF and World Bank, including their legacy of Third World loans and conditional structural adjustment programmes.

Stiglitz defines globalisation as 'the closer integration of the countries and peoples of the world . . . brought about by the enormous reduction of costs of transportation and communication and the breaking down of artificial barriers to the flows of goods, services, capital, knowledge and (to a lesser extent) people across international borders'. The process is not inherently bad, but has been accompanied by a litany of policies that have caused more harm than good in developing countries, including: fiscal austerity, high interest rates, trade liberalisation, capital markets liberalisation, privatisation and financial market restructuring.

Stiglitz believes that these policies are the result of an ideological commitment to free markets that is almost dogmatic, especially within the IMF. Stiglitz believes that the IMF tends to act in the interests of creditors and rich elites at the expense of the poor and the IMF is not sufficiently open to the views and perspectives of the poor. After all, it was this blinkered ideology, combined with 'bad economics' and 'thinly veiled special interests', that resulted in the Russian 'shock therapy' transition, which was the economic equivalent of the Wild West. By contrast, China has adopted its own form of gradualism with much greater success.

Stiglitz calls for a number of systemic reforms, including:

1. *Acknowledgement of the dangers of capital market liberalization*: 'hot money' imposes huge costs on those not directly party to the transactions;

2. *Bankruptcy reforms and standstills*: a 'super-Chapter 11' is needed to address bankruptcies that occur due to macroeconomic disturbances;

3. *Less reliance on bailouts*: via the 'moral hazard' mechanism, they encourage rather than discourage the continuation of risky investment;

4. *Improved banking regulation*: in both developed and less developed countries;

5. *Improved risk management*: developing countries and financial institutions should structure loans in ways that mitigate the risks of large fluctuations;

6. *Improved safety nets*: these are inadequate in developing countries overall, and in specific sectors of developed economies such as agriculture and small business; and

7. *Improved response to crises*: the interests of workers and small businesses have to be balanced against the concerns of creditors.

Beyond this, Stiglitz proposes that in future the IMF should 'limit itself to its core area, managing crises; it should no longer be involved (outside crises) in development or the economies of transition'. Developing economies and those transitioning from communism are better served by crafting country-specific, home-grown solutions in partnership with, rather than under the imperious supervision of, international financial institutions. The patients must heal themselves.

From the book

- [The IMF] was not participating in a conspiracy, but it was reflecting the interests and ideology of the Western financial community.

- Decisions were made on the basis of what seemed a curious blend of ideology and bad economics, dogma that sometimes seemed to be thinly veiling special interests.

- While misguidedly working to preserve what it saw as the sanctity of the credit contract, the IMF was willing to tear apart the even more important social contract.

- There is money to bail out banks but not to pay for improved education and health services, let alone to bail out workers who are thrown out of their jobs as a result of the IMF's macroeconomic mismanagement.

- Globalization can be reshaped, and when it is, when it is properly, fairly run, with all countries having a voice in policies affecting them, there is a possibility that it will help create a new global economy in which growth is not only more sustainable and less volatile but the fruits of this growth are more equitably shared.

About the author

Joseph E. Stiglitz (born 1943) is an American economist, best known for his work on the economics of information and the impacts of globalisation.

Stiglitz, a graduate of Amherst College, received his PhD from MIT in 1967, became a full professor at Yale in 1970, and in 1979 was awarded the John Bates Clark Award, given biennially by the American Economic Association to the economist under 40 who has made the most significant contribution to the field. He has taught at Princeton, Stanford, MIT and was the Drummond Professor and a fellow of All Souls College, Oxford. He is now University Professor at Columbia University in New York and Chair of Columbia University's Committee on Global Thought. He is also the co-founder and Executive Director of the Initiative for Policy Dialogue at Columbia and Director of Graduate Summer Programs at the Brooks World Poverty Institute.

Stiglitz was a member of the Council of Economic Advisers from 1993 to 1995, during the Clinton administration, and served as CEA chairman from 1995 to 1997. He then became Chief Economist and Senior Vice-President of the World Bank from 1997 to 2000.

In 2001, he was awarded the Nobel Prize in economics for his analyses of markets with asymmetric information. His work has helped explain the circumstances in which markets do not work well, and how selective government intervention can improve their performance.

In his own words
(2008 interview)

Reflections on the book

I had been Chief Economist at the World Bank, Senior Vice-President, and had been involved in a whole series of major issues: the transition of communist countries towards the market, the East Asia crisis, the global financial crisis of '97–'98, as well as the attempt to create a trade regime that was favourable or at least fair to the developing countries. My dissatisfaction with the way each of those crises was managed motivated me to write the book in the hope that, by exposing the problems, maybe something would be done to the democratic processes.

These were not inherent problems of globalisation, but the way globalisation was managed was disadvantageous to the developing countries, even disadvantageous to many people in the developed countries. One of the paradoxes was that, while in principle everybody was supposed to be better off as a result of globalisation, in practice the opposition to globalisation rose from both the North and the South. It had unified so much of the world against it because of the way it was managed. There were some winners but there were a lot more losers.

The role of business

I think there's a wide range of corporate behaviours, some of them very good some of them very bad. I was involved in Alaska and most of the oil companies operating in the state tried to cheat the state. At the other extreme you have companies like Hydro in Norway who not only are trying to push the agenda of transparency but also of human rights. Now that is an important contribution to corporate responsibility. Some think that corporate responsibility is a good web page; some really are trying to do something about it.

We should recognise there are some companies who are trying to enhance the productivity of poor people and there are some who recognise that you can take advantage of poor people. In the United States we've had the sub-prime mortgage crisis. American banking institutions saw that there was money at the bottom of the pyramid and they said, 'We have to take it for ourselves as corporate profits.' And they did. And now millions of Americans are losing their homes and with it their life savings.

As people started looking at what happened at the IMF and World Bank and failures of regulation of the global financial markets, there was a widespread recognition that something's not worked well. So understanding there is a problem is necessary before you're going to change. On the other hand, there are some people who benefit from the system as it works today and they are going to make it difficult to make the changes that we have to make. Overall there are some big opportunities in globalisation for gains to both the developed and developing countries, but special interests play an important role.

Looking to the future

Before the Seattle riots, there was an enthusiasm that was not tempered by reality.

OTHER BOOKS (SELECTION)

Whither Socialism? (MIT Press, 1996)

The Roaring Nineties: A New History of the World's Most Prosperous Decade (W.W. Norton & Co., 2003)

Fair Trade for All: How Trade Can Promote Development (with Andrew Charlton; Oxford University Press, 2005)

Making Globalization Work (W.W. Norton & Co., 2006)

The Three Trillion Dollar War: The True Cost of the Iraq Conflict (Allen Lane, 2008)

MORE INFORMATION

Joseph Stiglitz's official website:
www2.gsb.columbia.edu/faculty/jstiglitz

Columbia's Initiative for Policy Dialogue:
www0.gsb.columbia.edu/ipd

38
The Corporation
Joel Bakan

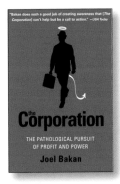

1st edn
**The Corporation:
The Pathological Pursuit
of Profit and Power**
Constable, 2004; 240pp,
pbk; 978-1845290795

Current UK edn
**The Corporation:
The Pathological Pursuit
of Profit and Power**
Robinson Publishing,
2005; 240pp, pbk, rev.
expanded edn;
978-1845291747

Current US edn
**The Corporation:
The Pathological Pursuit
of Profit and Power**
Free Press, 2005;
240pp, pbk;
978-0743247467

Key ideas

▶ Corporations are required by law to elevate their own interests above those of others, making them prone to prey on and exploit others without regard for legal rules or moral limits, which are the same traits as a psychopath.

▶ Corporate social responsibility, though sometimes yielding positive results, most often serves to mask the corporation's true character, not to change it.

▶ The corporation's unbridled self-interest victimises individuals, the environment and even shareholders, and can cause corporations to self-destruct, as recent Wall Street scandals reveal.

▶ Despite its flawed character, governments have freed the corporation from legal constraints through deregulation, and granted it ever greater power over society through privatisation.

▶ We urgently need a restoration of the corporation's original purpose, to serve the public interest, and re-establishment of democratic control over the institution.

Synopsis

The Corporation begins by reminding us that, originally, corporations (meaning large Anglo-American publicly traded businesses) were established with the explicit purpose of serving the public good (enshrined in a charter), with liable shareholders. Today, however, corporations have a legal obligation to pursue profits above all else, which becomes a pathological (i.e. valueless) mission that overrides the values of the individual executives working for corporations or the values of society.

Bakan explains that the nature of the corporation changed when the US Supreme Court ruled that a corporation should have the same rights as individuals, thus making it a legal person. However, it is a 'person' with no moral conscience and an exclusive focus on the benefits of shareholders. This results in a pattern of social costs imposed by business in exchange for private gains for its executives and owners.

Citing the World Health Organisation definition, Bakan argues that corporations embody all of the following characteristics of a psychopath: callous unconcern for the feelings of others; incapacity to maintain enduring relationships; reckless disregard for the safety of others; deceitfulness with repeated lying and conning for personal gain; incapacity to experience guilt; and failure to conform to social norms with respect to lawful behaviours.

Bakan justifies this view by quoting numerous examples of corporate misdemeanour, from layoffs, union busting and factory accidents, to sweatshops, chemical pollution and marketing-driven manipulation. He criticises privatisation as 'flawed philosophically because it rests upon a distorted and incomplete conception of human nature. Self-interest and materialistic desire are parts of who we are, but not all. At a practical level, privatization is flawed for its reliance on for-profit corporations to deliver the public good.'

Bakan expresses concern that capitalism's protagonists and players are the new high priests of our day. Industry and government have become intertwined to the extent that it's hard to tell when one ends and the other begins. Consequently, citizens are resisting and protesting their dissent to the centralisation of power in corporate hands. Business has typically responded with corporate social responsibility (CSR) programmes. This is good in some ways, but is often dishonest – a façade for covering up other activities that corporations are involved in, such as the minimisation of legislation that protects the environment and citizens.

Ultimately, Bakan argues, regulation is needed in order to force companies to internalise costs, ranging from protection of the environment and people's health and safety to the human rights of workers, consumers and communities. Regulation should be made more effective by staffing enforcement agencies, setting fines sufficiently high to deter corporations from committing crimes, strengthening the liability of top directors and managers for their corporations' illegal behaviours, barring repeat offender corporations from government contracts, and suspending the charters of corporations that persistently violate public interest.

Bakan concludes with a call to challenge international neoliberalism. 'We must remember that corporations are our creations. They have no lives or powers, and no capacities beyond what we, through our governments, give them.'

From the book

- The corporation's legally defined mandate is to pursue, relentlessly and without exception, its own self-interest, regardless of the often harmful consequences it might cause to others.

- Corporations now govern society, perhaps more than governments themselves do; yet ironically, it is their very power, much of which they have gained through economic globalization, that makes them vulnerable. As is true of any ruling institution, the corporation now attracts mistrust, fear, and demands for accountability from an increasingly anxious public.

- The corporation itself may not so easily escape the psychopath diagnosis, however. Unlike the human beings who inhabit it, the corporation is *singularly* self-interested and unable to feel genuine concern for others in any context.

- We have over the last three hundred years constructed a remarkably efficient wealth-creating machine, but it is now out of control.

- Corporate rule must be challenged in order to revive the values and practices it contradicts: democracy, social justice, equality, and compassion.

About the author

Joel Conrad Bakan (born 1959) is a Canadian lawyer and writer.

Bakan was born in Lansing, Michigan, and raised for most of his childhood in East Lansing, Michigan, where his parents, Paul and Rita Bakan, were both long-time professors in psychology at Michigan State University. In 1971, he moved with his parents to Vancouver, British Columbia. He was educated at Simon Fraser University (BA, 1981), University of Oxford (BA in law, 1983) and Dalhousie University (LLB, 1984).

He served as a law clerk to Brian Dickson in 1985; during his tenure as clerk, Chief Justice Dickson authored the judgment *R. v. Oakes*, which allows reasonable limitations on rights and freedoms through legislation if it can be 'demonstrably justified in a free and democratic society', among others. He then pursued a Master's degree at Harvard Law School. After graduation, he returned to Canada, where he has taught law at Osgoode Hall Law School of York University and the University of British Columbia.

The Corporation, published in 2004, was made into a film the same year and won 25 international awards. He is also the author of a number of books on Canadian constitutional law. He established the Marlee

Klein Memorial Lectures in Social Justice to commemorate his first wife's contributions to Canadian law and feminist legal theory, after she died of leukaemia in 2001. He is now married to Canadian actress and singer Rebecca Jenkins.

In his own words (2008 interview)

Reflections on the book

The history of the corporation is an interesting one, especially when you look primarily at Anglo-American law, which I did in the book. What you see is the watershed moment legally and economically in the mid-19th century. It's around that time in the United States and United Kingdom that you begin to see legislative changes that

are responsive to lobbying. That creates the modern corporation as we know it today, as an entity that is separate from the owners of the business.

The original notion of the corporation was that the sovereign would grant the status of corporation to a group of business people in order to acquit themselves of some responsibility to create something that was in the public good. For example, an early corporation in London in the 17th century was established to transport water . . . The notion that this was simply about creating wealth for the owners of the company was alien. It was really about serving some public interest, some sovereign interest.

The role of business

The so-called social responsibility that we hear about is a bit of an oxymoron, because legally a corporation can't really have a responsibility to society, unless it can justify the presence of such a responsibility as somehow ultimately serving its own interests in creating wealth. And that's where the pathology lies. The law creates this 'person' in the form of a corporation and then it requires the person always to act within its own self-interest.

The fundamental difficulty with social responsibility remains the fact that we haven't changed the nature of the corporation: it is, and continues to be, pathologically constituted, in the sense that it still must put its own interests above all others. And that makes it a very unstable kind of institution for achieving public goals, and for self-regulating.

Looking to the future

My scepticism about social responsibility is really driven by my sense that there's a better alternative, and that alternative is democratic government. I believe we have a better option in the form of not trying to *persuade* companies to be socially responsible, but just *demanding* that they be so through laws, through regulation.

Should we change the actual structure, the legal DNA, of the company? Or should we leave it as it is and regulate it from outside? I suppose in an ideal world I would like to see the legal structure of the company change, so that the best interests of the company would be understood as including the best interests of the community in which it's situated. But in the present I don't see much movement towards that. What we *do* have in existence is a very defensible, laudable and quite idealistic system of governance in Western democracies. So rather than try to change the actual structure of the company in the short term, we should try to reclaim these institutions.

OTHER BOOKS (SELECTION)

Social Justice and the Constitution: Perspectives on a Social Union for Canada (with David Schneiderman; Carleton University Press, 1993)

Just Words: Constitutional Rights and Social Wrongs (University of Toronto Press, 1997)

MORE INFORMATION

The Corporation film:
www.thecorporation.com

39
Presence
Peter Senge, C. Otto Scharmer, Joseph Jaworski and Betty Sue Flowers

1st edn
Presence
Human Purpose and the Field of the Future
Society for Organizational Learning, 2004; 289pp, hbk; 978-0974239019

Current UK edn
Presence:
An Exploration of Profound Change in People, Organizations and Society
Nicholas Brealey Publishing, 2005; 304pp, pbk; 978-1857883558

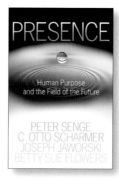

Current US edn
Presence:
Human Purpose and the Field of the Future
Doubleday, 2008; 304pp, pbk, repr. edn; 978-0385516303

Key ideas

▶ Personal and organisational change cannot rely on dispassionate analytical rationalism.

▶ For deep organisational and societal change to occur, there must be an ongoing synergy between the personal change and the collective, so that it becomes a co-creation.

▶ The process of personal and organisational transformation can be described as a 'U-Process', from sensing (changing our perceptions) through presencing (reaching a state of clarity and connection) to realising (experiencing the world as unfolding through us).

▶ The end point of the U-Process comes when innovation is institutionalised, i.e. when what we've learned becomes part of how we do things.

▶ We need (individually and collectively) to find ways to see the wholeness of life and to use our hearts and our intuition to become 'part of a future that is seeking to unfold'.

Synopsis

Presence presents a new model of personal and organisational change. Much of the book comprises transcripts of conversations between the authors, on subjects including science, business, leadership and spirituality. The authors' central question is: how do we individually and collectively bring about useful change in circumstances where the past, and established ways of thinking, are not good guides to the future?

Their answer is presented as a new 'Theory U' of change, comprising a 'U-Process', which is informed by an intuitive and holistic view of the world, rather than a rational and mechanistic one. First, to arrive at the deeper experience of presencing, we must first cultivate a deeper kind of observation, called Sensing. Visually depicted as moving down the left-hand side of the 'U', this involves a specific set of experiential capacities called Suspending, Redirecting and Letting Go.

Suspending is the ability to pause one's habitual flow of 'ideation' and mental models built up in the past, in the service of opening up a space of consciousness that is free from already-formed concepts. Redirecting, also described as the ability to 'see from the whole to the part', is essentially a psycho-spiritual capacity to dissolve the boundaries between seer and seen, subject and object. Letting Go is the capacity to 'surrender our perceived need to control', acting as the antidote to fixed views and attachments, self-concepts, and even ideas that form during the process of innovation.

The bottom of the 'U' is Presencing, the mysterious, transformative moment of 'field shift' – a deeply felt paradigm shift in which participants' sense of who they are alters in synchronicity with the arising of new, previously unimaginable options for action. The authors give dramatic examples of this moment, drawn from both individual and group experiences.

The final movement of the 'U' (visually, moving up the right-hand side) is Realising, a three-stage process of Crystallising (envisioning what seeks to emerge), Prototyping (embodying living microcosms) and Institutionalising (embodying the new). Hence, the third stage involves operationalising the radical learning achieved in Sensing and Presencing. A key injunction here is that, after the slowing-down and deepening of the earlier stages, Realising must be executed with swiftness and courage, using a method called 'rapid prototyping' – quickly enacting innovative ideas as small-scale, real-world experiments. The end point of the U comes when innovation is institutionalised, i.e. embedded in its own routines, practices and institutional laws.

The authors argue that the U-Process involves a fundamentally different approach to co-creation, in which we recognise that the self and the world are inescapably linked. The most profound work occurs at the bottom of the 'U'. This experience has been termed Presencing because it is about becoming totally present – to the larger space or field around us, to an expanded sense of self, and, ultimately, to what is emerging through us. Once we have achieved that stance, as individuals and as a team, moving up the 'U' involves acting in service of bringing that emerging reality into being.

From the book

- As long as our thinking is governed by industrial, 'machine age' metaphors such as control, predictability, and 'faster is better', we will continue to re-create institutions as we have, despite their increasing disharmony with the larger world.

- The basic problem with the new species of global institutions is that they have not yet become aware of themselves as living. Once they do, they can become a place for the presencing of the whole as it might be, not just as it has been.

- The U-Theory suggests that the central integrating thought will emerge from building three integrated capacities: a new capacity for observing that no longer fragments the observer from what's observed; a new capacity for stillness that no longer fragments who we really are from what's emerging; and a new capacity for creating alternative realities that no longer fragments the wisdom of the head, heart and hand.

- What's emerging is a new synthesis of science, spirituality and leadership as different facets of a single way of being.

- When all is said and done, the only change that will make a difference is the transformation of the human heart.

About the authors

Peter M. Senge (born 1947) is a Senior Lecturer in systems dynamics at the Massachusetts Institute of Technology. He is also Founding Chair of SoL, the Society for Organizational Learning, a global community of corporations, researchers and consultants dedicated to the 'interdependent development of people and their institutions'.

Senge received a BS in engineering from Stanford University, an MS in social systems modelling and a PhD in management from MIT. Following the publication of his million-copy bestselling book, *The Fifth Discipline: The Art and Practice of the Learning Organization* (1990), Senge has lectured extensively throughout the world, translating the abstract ideas of systems theory into tools for better understanding of economic and organisational change.

The *Journal of Business Strategy* named Senge as one of the 24 people who had the greatest influence on business strategy over the last 100 years. The *Financial Times* (2000) and *BusinessWeek* (2001) have named him as one of the world's 'top management gurus'.

In addition to several books, Senge has authored many articles published in both academic journals and the business press on systems thinking in management.

Peter M. Senge

C. Otto Scharmer

C. Otto Scharmer is a Senior Lecturer at MIT, the founding chair of the Presencing Institute, and a founding member of the MIT Green Hub.

Scharmer holds a PhD in economics and management from Witten-Herdecke University in Germany. His article 'Strategic Leadership within the Triad Growth–Employment–Ecology' won the McKinsey Research Award in 1991.

He introduced the theoretical framework and practice called 'presencing' in his book *Theory U: Leading from the Future as it Emerges* (2007), and in *Presence*. With his colleagues, Scharmer has used presencing to facilitate profound innovation and change processes both within companies and across societal systems.

Scharmer has consulted with global companies, international institutions, and governments in North America, Europe, Asia and Africa. He has co-designed and delivered award-winning business leadership programmes and also facilitates cross-sector programmes for leaders in business, government and civil society that focus on

Joseph Jaworski

Betty Sue Flowers

building people's collective capacity to achieve profound innovation and change.

Scharmer is also founding chair of ELIAS (Emerging Leaders for Innovation Across Sectors), an initiative focused on developing profound system innovations for a more sustainable world. ELIAS links 20 leading institutions across three sectors of business, government and civil society.

Joseph Jaworski is the founder and chairman of both Generon International and the Global Leadership Initiative.

Jaworski began his professional career as an attorney, specialising in domestic and international litigation at Bracewell & Patterson, a large Houston-based law firm where for 15 years he was a senior partner and member of the executive committee. In 1975 he was elected as a fellow of the American College of Trial. In addition, he

ran a successful horse-breeding operation (Circle J Enterprises), and helped found several organisations, including a life insurance company and a refining company.

In 1980, Joseph founded the American Leadership Forum, a non-governmental organisation responsible for developing collaborative leadership. Ten years later, he was invited to join the Royal Dutch/Shell Group of companies in London, to lead Shell's renowned team of scenario planners. Thereafter he returned to the US as a senior fellow and a member of the Board of Governors of the MIT Center for Organizational Learning, and was a founding member of the Society for Organizational Learning.

Jaworski is the author of the critically acclaimed book *Synchronicity* (1996), an explication of generative leadership based on his lifelong work and experience.

Betty Sue Flowers is the Director of the Johnson Presidential Library and Museum in Austin, Texas, a position she was appointed to in 2002.

Prior to that, she was the Kelleher Professor of English and member of the Distinguished Teachers Academy at the University of Texas at Austin. She is a Senior Research Fellow of the IC2 Institute, an Honorary Fellow of British Studies, a recipient of the Pro Bene Meritis Award, and a Distinguished Alumnus of the University of Texas.

Flowers is also a poet, editor and business consultant, with publications ranging from poetry therapy to the economic myth, including two books of poetry and four television tie-in books in collaboration with Bill Moyers. She hosted *Conversations with Betty Sue Flowers* on the Austin PBS-affiliate and has served as a moderator for executive seminars at the Aspen Institute for Humanistic Studies, consultant for NASA, member of the Envisioning Network for General Motors, Visiting Advisor to the Secretary of the Navy, and editor of Global Scenarios for Shell International in London and the World Business Council in Geneva.

Flowers received her BA and MA from the University of Texas and her PhD in English Literature from the University of London.

In their own words
(2008 interviews)

C. Otto Scharmer

Reflections on the book

One key insight that emerged was that there are two different sources of learning. One is learning from the past and the other is learning from the emerging future. We know everything about the first one and we know almost nothing about the second one . . . Over the years, I came to call the second learning process 'presencing' – it is a blending between two words: 'sensing', which means to sense an emerging future possibility and 'presence', which means to begin to operate from that possibility in the 'now'.

The role of business and leadership

The experience of being a victim of forces you can't control is pervasive in our current global system. It actually goes all the way up, including to the boardroom levels where you are chased by Wall Street . . . At the same time, I am finding another current reality which is where you experience that you can make a difference on something that matters for you. As a leader, can you create this other reality, this innovation space for yourself that keeps your spirit uplifted, that keeps you on this other energy loop . . . That's what I try to describe with 'presencing'.

Even if I work in very conservative business organisations and industries, I notice, particularly in younger leaders, how great the openness is to go into their deeper space. Why? Not only because it allows you to become a more effective leader, but also because it allows you to connect with the essence of who you really are. For those in leadership situations in business or government, the demands are so enormous that this deeper space of reflection becomes one of the anchor points that you use every day to be more effective.

Looking to the future

We know from the tipping point phenomenon that you have windows of potential radical change where the whole system can jump to another level of awareness and way of operating . . . I think we are in such a time now, where a small difference can have a big impact on where the whole system is going. And, in that regard, what we have seen in the past is not necessarily a good guide for what's going to happen in the future. We need to come up with new responses and new ways of addressing these challenges.

If we look at the evolution of capitalism, we have three coordination mechanisms that have evolved over the past 200 years: regulation and hierarchy; market and competition; and dialogue and stakeholder negotiations. What we need is more of these three plus a fourth one. The fourth one is disruptive and we can see it particularly in the area of sustainability and climate change on a small scale. That has to do with a fourth coordination mechanism which is called 'seeing and operating from the whole'. It means that the coordination is not the market mechanism or regulation, it is what spontaneously happens.

Betty Sue Flowers

Reflections on the book

The book started not with science, but with imagination. What if we could really, really feel and imagine and come to terms with the idea that the human race, because of our own activities, might die out. Would we behave differently, the way people tend to behave differently when told they only have a short time to live? What would it take? And how do you make large-scale change which requires a systemic level of understanding and action in groups? How do you have leadership in groups across boundaries, multinationally? So I think the book is connected to sustainability in these two ways. First, what is the act of imagination that would actually grab us enough to change our behaviour? And, secondly, how do you do this given the necessity to work across boundaries and in groups?

The role of economics and leadership

The economic myth – and by myth I don't mean something untrue, I mean a large story of reality that we swim in, the way the fish swim in the sea unconsciously – has, at its basis, growth, but it doesn't take into account quality. The strength of the economic myth is that economics is about interconnectedness and at its basis a fundamental equality: that is, my dollar is as good as your dollar. But what I call the ecological myth could evolve from the economic myth, because it too is about interconnectedness, but interconnectedness of quality not of quantity.

Leadership becomes important in setting the values of a company. On the other hand, people at different levels can themselves find kindred spirits to suggest or initiate actions that companies can take that gradually influence the culture of the company. So you can work at both grassroots and the leadership level and in fact both need to take responsibility: that's one of the things the ecological myth makes clear.

Looking to the future

We're destroying our home, the globe, the planet – that's a pretty deep story. What makes it an interesting deep story is the understanding that we all have a role to play in this. With everything from individual decisions in your own home to global decisions to cut emissions, from light bulbs to cocoa and beyond, there's a sense that we're all in this together and that in itself is a new kind of myth. The capitalistic or economic myth didn't really have a sense that we're all in this together.

If you attempt to scare people with the enormity of the problems, the tendency is simply to give up. When you dispirit people, when you remove the spirit, you also remove the capacity to change. But perhaps we can perform a positive function in the world if we were only to imagine a role as stewards. The result of that imagination should be the impetus to change not out of fear but out of love.

OTHER BOOKS (SELECTION)

The Fifth Discipline: The Art and Practice of the Learning Organization (Peter Senge; Doubleday/ Currency, 1994)

Synchronicity: The Inner Path of Leadership (Joseph Jaworski; Berrett-Koehler, 1998)

The Dance of Change: The Challenges of Sustaining Momentum in Learning Organizations (Peter Senge and Art Kleiner; Nicholas Brealey, 1999)

The Necessary Revolution: How Individuals and Organisations Are Working Together to Create a Sustainable World (Peter Senge; Nicholas Brealey Publishing, 2008)

Theory U: Learning from the Future as it Emerges (C. Otto Scharmer; Berrett-Koehler, 2009)

MORE INFORMATION

C. Otto Scharmer's official website: www.ottoscharmer.com

Presencing Institute: presencing.com

Society for Organizational Learning: www.solonline.org

40
The Fortune at the Bottom of the Pyramid
C.K. Prahalad

1st edn
The Fortune at the Bottom of the Pyramid: Eradicating Poverty through Profits
Wharton School Publishing, 2004; 432pp, hbk; 978-0131467507

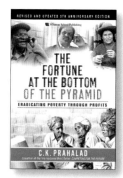

Current edn
The Fortune at the Bottom of the Pyramid: Eradicating Poverty through Profits
Wharton School Publishing, 2009; hbk; 978-0137009275; rev. and updated 5th anniversary edn

Key ideas

▶ We need to think of the poor as entrepreneurs and consumers, not victims needing handouts or charity.

▶ The poor, by virtue of their collective size and purchasing power, represent a significant market.

▶ However, this market has remained unserved or under-served because companies have failed to adapt their business model to suit the market conditions.

▶ Successfully serving the four billion people at the 'bottom of the pyramid' requires innovation in product design, marketing and distribution.

▶ It also requires debunking various myths about the poor, such as that they are a poor credit risk, or are only interested in low-cost, low-quality products.

Synopsis

The 'bottom of the pyramid' (BOP) refers to the global income distribution pyramid, where roughly four billion people live on less than $2 a day. The thesis of the book is that, although the per capita disposable income is low among the poor, collectively they represent a large market. The challenge, therefore, is to develop a business model that allows companies to serve this market profitably. Prahalad argues that this is not only possible, but imperative if we are going to make progress in tackling poverty.

The book begins by challenging many falsely held business assumptions about the poor, such as: the poor are not our target customers; they cannot afford our products or services; they do not have use for products sold in developed countries; only developed countries appreciate and pay for technological innovations; and the BOP market is not critical for long-term growth and vitality of multinational corporations.

The key is not whether BOP markets represent a massive opportunity, but rather how to capitalise on that opportunity. Prahalad suggests that companies must create the capacity to consume. This is based on three principles:

1. *Affordability*: without sacrificing quality or efficacy. This is not just about lower prices. It is about creating a new price–performance envelope;

2. *Access*: distribution of products and services must take into account where the poor live and work as well as their work patterns/schedules. This calls for geographical intensity of distribution; and

3. *Availability*: distribution efficiency is critical. BOP consumers cannot defer decisions since they purchase based on the cash they have on hand at the given moment.

To be successful in BOP markets, businesses need a new philosophy of innovation and product and service delivery. Managers need to re-examine assumptions about form and functionality, about channels and distribution costs. Furthermore, BOP consumer problems cannot be solved with old technologies. Most scalable, price–performance-enhancing solutions need advanced and emerging technologies that are creatively blended with the existing and rapidly evolving infrastructures.

National and local governments can act as enablers of the growth in BOP markets. Prahalad calls this the Transaction Governance Capacity (TGC). A social revolution is also required, since the emancipation of women is an important part of building markets at the BOP. Empowered, organised, networked and active women are key agents, entrepreneurs and consumers among the poor.

Prahalad concludes that 'a measure of development is the number of people in a society who are considered middle class. More important, social transformation is about the number of people who believe that they can aspire to a middle-class lifestyle. Our goal is to rapidly change the pyramid into a diamond.'

From the book

- Doing more of the same, by refining the solutions of the past . . . is important and has a role to play, but has not redressed the problem of poverty.

- We are all prisoners of our own socialization. The lenses through which we perceive the world are colored by our own ideology, experiences, and established management practices. Each one of the groups that is focusing on poverty alleviation – the World Bank, rich countries providing aid, charitable organizations, national governments, and the private sector – is conditioned by its own dominant logic.

- If we stop thinking of the poor as victims or as a burden and start recognizing them as resilient and creative entrepreneurs and value-conscious consumers, a whole new world of opportunity will open up.

- Charity might feel good, but it rarely solves the problem in a scalable and sustainable fashion.

- When the poor are converted into consumers, they get more than access to products and services. They acquire the dignity of attention and choices from the private sector that were previously reserved for the middle-class and rich.

- Both sides – the large firms and the BOP consumers – have traditionally not trusted each other. The mistrust runs deep. However, private-sector firms approaching the BOP market must focus on building trust between themselves and the consumers.

- The capabilities to solve the perennial problem of poverty through profitable businesses at the BOP are now available to most nations. However, converting the poor into a market will require innovations.

About the author

Coimbatore Krishnao (C.K.) Prahalad (born 1941) is an Indian academic, management consultant and author, best known for his work on strategy.

Prahalad studied physics at the University of Madras (now Chenai). He worked as a manager in a branch of the Union Carbide battery company, before continuing his education in the United States, and earning a PhD from Harvard. He taught in India and America, eventually joining the faculty of the University of Michigan's Ross School of Business, where he is the Paul and Ruth McCracken Distinguished University Professor of Corporate Strategy and holds the

Harvey C. Fruehauf chair of Business Administration.

Prahalad is particularly well known for his groundbreaking work on corporate strategy, including on 'core competencies' (with Gary Hamel) and the 'bottom of the pyramid' (with Stuart Hart). His book with Hamel, *Competing for the Future,* was named the Bestselling Business Book of the Year in 1994. Less well known is that Prahalad was co-founder and became CEO of Praja Inc. ('praja' means 'citizen' or 'common people') before it was sold to TIBCO. He is still on the board of TiE, The Indus Entrepreneurs.

Prahalad has won numerous awards and is frequently cited as a 'top ten management thinker'. He is a member of the blue ribbon commission of the United Nations on Private Sector and Development and the first recipient of the Lal Bahadur Shastri Award for Contributions to Management and Public Administration presented by the President of India in 2000.

OTHER BOOKS (SELECTION)

The Multinational Mission: Balancing Local Demands with Global Vision (with Yves L. Doz; Macmillan, 1987)

Competing for the Future (with Gary Hamel; Harvard Business School Press, 1994)

Strategic Flexibility: Managing in a Turbulent Economy (ed. with Gary Hamel, Howard Thomas and Don O'Neal; Wiley, 1998)

The Future of Competition: Co-creating Unique Value with Customers (with Venkat Ramaswamy; Harvard Business School Press, 2004)

The New Age of Innovation: Driving Cocreated Value through Global Networks (with M.S. Krishnan; McGraw-Hill, 2008)

MORE INFORMATION

Base of the Pyramid Protocol:
www.bop-protocol.org

NextBillion:
www.nextbillion.net

41
The River Runs Black
Elizabeth C. Economy

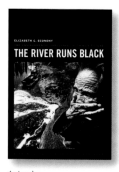

Current edn
**The River
Runs Black:**
**The Environmental
Challenge to
China's Future**
Cornell University
Press, 2005; 368pp,
pbk; 978-0801489785

1st edn
**The River
Runs Black:**
**The Environmental
Challenge to
China's Future**
Cornell University
Press, 2004; 272pp,
hbk; 978-0801442209

Key ideas

▶ China's spectacular economic growth over the past two decades has dramatically depleted the country's natural resources and produced dangerous levels of pollution.

▶ Environmental degradation has in turn contributed to significant public health problems, mass migration, economic loss and social unrest.

▶ China's current approach to environmental protection mirrors the one embraced for economic development, devolving authority while retaining only weak central control.

▶ The result has been a patchwork of environmental protection, mostly in a few wealthy regions with strong leaders, while most of the country continues to deteriorate.

▶ Proactive policies backed by effective local enforcement could still avert an environmental crisis, but only if China changes course.

Synopsis

The River Runs Black, as the title suggests, paints a fairly bleak picture of China's state of the environment. The book quotes 2002 figures, in which China had six of the world's ten most polluted cities, more than 300,000 people dying annually from air-pollution-related ailments, more than 75% of China's rivers being so polluted that the water is undrinkable and cannot support fish, and desert covering 25% of the country as a result of continued deforestation and grassland degradation.

Economy concedes that the Chinese government has not been unaware or inactive in responding to these issues. In the 1980s, it introduced many environmental laws and by the late 1990s publicly embraced environmental issues, especially after Beijing's successful Olympic bid. In the cities, they have also been replacing coal-heated systems with natural gas. Despite these efforts, however, China's environmental problems continue to get worse, rather than better, not least due to the rapid increase in private automobile ownership.

Economy argues that China's well-intended attempts to promote sustainable development ultimately are hampered by inappropriate policies and ineffective local implementation; furthermore, that China's environmental problems are not simply a crisis born of the past 20 years of rapid economic development, but rather from centuries of war, economic development and population pressures. Hence, there are deep-seated cultural and historical barriers to overcome.

While China's cities have among the worst air quality in the world, Economy believes water actually may be the country's most serious environmental problem, where 60 million Chinese residents have difficulty finding adequate drinking water sources, while ten times that number regularly consume contaminated water. Water scarcity continues to grow as demand for the resource increases 5% annually.

The magnitude of China's increasingly degraded environment has implications for the country's economic development, public health and social stability. According to the World Bank, environmental problems cost the country 8–12% of its GDP each year. Western China is creating rural eco-refugees, whose migration to the east coast places stress on already burgeoning urban centres. Government officials acknowledge that environmental problems are one of the four major sources of social unrest in China.

One barrier to overcoming China's environmental challenges is the lack of appropriate resources. Though the country's environmental agency has many forward-thinking individuals, it has a workforce of only 270 people. Furthermore, China invests only 1.3% of its GDP in environmental protection efforts, while Chinese environmental scientists contend the country needs to spend at least 2.2% just to maintain the current level of air and water quality.

Environmental NGOs, since the first one was established in 1994, are increasingly having an impact. For instance, the network of environmental groups has had enough popular support to derail plans for two major dam projects in southwest China. Their growing activism forms part of Economy's most optimistic scenario for China's future (China Goes Green), as compared with a continuation of the status quo (Inertia Sets In), and further environmental deterioration (Environmental Meltdown).

From the book

- Throughout the country, centuries of rampant, sometimes willful destruction of the environment have produced environmental disasters.

- In virtually every respect, China's environment overall has deteriorated.

- Each element of the bureaucratic apparatus exhibits fundamental structural weaknesses that undermine the best of intentions.

- Attitudes, institutions, and policies evolved from traditional folk understandings and philosophical thought, such as Confucianism, which most often promoted man's need to use nature for his own benefit.

- China's leaders face a daunting task. With one-quarter of the world's population, centuries of grand-scale campaigns to transform the natural environment for man's benefit, intensive and unfettered economic development, and – most recently – its entry into the global economy, China has laid waste to its resources.

- With roughly five times the population of the United States, China possesses a central environmental protection bureaucracy only one-twentieth as large.

- 'If you don't have democracy you can't have real environmental protection' (quoting environmental activist Tang Xiyang).

About the author

Elizabeth C. Economy (born 1962) is a researcher and author on Chinese domestic and foreign policy, Sino–US relations, and global environmental issues.

Economy received her PhD from the University of Michigan, her MA from Stanford University and BA from Swarthmore College. She has taught undergraduate- and graduate-level courses at Columbia University, Johns Hopkins University's Paul H. Nitze School of Advanced International Studies, and the University of Washington's Jackson School of International Studies.

Economy is currently the C.V. Starr senior fellow and director of Asia studies at the Council on Foreign Relations in New York. She serves on the board of the China–US Center for Sustainable Development and the advisory board for *Issues and Studies*, an international journal on Chinese, Taiwanese and East Asian affairs.

Economy has published widely on both Chinese domestic and foreign policy. *The River Runs Black* was named one of the top ten books of 2004 by *The Globalist* and won the International Convention on Asia

Scholars Award for the best social sciences book published on Asia in 2003 or 2004.

Economy is a frequent guest on nationally broadcast radio and television programmes, has testified before Congress on numerous occasions, and regularly speaks at international conferences such as the World Economic Forum in Davos and the Fortune Global Forum.

In her own words
(2008 interview)

Reflections on the book

The environment was sort of a lost issue in China's development. And I don't think many people were paying attention to it in the mid-1990s. But Al Gore, when he went to China in 1997, did put the issue of China and climate change on the map. And to a certain extent that helped to elevate my work.

One of the things we've seen just in the past year that's quite interesting and is not in my book because it's just beginning to happen, is that we've seen the protests in China, of which there are some 50,000 on the environment alone, according to China's Minister of Environmental Protection.

The role of business

The story of multinationals and their environmental practices in China is a mixed one. Up until a few years ago, the story was largely positive for European, American and Japanese multinationals. They were generally regarded as environmental leaders within China, and welcomed for their best practices. But a few years ago an environmental activist named Ma Jun put together a water pollution map, where he detailed about 3,300 factories throughout the country that had failed to address their pollution problems, and about 1% could be traced back to multinationals. So the general tenor of the debate within China with regard to multinationals has changed. There's far more emphasis now on the negative role that multinationals play in China; the sense that they have simply offloaded their most polluting industries into China, that they are not in fact transferring the best technologies and that they're taking advantage of China's relatively weak environmental enforcement.

There are some initial efforts by companies like Wal-Mart to begin to trace all their products down the supply chain. But I think this is going to be a long process of transforming the way that China and Chinese factories do business. And it's going to have to be done hand in hand with local environmental protection bureau officials and the multinational actors.

Looking to the future

It's very difficult to see how much progress China is going to be able to make in an overwhelmingly coal-based economy in which the Premier Wen Jiabao says, 'We need to quadruple our economy by 2020.' I just don't know how that's done in an environmentally sustainable way.

You have some parts of the country that are moving ahead, primarily the wealthier parts, with strong engagement with the international community. You have environmental NGOs increasing their activism and the range of issues that they're trying to tackle. You have the media interested; not always able to participate in the way that they would like, but trying very hard to play an important role in environmental protection. And you have some important environmental leaders within the Chinese government. But overwhelmingly still, despite all the rhetoric – the talks about environmental protection and the need for environmental protection in China – growth and rapid growth remains the imperative.

I take all of my inspiration and hope for the work that I do – and certainly for the future of China – from China's environmental activists and from the Chinese people themselves. I have the most profound respect for these people, because they're pioneers, and every day any one of them is pushing the boundaries and challenging a system that in many ways is antithetical to strong and good environmental protection. They're pushing it in terms of those issues of transparency and the rule of law and accountability and putting their lives on the line in some cases. There are environmental activists in jail today. Some of them are award-winning, prize-winning environmental activists who are sitting in jail cells in China. And so I just have enormous respect for the energy and effort that these people bring to their work every single day of their lives, and for what they're willing to risk for the cause of improving their country's environment and that of the rest of the world.

OTHER BOOKS (SELECTION)

The Internationalization of Environmental Protection (ed. with Miranda Schreurs; Cambridge University Press, 1997)

China Joins the World: Progress and Prospects (with Michel Oksenberg; Council on Foreign Relations Press, 1999)

MORE INFORMATION

Council on Foreign Relations: www.cfr.org

42
Capitalism as if the World Matters
Jonathon Porritt

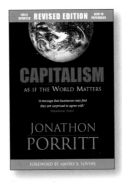

1st edn
Capitalism as if the World Matters
Earthscan Publications, 2005; hbk; 978-1844071920

Current edn
Capitalism as if the World Matters
Earthscan Publications, 2007; pbk, rev. edn; 978-1844071937

Key ideas

▶ It is impossible to deny the need for profound change in the face of today's ecological crises, which threaten the economy and the well-being of global society.

▶ The pace and scale of change to date has been inadequate and conventional environmentalism has failed to win over hearts and minds.

▶ Change has to be seen as desirable (i.e. about creating a better future) and will not come about by threatening people with ecological doom.

▶ We should embrace capitalism as the only overarching system capable of both reconciling ecological sustainability and reforming it.

▶ However, we need an evolved, intelligent and elegant form of capitalism that puts the Earth at its centre and ensures that all people are its beneficiaries.

Synopsis

Capitalism as if the World Matters starts with the sobering message that, despite growing interest in sustainability, things are still going from bad to worse. This is caused by population growth, a consumption-driven economy and our inability to accept that there are ecological limits. According to Porritt, this reflects the prevailing culture of denial within business and government – 'not so much denial of the empirical and social data, but denial of the implications of that data'. He cites corporate social responsibility (CSR) as a typical 'band aid' approach, rather than a strategic commitment to becoming genuinely sustainable.

Porritt also acknowledges the failure of the environmental movement to move beyond a single-issue focus. Often it gets caught up in technical discussions and campaigns and fails to engage with all of us on the level of values and beliefs. Conventional environmentalism has so far failed to win over hearts and minds either within the electorate at large or within today's political elites. So profound change is needed, but it will succeed only if we adopt a different approach from that of the past. And, since capitalism 'is the only game in town', this should be the focus of our efforts, rather than pursuing utopian dreams.

Porritt proposes two strategies for reforming capitalism: extending the concept of capital, and changing sustainability into a positive agenda. The first involves reinterpreting capital to mean more than financial and manufacturing capital. Hence, we must also take into account natural capital, which is any stock or flow of energy and material that produces goods and services, human capital, consisting of people's health, knowledge, skills and motivation, and so-cial capital, which concerns the institutions that help us maintain and develop human capital in partnership with others.

Regarding the second reform strategy, Porritt argues that we cannot scare people into change. Sustainability needs to be re-framed as a positive agenda. It must be as much about new opportunities for responsible wealth creation as about outlawing irresponsible wealth creation; it must draw on a core of ideas and values that speaks directly to people's desire for a higher quality of life, emphasising enlightened self-interest and personal well-being of a different kind.

A key part of this change is to begin focusing the sustainability discussion more on well-being. Hence, governments should be measuring and reporting 'progress' in terms of total well-being, rather than just growth that brings benefits but also unwanted social and environmental costs. The public should also be made aware that individuals who are focused on extrinsic goals (money, power, affluence) tend to have a lower quality of life than those driven by intrinsic goals (good relationships, personal growth, a meaningful job, being useful to others).

Porritt concludes that only this message – of economic opportunities and human well-being despite natural limits – is likely to provide any serious political alternative to today's economic and political orthodoxy. And, unless it aligns with this kind of progressive political agenda, conventional environmentalism will continue to decline, as will our quality of life and the Earth's life-support systems.

From the book

- We've wasted the best part of 20 years pursuing to the point of utter exhaustion a model of capitalism that can only succeed by liquidating the life-support systems that sustain us, and systematically widening the 'inequity gaps' upon which any kind of social cohesion depends in the long run.

- Servitude to detached and indifferent shareholders . . . has led to a pattern of self-serving, irresponsible and illegal [corporate] behaviour that would beggar belief if it was not such a logical consequence of everything that's been going on.

- The very fact that the majority of companies still opt for CSR as the self-contained box into which to pack all their 'good stuff', while they continue to pursue their core business without the remotest likelihood that they or their products/services will ever become genuinely sustainable, reveals all one really needs to know about the empty, seductive illusion that is CSR.

- The notion of 'capitalism as if the world mattered' demands a reform agenda, not a revolutionary one. But it requires a different level of engagement and a much greater readiness to confront denial, to challenge the slow, soul-destroying descent into displacement consumerism, and to take on today's dominant 'I consume, therefore I am' mindsets and lifestyles.

- We are so preoccupied with avoiding nightmares in the future that we have pretty much given up on offering our dreams of a better world today.

- If we don't learn to live sustainably within the natural systems and limits that provide the foundations for all life forms, then we will go the same way as every other life form that failed to adapt to those changing systems and limits. Deep down in our collective psyche, after hundreds of years of industrialisation that systematically suppressed a proper understanding of our continuing and total dependency upon the natural world, that atavistic reality is beginning to resurface.

About the author

Jonathon Porritt (born 1950) is an English writer, broadcaster and commentator on sustainable development.

Porritt was educated at Eton College and Magdalen College, Oxford. Despite training as a barrister, he decided to become an English teacher at St Clement Danes Grammar School (later Burlington Danes School) in Shepherd's Bush, west London, in 1974. He was chair of the UK Ecology Party (now the Green Party) from 1978 to 1984 and, in

1984, gave up teaching to become Director of Friends of the Earth in Britain, a post he held until 1990.

In 1996, Porritt co-founded Forum for the Future, one of the UK's leading sustainable development charities, where he currently serves as Founder Director. In 2000, he was appointed by the Prime Minister as Chairman of the UK Sustainable Development Commission, a post he held until 2009. In addition, he has been a member of the Board of the South West Regional Development Agency since December 1999, and is Co-director of The Prince of Wales's Business and Environment Programme.

In 2005 he became a non-executive director of Wessex Water, and a trustee of the Ashden Awards for Sustainable Energy. He is also Vice-President of the Socialist Environment Resources Association (SERA). He was formerly Chairman of UNED-UK (1993–96), Chairman of Sustainability South West, the South West Round Table for Sustainable Development (1999–2001) and a Trustee of WWF UK (1991–2005).

In his own words
(2008 interview)

Reflections on the book

The purpose of [my first book] *Seeing Green* was really to demonstrate that green politics was a distinct, radical, progressive way of looking at the challenges at the time . . . *Capitalism as if the World Matters* was a much more ambitious endeavour, which was to try and open up the investigation around the degree of compatibility between sustainable development and capitalism.

The book is a pragmatic acceptance that, looking at people all over the world today, rich and poor, they are not remotely close to a state of mind that would call for anything revolutionary. There's no vast upheaval of people across the world saying, 'This system is completely and utterly flawed and must be overturned and we must move towards a different system.'

This is not the time for revolution, so what do we do? The dominant system is capitalism. The choice, therefore, if you're not going to erect barricades and overthrow capitalism, is to firstly explore what sustainable capitalism would look like, and then commit wholeheartedly to a set of radical reform processes that would convert today's capitalism into a kind of capitalism that would deliver a sustainable world.

The role of business and policy

The new energy source is about coupling up with the business community's interest in sustainable wealth creation, and combining with politicians' emergent realisation that the progress model they have to offer isn't really cutting it for people today. We do not have hundreds of millions of happy bunnies all over the world. If those things can be brought together, then you could see how you could aggregate up to a tipping-point moment which would provide a new kind of momentum. Whether we can get there building gradually over a period of time, or whether we need some shocks in the system to accelerate that, that is still a hard one to call.

Looking to the future

There are some breathtakingly inspiring people who have very powerful visions of a better world. However, we have not collectively articulated what this better world looks like: the areas in which it would offer such fantastic improvements in terms of people's quality of life, the opportunities they would have, the chance to live in totally different ways to the way we live now. We haven't done that. Collectively we've not made the alternative work emotionally and physically, in terms of economic excitement. We've just not done it. So my feeling is we're going to have to get a lot smarter at that, because otherwise all we'll have is this rather half-hearted set of incoherent thoughts about what living in a sustainable world would look like. They won't be substantive enough to persuade people that this is much better than the way we're living now. And that means we'll drift until disaster compels an emergency response, which won't be pretty.

OTHER BOOKS (SELECTION)

Seeing Green: The Politics of Ecology Explained
(Cambridge University Press, 1984)

MORE INFORMATION

Forum for the Future:
www.forumforthefuture.org.uk

43
Capitalism at the Crossroads
Stuart L. Hart

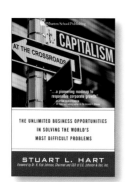

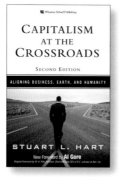

1st edn
Capitalism at the Crossroads: The Unlimited Business Opportunities in Solving the World's Most Difficult Problems
Wharton School Publishing, 2005; 288pp, hbk; 978-0131439870

Current edn
Capitalism at the Crossroads: Aligning Business, Earth and Humanity
Wharton School Publishing, 2007; pbk, 2nd edn; 978-0136134398

Key ideas

▶ Global capitalism is at a crossroads. Without a significant change of course, the future of economic globalisation, free trade and multinational corporations appears increasingly bleak.

▶ Business must respond if it wants its operating environment to remain stable. Hence, it is in companies' self-interest to seek a more benign form of capitalism.

▶ If it succeeds, and truly creates a sustainable global enterprise, then the business community and the planet can prosper.

▶ Among the best examples of a new type of capitalism are business experiments taking place at the 'base of the pyramid'.

▶ Part of the solution is for companies to discover what it means to be 'indigenous', i.e. truly integrated into and responsive to local communities.

Synopsis

Capitalism at the Crossroads begins by showing why our current model of capitalism is unsustainable. The book takes 'the contrarian's' view that business is uniquely equipped to lead us toward a sustainable world. Properly focused, the profit motive can accelerate (not inhibit) the transformation toward global sustainability, with non-profits, governments and multilateral agencies all playing crucial roles as collaborators.

Hart 'foresees massive opportunities for companies both to make money and to make the world a better place, particularly among the four billion poor at the base of the economic pyramid'. This view is a deliberate challenge to what he calls the 'Great Trade-Off Illusion': the belief that firms must sacrifice financial performance to meet societal obligations. Such thinking is the outmoded legacy of the 1970s and early 1980s, where command-and-control regulation turned environmental issues into a cost, requiring end-of-pipe solutions.

By the late 1980s, with the advent of pollution prevention and the coming-together of the quality and environmental management, we saw the age of 'Corporate Greening', where companies started to see financial and strategic advantages in creating societal value. Since the late 1990s, corporations have been challenged to move beyond greening, by pursuing new technologies that have the potential to be inherently clean and by bringing the benefits of capitalism to the four billion at the 'bottom of the pyramid'.

The next stage in the evolution of sustainable enterprise is what Hart calls becoming 'indigenous': 'Doing so will require that they first widen the corporate bandwidth by admitting voices that have, up to now, been excluded; this means becoming radically transactive rather than just radically transparent. It will also entail the development of new "native" capabilities that enable a company to develop fully contextualized solutions to real problems in ways that respect local culture and natural diversity.'

Hart presents a Sustainable Value Framework, in which companies can create sustainable value by:

1. Reducing the level of material consumption and pollution associated with rapid industrialisation;

2. Operating at greater levels of transparency and responsiveness, across the entire life-cycle of the product system;

3. Developing new, disruptive technologies that hold the potential to greatly shrink the size of the human footprint on the planet; and

4. Meeting the needs of those at the bottom of the world income pyramid in a way that facilitates inclusive wealth creation and distribution.

As well as drawing on his own seminal work (with C.K. Prahalad) on the 'base of the pyramid', Hart applies Schumpeter's concept of 'creative destruction', arguing that 'Today's corporations can seize the opportunity for sustainable development, but to do so, they must look beyond the incremental improvements associated with pollution prevention and product stewardship in the current business. Instead, companies must make obsolete the very technologies and product systems upon which they currently depend.'

From the book

- Global capitalism is at a crossroads. Without significant change of course, the future of economic globalization, free trade, and multinational corporations appears increasingly bleak.

- By creating a new, more inclusive brand of capitalism, one that incorporates previously excluded voices, concerns and interests, the corporate sector could become the catalyst for a truly sustainable form of development, and prosper in the process.

- By moving beyond greening, companies hope not only to address mounting social and environmental concerns, but also to build the foundation for innovation and growth in the coming decades.

- The time is now for the birth of a new, more inclusive form of commerce, one that lifts the entire human family while at the same time replenishing and restoring nature.

- The path to a sustainable world will be anything but smooth. It will be a bumpy ride strewn with the remains of companies that variously dragged their feet, made promises they could not keep, bet on the wrong technology, collaborated with the wrong partners, and separated their social and business agendas. Only those companies with the right combination of vision, strategy, structure, capability, and audacity will succeed in what could be the most important transition period in the history of capitalism.

About the author

Stuart L. Hart (born 1952) is one of the world's leading academics on the implications of sustainable development and environmentalism for business strategy.

Hart obtained a Bachelor of Arts in General Science from the University of Rochester in 1974, a Master of Forestry Science in Environmental Management from Yale University in 1976 and a PhD in Planning and Strategy from the University of Michigan in 1983.

Hart is the Samuel C. Johnson Chair in Sustainable Global Enterprise at Cornell University. Before coming to the Johnson School, he taught strategic management and founded both the Center for Sustainable Enterprise (CSE) at the University of North Carolina's Kenan-Flagler Business School, and the Corporate Environmental Management Program (CEMP) at the University of Michigan. He has consulted or served as management educator for many corporations and organisations throughout the world.

Hart has published over 50 papers and authored or edited five books. He wrote the seminal article 'Beyond Greening: Strate-

In his own words
(2008 interview)

Reflections on the book

The 19th century dis-embedded the economy from society, produced a whole new organisational form called the large corporation which didn't previously exist, and took capitalism in a direction that no one could have anticipated. It solved a lot of problems; there's a lot of good that came from that. But it also has had a huge dark side and we haven't resolved the dark side of 19th-century industrial capitalism. But I'm absolutely convinced that what we're in the midst of is the next transformation, just like capitalism transformed in a fundamental way between 1850 and 1890.

The role of business

The presumption is that, if the environment really paid, then everybody would be doing it and everybody would be successful at it. That's not the way the competitive system works. Not everybody is going to be able to do it and not everybody is going to be successful at it. That's why some companies are going to gain competitive advantage and out-compete the others, and hopefully drive them out of business. That the sustainable companies drive the unsustainable ones out of business – that's the objective.

What makes the world of commerce interesting in my mind is its ability to creatively destroy itself. And, when the conditions are right, capitalist institutions, companies and the competitive process can generate change in a hurry. And that's what we desperately need. So I think if we're able to

gies for a Sustainable World', which won the McKinsey Award for Best Article in *Harvard Business Review* in 1997, and helped launch the movement for corporate sustainability. With C.K. Prahalad, Hart also wrote the groundbreaking 2002 article 'The Fortune at the Bottom of the Pyramid', which provided the first articulation of how business could profitably serve the needs of the four billion poor in the developing world.

turn this ship to reframe what capitalism might look like in the 21st century, then we have a mechanism through which this change could unfold at the rate that it needs to in order to move us towards a sustainable world before it's too late.

I'm not yet convinced that publicly owned companies wouldn't ultimately be rewarded for sustainability. I think it is just fear on the part of the senior leadership that if they really came forward and spoke their mind about these issues, that their head would roll and there would be uniform discontent on Wall Street. I'm not sure that's true . . . If you can make a persuasive case for why you're doing it and what the opportunity is, I think Wall Street is with you . . . It's not like falling off a log. Some companies are going to do this more effectively than others.

Looking to the future

If there are sustainable innovations that are disruptive, then it may well be that the biggest opportunities are in the under-served markets, places where you don't have established infrastructure in place, where you can bring in renewable energy and distributed generation. So scaling can take care of itself because two-thirds of humanity is still fundamentally under-served or un-

served. There is not a scale problem there. The problem is with having the imagination and the capability in order to understand how to do it.

There's the big old locomotive powered by coal on one track, and it's big and it's puffing away. But then there's also the 'little train that could' on this little track that's just emerging, called clean tech or sustainable innovation. You look at places like China and India and it's where some of the most exciting next-generation, potentially clean, green technologies are really taking root and taking root the fastest. And so it's this paradox, and the question is which one's going to win? We've got to put a lot of chips on that 'little train that could', and hope that it can get a lot bigger in a hurry and outrun the other one.

The simple truth is that there are no companies that are sustainable in the world today; there are none. What we have are companies that are experimenting with pieces of the puzzle. When you look at companies that are interesting for different reasons, they have different pieces. And, if you could begin to create a mosaic of those pieces, you could perhaps begin to imagine a company that would move you more closely to [sustainability] in its totality.

OTHER BOOKS (SELECTION)

Green Goals and Greenbacks: State-Level Environmental Review Programs and their Associated Costs (with Gordon A. Enk; Westview Press, 1980)

Improving Impact Assessment: Increasing the Relevance and Utilization of Scientific and Technical Information (with Gordon A. Enk and William F. Hornick; Westview Press, 1984)

MORE INFORMATION

Base of the Pyramid Protocol:
www.bop-protocol.org

Center for Sustainable Global Enterprise:
www.johnson.cornell.edu/sge

Enterprise for a Sustainable World:
www.e4sw.org

44
Collapse
Jared Diamond

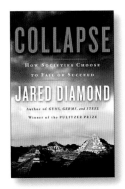

1st edn
Collapse:
How Societies Choose
to Fail or Succeed
Viking Books, 2005;
592pp, hbk;
978-0670033379

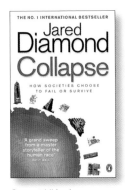

Current US edn
Collapse:
How Societies Choose
to Fail or Succeed
Penguin Press, 2005;
592pp, pbk;
978-0143036555

Current UK edn
Collapse:
How Societies Choose
to Fail or Survive
Penguin Press, 2006;
592pp, pbk;
978-0140279511

Key ideas

▶ Societies have failed and succeeded in the past due to human environmental impact; climate change; enemies; friends; and societies' institutions.

▶ The role of the elites is crucial: if they see themselves as separate from the environment and society, they will fail to recognise the urgency of the situation and to act accordingly.

▶ Modern society is in danger of collapse due to its population size, inappropriate use of technology and the inequities of globalisation.

▶ We can avoid such a collapse by learning from history, especially with regard to environmental impacts, (communications) technology and institutional structures.

▶ The focus on just one threat (e.g. climate change) or one culprit (e.g. the USA) is not useful or accurate, as many issues and solutions are interrelated.

Synopsis

Collapse examines various societies throughout history that have collapsed (Easter Island, Pitcairn, the Maya, Anasazi, the Vikings/Norse in Greenland) and compares these to societies that faced similar conditions and yet succeeded (Japan, New Guinea Highlands, the Vikings/Norse in Iceland). Diamond identifies five factors that define collapse or success:

1. *Human environmental impact*: societies tend to over-exploit resources on which they depend and thereby commit ecological suicide, or 'ecocide';

2. *Climate change*: both natural and human-induced climate change can push a society over the brink or help it last longer, depending on the ability to adapt;

3. *Enemies*: if a community or nation gets weakened due to various factors, there is a high risk that hostile (or ambitious) neighbours will either eliminate or take over that society;

4. *Friends*: friendly neighbours are an important survival strategy, since virtually no society is entirely independent or invulnerable; and

5. *Societies' institutional response to threats*: the effectiveness of a society's economic or social institutions and cultural values will allow it either to perceive and solve problems, or not.

Looking specifically at environmental impacts, Diamond identifies various forms of historical 'ecocide', including deforestation and habitat destruction, soil problems (erosion, salinisation and loss of soil fertility), water management problems, overhunting, overfishing, the effects of introduced species on native species, human population growth and increased per capita impact of people. There is evidence of all of these dangers in modern society.

Diamond suggests a number of lessons that we can learn from societies that have collapsed. First, we need to take environmental problems seriously. They have dragged down societies in the past and are doing so today. Second, pay attention to the behaviour of the elite. If they are able to insulate themselves from the consequences of their actions (as the Maya kings did), there will be an inadequate response to crises until it is too late. Diamond argues that, in the US, Europe and Japan, politicians are often insulated and even their population act like a gated community that is insulated from impacts in the Third World.

Diamond concedes that our modern society is very different from past societies, but that some of these differences make us much more prone to collapse. For example, there are more people with more destructive technology, so 'bad' things can happen at a much larger scale. Also, our interconnectedness through globalisation makes us more vulnerable to terrorism and disease pandemics. On the other hand, the information and communications revolution means that we are more informed and able to act accordingly.

Diamond sees an important role for business, but places responsibility for change in the hands of the public and subsequently government, rather than expecting moral behaviour from business. His parting message is one of optimism: 'Because we are the cause of our environmental problems, we are the ones in control of them, and we can choose or not choose to stop causing them and start solving them.' However, this will require long-term planning and a willingness to reconsider our core values.

From the book

- In the first decade of the Third Millennium, life on planet Earth faces challenges unprecedented since the end of the Cretaceous period, about 65 million years ago.

- People often ask, 'What is the single most important environmental/population problem facing the world today?' A flip answer would be, 'The single most important problem is our misguided focus on identifying the single most important problem!'

- If environmentalists aren't willing to engage with big business, which are among the most powerful forces in the modern world, it won't be possible to solve the world's environmental problems.

- The societies that ended up collapsing were (like the Maya) among the most creative and (for a time) advanced and successful of their times.

- Past peoples were neither ignorant bad managers who deserved to be exterminated or dispossessed, nor all-knowing conscientious environmentalists who solved problems that we can't solve today. They were people like us, facing problems broadly similar to those that we now face. They were prone either to succeed or to fail.

About the author

Jared Mason Diamond (born 1937) is an American evolutionary biologist, physiologist, biogeographer, lecturer and non-fiction author.

Diamond was born in Boston to a physician father and a teacher/musician/linguist mother. After training in laboratory biological science at Harvard College, the University of Cambridge (England), and the Max Planck Institute for Biochemistry in Munich (Germany), he became Professor of Physiology at UCLA Medical School in 1966. However, even while still in his twenties, he also developed a second parallel career in the ecology and evolution of New Guinea

birds. That led him to explore some of the most remote parts of that great tropical island, and to rediscover New Guinea's long-lost Golden-Fronted Bowerbird. In his fifties he gradually developed a third career in environmental history, sealed by his switching his appointment at age 65 to become Professor of Geography and of Environmental Health Sciences at UCLA.

Jared Diamond is known for over 500 technical articles and numerous books that have won him a range of honours, including the National Medal of Science, the Tyler Prize for Environmental Achievement, and research prizes of the American Physiological

Society, American Gastroenterological Society and American Ornithologists Union, as well as election to the National Academy of Sciences. His book *Guns, Germs, and Steel* won the 1998 Pulitzer Prize for Non-fiction, as well as the Phi Beta Kappa Award in Science.

OTHER BOOKS (SELECTION)

45
The End of Poverty
Jeffrey D. Sachs

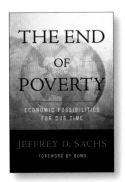

1st edn
The End of Poverty:
Economic Possibilities
for Our Time
Penguin Press, 2005;
416pp, hbk;
978-1594200458

Current UK edn
The End of Poverty:
How We Can Make It
Happen in Our Lifetime
Penguin Press, 2005;
416pp, pbk;
978-0141018669

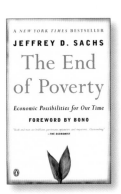

Current US edn
The End of Poverty:
Economic Possibilities
for Our Time
Penguin Press, 2006;
416pp, pbk, repr.;
978-0143036586

Key ideas

▶ If we learn from the past 50 years of development efforts and focus on what works, we can end extreme poverty by 2025.

▶ There are objective reasons that prevent economies from developing, and proper analysis suggests numerous workable solutions.

▶ Poor countries do not have the necessary capital to escape the poverty trap. Hence, the main barrier to development is the lack of aid investment from wealthy countries.

▶ Wealthy countries spend more on defence budgets than aid, failing to see that continued poverty exacerbates global security problems.

▶ Because it is possible to end poverty, it is morally necessary. We must not shy away from our moral responsibilities as Western societies and individuals.

Synopsis

The End of Poverty argues that extreme poverty, defined by the World Bank as having an income of less than $1 a day, is 'the poverty that kills'. However, it is almost entirely preventable and solvable (as has been shown in developed countries and many developing countries) through the provision of basic services in water, sanitation, healthcare and food. Hence, the end of poverty is not only possible, but also morally imperative.

Sachs challenges the wholly pessimistic view of poverty, pointing out that five-sixths of the world have escaped extreme poverty due to the scientific and industrial revolution, which has raised living standards and life expectancy. This shows that development does work, and that the remaining one billion poor are not inevitably condemned to remain destitute.

All forms of poverty, Sachs argues, have practical solutions, but we 'just don't do them'. For example, malaria kills about three million per year, even though it is preventable if treated. It can be avoided if you get a bed-net for $5 per year. The poor cannot afford this, but the wealthy countries can. Similar low-cost solutions exist for water management, crop management, livestock management, soil management and improving school attendance.

Sachs takes issue with the glib explanation of politicians and bureaucrats for the failure of development efforts over the past 50 years: namely, that it is the result of Third World corruption and mismanagement. This, he believes, is an unjustified and untrue stereotype. Many countries with relatively good levels of governance (e.g. Ghana, Malawi, Mali and Senegal) have failed to prosper, while others with extensive corruption have prospered (e.g. Bangladesh, Indonesia, Pakistan).

The real explanation is more complex and often driven by other factors such as geography, climate and terms of trade. Hence, the poor are not poor because they are lazy or their governments are corrupt. The poor face structural challenges that keep them from getting even their first foot on the ladder of development.

Sachs lists the 'big five' development priorities as: boosting agriculture, improving basic health, investing in education, bringing power, and providing clean water and sanitation. The cost of achieving this is calculated at only $70 per person per year. This means that a country like Kenya would need $15 billion, while international donors currently donate less than $100 million. For 35 years, the rich have promised to give 0.7% in official development assistance and failed to do so. In the US, $15 billion is allocated to development aid, compared to $500 billion in military spending. As a consequence the world is becoming more unstable and divided, while the solutions are at hand.

Sachs concludes with nine steps to end poverty: commit to the task (of 'making poverty history'); adopt a plan of action (linked to the Millennium Development Goals); raise the voice of the poor; redeem the US role in the world; rescue the IMF and the World Bank; strengthen the UN; harness global science; promote sustainable development; and make a personal commitment.

From the book

- I have strived to be clear about what is needed, and have paid much less attention to what I am told is 'politically possible'. When something is needed it can and must become possible!

- I do not take as a given what is considered politically impossible, but rather I am prepared to argue incessantly, and annoyingly, for what needs to be done, even when it is claimed to be impossible.

- Extreme poverty can be ended, not in the time of our grandchildren, but our time.

- It's quite possible to arrive in the year 2030 where people are no longer dying of poverty. We could actually help lead a global end – not a reduction, but an end – to absolute poverty.

- Great social forces are the mere accumulation of individual actions. Let the future say of our generation that we sent forth mighty currents of hope, and that we worked together to heal the world.

About the author

Jeffrey D. Sachs (born 1954) is a leading international economic advisor on the challenges of economic development, poverty alleviation and enlightened globalisation.

Sachs was born in Detroit and received his BA, summa cum laude, from Harvard College in 1976, and his MA and PhD from Harvard University in 1978 and 1980 respectively. He joined the Harvard faculty as an Assistant Professor in 1980, and was promoted to Associate Professor in 1982 and Full Professor in 1983. Prior to his arrival at Columbia University in July 2002, Sachs spent over 20 years at Harvard University, most recently as Director of the Center for International Development and Galen L. Stone Professor of International Trade.

Sachs is now the Director of the Earth Institute, Quetelet Professor of Sustainable Development, and Professor of Health Policy and Management at Columbia University. He is also Special Advisor to United Nations Secretary-General Ban Ki-moon. From 2002 to 2006, he was Director of the UN Millennium Project and Special Advisor to United Nations Secretary-General Kofi Annan on the Millennium Development Goals. Sachs is also President and Co-founder of Millennium Promise Alliance, a non-profit organisation aimed at ending extreme global poverty.

Sachs is author of hundreds of scholarly articles and several bestselling books. In 2004 and 2005, he was named as one of the 100 most influential people in the world by *Time* magazine. He is the recipient of many awards and honours from around the world.

In his own words
(2008 interview)

Reflections on the book

If you take the big picture of development, it's been a resounding success. For the vast proportion of human history, societies were economically stagnant, and the overwhelming majority was living at the edge of survival. And during the last 50 years almost all the world has gotten off of the edge. The whole point of the book is that, with about a sixth of the world's population still stuck in extreme poverty, but with the tools to end that extreme poverty at hand, we have the makings of the completion of what has been a very broad success of economic development, bringing it to those remaining parts of the world that have not yet experienced the sustained economic take-off.

UN Photo/Mark Garten

The role of business

Business is far more effective than government at scaling, at speed, at achieving a bottom line, if there really is a fortune at the bottom of the pyramid. Business has scalability, information and management systems and it holds the technology. But, if there's no market at the end for the public good that we need, then at a minimum we need a public–private partnership, where business does what it does, but government makes the market, or provides the financing to get the job done.

I love markets wherever they work, but I spend a tremendous amount of time also emphasising markets don't work for everything. With cell phones, you may be able to reach 25%, 30%, even 40% penetration in Africa, and it's phenomenal; it's world-changing. But 25% to 30% or 40% penetration for immunisations won't do it. If you leave 60% of the population unimmunised you've got epidemics and mass death. So you can't apply the same model that you would for a cell phone to immunisation.

Looking to the future

Every time I turn around, whether it's in India, China, Malaysia or Tanzania, there's no shortage of reasons for optimism – the power of our technologies, the wonders of our information linkages now, a world where isolation, which was the essence of poverty, has been broken, where a cell phone is within reach for just about any village around the world, thereby making a link for people who were desperately outside of the chain of information and are now part of markets and global knowledge – there's all the reason for optimism.

What is the hardest part of all is managing change and having the understanding of how crucial and how fruitful cooperation can be right now. The problem isn't our lack of tools; the problem is our ability to manage all these wonderfully powerful tools that we have to a human effect. We have a challenge of management and understanding, of learning and cooperation. We're going to solve these problems: extreme poverty will end by the year 2025. That's what I said in the book and I think that's what's going to happen.

OTHER BOOKS (SELECTION)

Developing Country Debt and the World Economy (ed.; University of Chicago Press, 1989)

Macroeconomics in the Global Economy (Prentice Hall, 1993)

Escaping the Resource Curse (ed. with Macartan Humphreys and Joseph E. Stiglitz; Columbia University Press, 2007)

Common Wealth: Economics for a Crowded Planet (Allen Lane, 2008)

MORE INFORMATION

The Earth Institute at Columbia University:
www.earth.columbia.edu

46
The Chaos Point
Ervin Laszlo

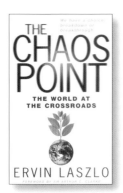

1st and current UK edn
**The Chaos Point:
The World at the
Crossroads**
Piatkus Books, 2006;
240pp, pbk;
978-0749927165

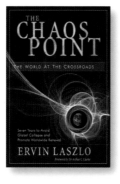

Current US edn
**The Chaos Point:
The World at the
Crossroads**
Hampton Roads
Publishing Company,
2006; 200pp, pbk;
978-1571744852

Key ideas

▶ Society is at a chaos (or crisis or bifurcation) point, which is a time of profound change and transition to a new state of organisation.

▶ Systems dynamics predicts that society will move to a new steady state, after either a breakdown or a breakthrough.

▶ Breakdown (regression to a lower standard of life across the world) will occur if we continue on our current environmentally, socially and economically destructive path.

▶ Breakthrough (evolution to a better world for all) will occur if we embrace the thinking of modern holistic sciences, such as systems thinking and ecological science.

▶ The closer we move towards the crisis point, the higher the likelihood of an abrupt change in collective consciousness, for better or worse.

Synopsis

The Chaos Point starts with the warning that society is headed for Breakdown, a scenario in which: the 'haves' and 'have-nots' become more polarised; violence and organised crime increase, as does military conflict and expenditure at the expense of investments in health and environmental care; dramatic famines and disease lead to death and mass migration; governments close off their borders, 'cleanse' unwanted populations and adopt a bunker mentality, leading to escalating conflict between nations, potentially with nuclear consequences. In short, the global system breaks down.

Despite this bleak picture, Laszlo is not a doomsayer. Drawing on complexity and chaos theory, he points out that humanity, like nature, is a dynamic system that is capable of 'abrupt change': that is, of ultra-rapid transformation. When such a system nears the point where the existing structures and feedbacks can no longer maintain the system's integrity, it becomes super-sensitive and responds even to a small impetus for change. Hence, 'butterfly effects' become possible, where the thinking, values, ethics and consciousness of a critical mass in society can cause rapid and fundamental change.

Laszlo believes humanity is nearing such a system-wide tipping point. For example, climate change may catalyse social breakdowns, spreading to political crises leading to escalating conflict and violence. This is a 'chaos point' – not necessarily a doorway to disaster, but the threshold beyond which there is no return to the previously established conditions. Although humanity is nearing a chaos point, the situation is far from hopeless. Even if the majority of political leaders refuse to face the need for fundamental change, an increasing number of people are becoming aware that they must do something to bring about real change. Society's awakening may soon reach the critical mass where rapid and fundamental transformation becomes politically realistic, and indeed unavoidable.

The key lies in two types of growth: *extensive* growth is characterised by Conquest, Colonisation and Consumption, and has been the type of growth we have seen in the past, which will lead to the Breakdown scenario. By contrast, *intensive* growth, characterised by Connection, Communications and Consciousness, is the type of growth we need in the future in order to achieve a Breakthrough. In order to nudge us in this direction, Laszlo concludes with the following advice:

- *Shed obsolete beliefs* that lead to irrational practices, including beliefs in economic rationality, the cult of efficiency, the equitable distribution of benefits by the market and equating consumption with progress and happiness;

- *Adopt a new morality* that can be accepted by all people, wherever they live, which links peoples and cultures based on beliefs and objectives they can share and adopt;

- *Dream your world and act on it*, as Bobby Kennedy put it: 'Some men see things as they are and say, *why;* I dream things that never were and say, *why not*'; and

- *Evolve your consciousness*, which will lead to the awareness that each individual and organisation has the power to change the world.

From the book

- A Chinese proverb warns, 'If we do not change direction, we are likely to end up exactly where we are headed'. Applied to contemporary humanity, this would be disastrous.

- We live in a chaotic system. Our task is not to predict what will happen, but to tip the system so that what will happen corresponds in some measure to what we would like to happen.

- We are presently entering the small but crucial window in time that decides whether the Chaos Point will lead to breakdown and the end of civilization or to a breakthrough that opens the path to a new civilization.

- Eventually, a point will be reached where even transformation-oriented measures become politically realistic.

- Ours is not a time for despair; it is a time for action.

About the author

Ervin Laszlo (born 1932) is a Hungarian scientist and leading writer on systems philosophy and general evolution theory.

Laszlo serves as president of the Club of Budapest and head of the General Evolution Research Group, which he founded. He is an advisor to the UNESCO Director General, ambassador of the International Delphic Council, member of the International Academy of Science, World Academy of Arts and Science, and the International Academy of Philosophy. He is the former president of the International Society for Systems Sciences.

Laszlo is the recipient of the highest degree in philosophy and human sciences from the Sorbonne, the University of Paris, as well as of the coveted Artist Diploma of the Franz Liszt Academy of Budapest. His numerous prizes and awards include four honorary doctorates. His appointments have included research grants at Yale and Princeton universities, professorships for philosophy, systems sciences and future sciences at the universities of Houston, Portland State and Indiana, as well as Northwestern University and the State University of New York.

Laszlo is the author or editor of 69 books translated into as many as 19 languages, and has over 400 articles and research papers and six volumes of piano recordings to his credit. He serves as editor of the monthly *World Futures: The Journal of General Evolution* and of its associated *General Evolution Studies* book series.

In his own words
(2008 interview)

Reflections on the book

I have been working with systems theory, especially with the way complex systems evolve over time, and I've recognised that this evolution is strongly non-linear. That means it goes through periodic quantum leaps and, if you apply this to human society, when you reach a critical threshold in the development of society, then a sudden non-linear change is likely to occur. We are approaching such a threshold, so it needs to be thought about, it needs to be anticipated as much as possible and prepared for. Because, even though it's unpredictable, it's not unguidable. You can still govern change like this, even though you can't predict it in advance.

The role of business

If you think of yourself as being separate from the world, if you think of the world as being material and mechanistic, then you try to manipulate it, to pursue your own interests independently of the interests of the others and to impose your own thinking and interests on others. This kind of mind-set is creating the problem. In business, it is creating the shareholder philosophy, whereby business is responsible only to its own shareholders and its responsibility to anything else is secondary, if it exists at all. The basis of the shareholder philosophy is that one business is separate from other businesses, separate from the communities in which it operates, separate from nature; it has only itself to account for because it is an entity purely in its own right. This is based on a concept of the world which has become obsolete and it is now dangerous in its consequences.

Looking to the future

At the tipping point, only two things are impossible: the status quo and going back. In the Breakdown scenario, you either want to maintain things the way they are or find a tried and tested method that takes you back to a stability that was there in the past. But these things don't work because they bring you to a tipping point; they bring you to a point of breakdown, due to unsustainability of the system. I think the system as a whole is structurally unsustainable. That means it has to be transformed. It can't be patched up.

I think an optimist is a dangerous person, in the sense that an optimist might believe that this is the best of all possible worlds. If you do that then you're not particularly motivated to change it. A pessimist is just as dangerous because he thinks you can't change this world. You have to be in between, you have to recognise that the world is changeable and that it's in need of change. I find that the world is in need of change and at the same time it's beginning to change, quite rapidly in fact. I find that the ideas that I put forward 15 years ago are having a larger resonance today, a larger effect than they had at the time that they were published.

OTHER BOOKS (SELECTION)

The Systems View of the World: A Holistic Vision for our Time (Hampton Press, 1996)

You Can Change the World: An Action Handbook for the 21st Century (Positive News Publishing, 2002)

The Connectivity Hypothesis: Foundations of an Integral Science of Quantum, Cosmos, Life, and Consciousness (State University of New York

Science and the Reenchantment of the Cosmos: The Rise of the Integral Vision of Reality (Inner Traditions Bear and Co., 2006)

Quantum Shift in the Global Brain: How the New Scientific Reality Can Change Us and Our World (Inner Traditions International, 2008)

MORE INFORMATION

Club of Budapest: www.clubofbudapest.org

47
Heat
George Monbiot

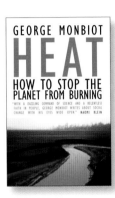

1st edn
Heat:
How to Stop
the Planet Burning
Allen Lane, 2006;
276pp, hbk;
978-0713999235

Current edn
Heat:
How to Stop
the Planet from Burning
South End Press, 2009;
pbk, repr. edn;
978-0896087873

Key ideas

▶ The world faces the prospect of not just disruptive, but catastrophic (possibly 'run-away') climate change.

▶ According to the scientists (rather than the economists or politicians), a 90% reduction in carbon emissions by 2030 is necessary to avert catastrophic climate change.

▶ It is possible to achieve the scale and speed of carbon reduction with existing technology solutions and policy instruments.

▶ The most significant barrier to achieving the necessary emission reductions is a lack of political will and personal responsibility.

▶ There is also still an active 'denial industry' which is seeking to confuse the public, delay the government and deny the science on climate change.

Synopsis

Heat begins by making a powerful and compelling case that climate change is a threat to be taken extremely seriously and is caused by human-made emissions. Exacerbating the problem is what Monbiot calls the 'denial industry': an active campaign of dissuasion by certain sectors of business, wealthy classes, media and governments to deny climate change with bold assertions based on poor science, often financed by the corporations. The result is that the public remains confused or sceptical and the politicians feel disempowered to take the bold action that is needed.

The book sets out to prove, using the UK as a test case, that we can achieve a 90% reduction in carbon emissions by 2030 (in contrast to Stern's 60% by 2050) while maintaining our standard of living. The basic strategy being advocated by Monbiot is 'contraction and convergence', where a national allocation of carbon is found by dividing the global CO_2 allowance at any given time by the number of inhabitants of the planet at that time. Multiplying this figure by the population of a country will give a national carbon allocation. For instance, the UK's required 90% requires an annual average reduction from 2.6 tonnes of greenhouse gas emissions per person to 0.33 tonnes.

Monbiot suggests each person be given a carbon allocation, which they could use or sell. This would create a new form of carbon rationing, with its own currency which Monbiot calls 'icecaps'. Simply creating this market is not enough. For this system to work and be equitable, the infrastructure balance between rich and poor will have to be redressed. Poor people tend to live in low-efficiency houses and drive old, low-efficiency vehicles, so the government will have to invest in better insulation, green building and an efficient transport infrastructure. Otherwise the poor will be faced with a choice between food and energy.

Monbiot also argues that we need to break the link between carbon and energy. A 90% cut in carbon will never be acceptable or feasible if it also requires a 90% cut in energy. What are therefore needed are means to reduce the carbon intensity of our energy use. In order to achieve this, Monbiot identifies a suite of existing technological, policy and public solutions that can be feasibly implemented across the housing, energy, transport and retail sectors. He is also critical of several strategies such as renewable energy (too little, too late) and carbon offsetting (which 'is like pushing the food around on your plate to create the impression that you have eaten it').

Monbiot cautions that we must beware of complacency by thinking that 'someone or something will save us. A faith in miracles grades seamlessly into excuses for inaction.'

Monbiot concludes that 'only regulation – that deeply unfashionable idea – can quell the destruction wrought by the god we serve, the god of our own appetites. Man-made global warming cannot be restrained unless we persuade the government to force us to change the way we live.' He therefore calls on people to force governments to reverse their policies, by 'joining what must become the world's most powerful political movement'.

From the book

- I have one purpose in writing this book: to persuade you that climate change is worth fighting. Failing that, I have one last hope: that I might make people so depressed about the state of the planet that they stay in bed all day, thereby reducing their consumption of fossil fuels.

- Until we have demonstrated that we are serious about cutting our own emissions we are in no position to preach restraint to the poorer countries.

- Perhaps the most intractable cause of global warming is 'love miles': the distance you must travel to visit friends and partners and relatives on the other side of the planet. The world could be destroyed by love.

- It is true that this effort will disrupt our lives. But it will cause less disruption that the alternative, which is to allow man-made global warming to proceed unhindered.

- I have sought to demonstrate that the necessary reduction in carbon emissions is – if difficult – technically and economically possible. I have not demonstrated that it is politically possible. There is a reason for this. It is not up to me to do so. It is up to you.

About the author

George Monbiot (born 1963) is a British journalist and bestselling author.

Monbiot writes a weekly column for the *Guardian* newspaper. During seven years of investigative journeys in Indonesia, Brazil and East Africa, he was shot at, beaten up by military police, shipwrecked and stung into a poisoned coma by hornets. He came back to work in Britain after being pronounced clinically dead in Lodwar General Hospital in north-western Kenya, having contracted cerebral malaria.

In Britain, Monbiot joined the roads protest movement. He was hospitalised by security guards, who drove a metal spike through his foot, smashing the middle bone. He helped to found The Land is Ours, which has occupied land all over the country, including 13 acres of prime real estate in Wandsworth belonging to the Guinness corporation and destined for a giant superstore.

He has held visiting fellowships or professorships at the universities of Oxford (environmental policy), Bristol (philosophy), Keele (politics) and East London (environmental science). He is currently Visiting Professor of Planning at Oxford Brookes University. In 1995 Nelson Mandela presented him with a United Nations Global 500 Award for outstanding environmental achievement. He has also won the Lloyds National Screenwriting Prize for his screenplay *The Norwegian*, a Sony Award for radio production, the Sir Peter Kent Award and the OneWorld National Press Award. In summer 2007 he was awarded an honorary doctorate by the University of Essex and an honorary fellowship by Cardiff University.

Photo: JK the Unwise

In his own words
(2008 interview)

Reflections on the book

I wrote *Heat* because there was a clear gap in our perception of the scale of the problem and the necessary solutions. The two simply did not match up. We were looking at the necessity for an 80% or 90% cut in carbon emissions, and all people were really talking about was solar panels on people's roofs and micro-wind turbines and changing of light bulbs and driving a more efficient car, which clearly was not going to get us anywhere near that, and did not represent a systematic programme for cutting emissions. So I set out to see how we could achieve a 90% cut in emissions without turning this into a very poor Third World country, and while sustaining much of what people consider to be their quality of life.

The role of business and government

There are some businesses that are now looking at environmental technology investments as being something that will make them rich for a very long time to come. But they have been held back by limitations in the degree of certainty about what governments are going to do. They see the price of carbon as being insufficiently certain to permit them to make those investments at the moment. At the same time, we are seeing massive investments in tar sands in Alberta, massive investments in coal to liquids, all sorts of incredibly destructive approaches which are going to have the opposite to the desired effect. If governments sent a clear enough signal about long-term policy, there is no way that companies would be contemplating those destructive investments. So what's lacking here is a clear and firm enough idea from government that they are serious.

Looking to the future

We need the innovation, though it has to be said that all the technologies we require to make a 90% cut already exist. We don't have to wait for some new miracle technology: it is all there; but we need it to be deployed. We need to see a massive substitution of current investment with a whole trench of new investments in the latest environmental technologies. This would create a great jobs boom and have all sorts of positive impacts, but for many industries which are already committed to the fossil-fuel economy it would have many negative impacts, so those industries are very resistant to change.

We have to make use of technology and we have to make sure that we use our money wisely to ensure that we get the most bang for our buck in terms of renewable energy. But that only works if you have a regulatory framework that says that we are having an overall cut in emissions and a cap which comes down every year. Without that you have your dieting conundrum, where you're still eating your fatty foods and eating your salad doesn't cancel them out. You have to get rid of the fossil fuels at the same time as you are producing your renewables.

OTHER BOOKS (SELECTION)

Amazon Watershed: The New Environmental Investigation (Michael Joseph, 1991)

Captive State: The Corporate Takeover of Britain

MORE INFORMATION

George Monbiot's blog:
www.monbiot.com

George Monbiot's Guardian columns:

48
An Inconvenient Truth
Al Gore

1st and current UK edn
**An Inconvenient Truth:
The Planetary Emergency of
Global Warming and What
We Can Do About It**
Bloomsbury Publishing,
2006; 336pp, pbk;
978-0747589068

1st and current US edn
**An Inconvenient Truth:
The Planetary Emergency
of Global Warming and
What We Can Do About It**
Rodale Books, 2006;
328pp, pbk;
978-1594865671

Key ideas

▶ There is overwhelming scientific evidence and consensus that human-caused global warming is a real and serious threat.

▶ The consequences of global warming, if left unchecked, will be disastrous for the planet and its population.

▶ There are solutions that could help us reduce the threat of global warming, but the political will is lacking to put these solutions into action.

▶ Besides lacking political will, there are some businesses who are actively pursuing a campaign of misinformation about the threat of climate change.

Synopsis

An Inconvenient Truth sets out to dispel numerous global warming misconceptions, in three areas: the science, the consequences and the solutions. In terms of the science, Gore explains how, by burning fossil fuels such as coal, gas and oil and clearing forests, we have dramatically increased the amount of carbon dioxide in the Earth's atmosphere and temperatures are rising. This represents the consensus of the vast majority of scientists and we are already seeing changes.

For example, the number of Category 4 and 5 hurricanes has almost doubled in the last 30 years; malaria has spread to higher altitudes in places like the Colombian Andes, 7,000 feet above sea level; the flow of ice from glaciers in Greenland has more than doubled over the past decade; and at least 279 species of plants and animals are already responding to global warming, moving closer to the poles.

If the warming continues, we can expect catastrophic consequences: deaths from global warming will double in just 25 years, to 300,000 people a year; global sea levels could rise by more than 20 feet with the loss of shelf ice in Greenland and Antarctica, devastating coastal areas worldwide; heatwaves will be more frequent and more intense; droughts and wildfires will occur more often; the Arctic Ocean could be ice-free in summer by 2050; and more than a million species worldwide could be driven to extinction by 2050.

In other words, humanity is sitting on a time bomb. If the vast majority of the world's scientists are right, we have just ten years to avert a major catastrophe that could send our entire planet's climate system into a tailspin of epic destruction involving extreme weather, floods, droughts, epidemics and killer heatwaves beyond anything we have ever experienced – a catastrophe of our own making. But there is hope. The technology that can help us dramatically reduce emissions already exists.

One example is the work that Socolow and Pacala have done on 'stabilisation wedges'. Examples include: more efficient use of electricity in heating and cooling systems; designing buildings and sites to use less energy; increased vehicle efficiency; improving transport efficiency through better design of cities; increased use of renewable energy; and capture and storage of excess carbon. There are also personal actions that can be taken: save energy in the home; get around on less (reduce transportation emissions); consume less, conserve more; and be a catalyst for change.

Hence, solutions do exist. But the political will is lacking to make change happen, and some special-interest groups funded by oil, coal and utility companies are actively trying to 'reposition global warming as theory, rather than fact', mirroring the tactics utilised by the tobacco companies in the last century. Despite this, we should be hopeful. Humanity has achieved amazing things against the odds: abolition of slavery, women's suffrage, beating fascism, stopping the spread of disease, reducing the hole in the ozone layer, landing on the moon. Global warming is simply our next major challenge.

From the book

- What gets us into trouble is not what we don't know. It's what we know for sure that just ain't so (quoting Mark Twain).

- Future generations may well have occasion to ask themselves, 'What were our parents thinking? Why didn't they wake up when they had a chance?' We have to hear that question from them, now.

- What we take for granted might not be here for our children.

- We have everything, save perhaps political will. But in America, I believe political will is a renewable resource.

- It is difficult to get a man to understand something when his salary depends upon his not understanding it (quoting Upton Sinclair).

- I don't really consider this a political issue; I consider it to be a moral issue.

- You see that pale, blue dot? That's us. Everything that has ever happened in all of human history, has happened on that pixel. All the triumphs and all the tragedies, all the wars all the famines, all the major advances . . . it's our only home. And what is at stake [is] our ability to live on planet Earth, to have a future as a civilization. I believe this is a moral issue, it is your time to seize this issue, it is our time to rise again to secure our future.

About the author

Albert Arnold 'Al' Gore, Jr (born 1948), received a degree in government with honours from Harvard University in 1969. After graduation, he volunteered for enlistment in the US Army and served in the Vietnam War. On returning from Vietnam, Al Gore became an investigative reporter with *The Tennessean* in Nashville, where he also attended Vanderbilt University's Divinity School and then Law School.

Gore was elected to Congress in 1976 and in 1984 moved up to the Senate and was re-elected in 1990. After running for the presidency in 1988, Gore was chosen by Clinton to be his 1992 running mate; the two were elected and then re-elected in 1996. Al Gore served for eight years as vice-president under Bill Clinton, then was the Democratic Party's nominee for president in 2000, but lost to George W. Bush.

An Inconvenient Truth, the film that preceded the book, was released in 2006 and won an Oscar for best documentary. The following year, Gore was jointly awarded the 2007

West Coast Green Conference 2008

Nobel Peace Prize (with the IPCC) for his work on climate change. In July 2007, Gore organised the Live Earth concert in an effort to raise awareness about climate change. At the time of writing, Gore was chairman of the American television channel Current TV, chairman of Generation Investment Management, a director on the board of Apple Inc., an unofficial advisor to Google's senior management, chairman of the Alliance for Climate Protection, and a partner in the venture capital firm Kleiner Perkins Caufield & Byers, heading that firm's climate change solutions group.

OTHER BOOKS

Earth in the Balance: Ecology and the Human Spirit (Houghton Mifflin, 1992)

The Assault on Reason: How the Politics of Fear, Secrecy and Blind Faith Subvert Wise Decision-making and Democracy (Bloomsbury, 2007)

MORE INFORMATION

Al Gore's official website:
www.algore.com

An Inconvenient Truth:
www.climatecrisis.net

49
When the Rivers Run Dry
Fred Pearce

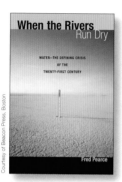

1st edn
**When the
Rivers Run Dry.
Water: The Defining
Crisis of the Twenty-first
Century**
Beacon Press, 2006;
324pp, hbk;
978-0807085721

Current US edn
**When the
Rivers Run Dry.
Water: The Defining
Crisis of the Twenty-first
Century**
Beacon Press, 2007;
324pp, pbk;
978-0807085738

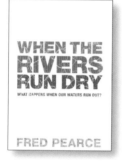

Current UK edn
**When the
Rivers Run Dry:
What Happens When
Our Water Runs Out?**
Eden Project Books,
2007; 368pp, pbk;
978-1903919583

Key ideas

▶ We are a heavily water-intensive society globally, and the planet has passed the point of having enough water, on current patterns of usage, for everyone.

▶ Engineering solutions (dams, reservoirs and canals) usually produce short-term gains and serious long-term problems.

▶ The traditional benefits of natural river systems (flooding, fertilisation, etc.) aren't well priced by planners and therefore are overlooked.

▶ The 'green revolution' has enabled us to feed most of our expanding global population but the water intensity has been high; we now need 'more crop per drop'.

▶ Although the outlook is bleak (already many areas are reverting to desert), there are promising simple, local (and often traditional) solutions, like harnessing and harvesting rainwater.

Synopsis

When the Rivers Run Dry sets out a case for water being as large and urgent an environmental challenge as climate change. Today, the world grows twice as much food as it did a generation ago, but it uses three times as much water. As a result, many of the waterways, lakes and rivers that we used to take for granted are under severe threat or already disappearing. Examples include the Aral Sea, the Colorado River, the Rio Grande or even the Yellow River.

In addition, aquifers containing underground water, which are essentially a non-renewable resource, are being drained at an alarming rate. 'Half a century of pumping on the high planes of the USA has removed water that will take two thousand years to replace. In India, farmers whose fathers lifted water from wells with a bucket now sink boreholes more than a kilometre into the rocks – and still they find no water.'

Like so many environmental problems, water is intimately linked with population. Population expansion has led to an increased demand for water, both directly through drinking, cooking and washing needs, and indirectly through agriculture and industry. For example, it takes between 2,000 and 5,000 litres of water to grow 1 kilogram of rice. It takes a thousand litres to grow a kilogram of wheat, 11,000 litres to grow the feed for enough cow to make a quarter-pound hamburger and between 2,000 and 4,000 litres for that cow to fill its udders with a litre of milk. Managing this 'virtual water' is as important as direct water consumption.

For decades, the most popular policy solutions have all been based on heavy engineering, especially dam building. However, Pearce argues that large-scale hydroelectric dams have been very ineffective in producing electricity, with a 'power density' of around a kilowatt per hectare, far worse than wind or solar. Furthermore, the benefits usually turn out to be short-term, and the rich gain far more than the poor. Indeed, at least 80 million worldwide have been forced to move from their homes to escape the areas the dams flood.

As an alternative, Pearce calls for a second agricultural revolution. We've had the 'green revolution' which increased harvests to feed a growing world population but at the expense of water supplies. Now we need a 'blue revolution' before the gains of the past generations are wiped out. This will require 'a new ethos for water: an ethos based not on technical fixes, but on managing the water cycle for maximum social benefit rather than narrow self-interest'. Managing water should become a model for how we deal with nature – not as something to be fought, but something to nurtured and worked with.

In practice, Pearce believes this means that solutions need to be much more local and small-scale. For example: going back to ancient ways, such as harvesting rain where it falls, providing local water for local needs; using high-tech irrigation to provide 'more crop for every drop'; and building fewer dams and rather using underground reservoirs more intelligently. If we are unsuccessful, water will increasingly be used as a political weapon, in some cases leading to war. If we are successful, we will make water (which is a fundamental human right) accessible to 6.5 billion people where and when they need it.

From the book

- Today the world grows twice as much food as it did a generation ago, but it uses three times as much water to grow it.

- Once, the world's river teemed with fish. Then, during the 20th century, most of the rivers were barricaded with dams and their wild flows tamed. Almost everywhere this has caused a drastic decline in fisheries.

- By 2025, economists say, water scarcity will cut global food production by 385 million tons a year. That is more than the current US grain harvest and the equivalent of a loaf of bread a week for every person on the planet.

- The water 'footprint' of western countries on the rest of the world deserves to become a serious issue. Whenever you buy a T-shirt made of Pakistani cotton, eat Thai rice or drink coffee from Central America, you are influencing the hydrology of these regions – taking a share of the River Indus, the Mekong or the Costa Rican rains. You may be helping the rivers run dry.

- Apart from global warming, there has been no more drastic human alteration of the landscape than the damming, regulation and diversion of the world's rivers. [But] the time when large dam projects provided a realistic answer to solving water problems is behind us.

- We will never run out of water, but we do need to learn to manage it, which means being able to have it where we need when we need it for 6.5 billion of us.

- We need to find ways of storing water without wrecking the environment; of restoring water to rivers and refilling lakes and wetlands without leaving people thirsty; and of sharing waters rather than fighting over them.

About the author

Fred Pearce (born 1951) is a British journalist, author and environmental consultant.

Pearce consults to *New Scientist* magazine and his fortnightly environment blog, 'Footprint', appears on its website. He is a regular contributor to the *London Daily Telegraph*, the *Independent*, *Guardian*, *Times Higher Education Supplement* and *Country Living*. He has also written for several US publications including *Foreign Policy*, *Audubon* magazine, *Seed*, *Popular Science* and *Time*. He has also written a wide range of books on environment and development issues published in both the UK and US.

His books have been translated into ten languages including French, German, Portuguese, Japanese and Spanish.

Pearce is a regular broadcaster and international speaker on environmental issues, and has given public presentations on all six continents in the past two years. Among his engagements have been the Edinburgh, Hay and Salisbury Book Festivals, the Ottawa and Melbourne International Writers Festivals, the Brisbane River Symposium in 2006, Yale and Cambridge universities, a speaking tour for the British Council in India, and presentations to business and financial groups, such as AngloAmerican in South Africa, Cathay Pacific in Hong Kong and UBS in London.

He has also written reports and extended journalism for WWF, the UN Environment Programme, the Red Cross, UNESCO, the World Bank, the European Environment Agency and the UK Environment Agency. He is a trustee of the Integrated Water Resources International.

In his own words
(2008 interview)

Reflections on the book

I suppose the intellectual trigger was just seeing a series of reports in the media: little one-paragraph stories saying the Yellow River has run dry, or the River Indus didn't flow this month, or there is a sand bar formed across the mouth of the Rio Grande, or the Colorado hasn't given any water to the Mexicans for two or three years. And it seemed to me it was an environmental issue that nobody had looked at. People were talking about the rainforest and spreading deserts and climate change, but nobody had looked at rivers and at water. So I wanted to explore that. Would these local crises add up into a global crisis?

The role of business

Business is starting to talk about their water footprint, which is a phrase that they would never have used even five years ago. But having thought about their carbon footprint and now realising that there are constraints on water and water prices are going up, they are thinking about it as regards to their bottom line. There have been some preliminary discussions within the European Union about having labelling on water footprints in the way that a few products now have carbon footprint labels on them: we are going to see more of that.

In principle, there is no reason why you can't develop a system that would allow companies to be water-neutral. That's the language of environmental debate now and one would expect that, in the same way that it has been played out in debates about the carbon cycle and climate change, that will be the language of discussions about water use.

Looking to the future

I think we have got fixated with large-scale, state-run, big water management schemes. And we need to probably go back to much smaller, locally managed schemes where possible. There are good hydrological reasons for doing that but there are good social reasons: people have more control over their resources; I think that is inherently a good thing. It also means that communities manage their water a lot better. If they're in control of it, if they capture it from the land and store it themselves and supply it to their fields themselves, they think rather harder about what crops they are going to grow.

We need some international governance. We clearly need treaties, for sharing out water on major rivers and underground water reserves that run across borders. But I think much of this is more local. At a government level we need sensible water pricing policies. We need to think about the kind of anarchy that we have in use of underground water reserves where anybody can just pump it up from underground, frequently without any limit at all. What kinds of systems of governance can we have to make sure that this isn't a classic tragedy of the commons?

Like a lot of resource issues, we have a question about whether the primary problem that we have is one of population in terms of numbers or consumption. And my strong feeling is that most resource issues are about consumption rather than absolute numbers. And that is increased by what is happening to world population numbers. World fertility rates are dropping fantastically fast throughout the world; families are getting much much smaller.

OTHER BOOKS (SELECTION)

Deep Jungle: Journey to the Heart of the Rainforest (Eden Project Books, 2005)

Last Generation: How Nature Will Take Her Revenge for Climate Change (Eden Project Books, 2006)

Earth Then and Now: Potent Visual Evidence of Our Changing World (Mitchell Beazley, 2007)

Confessions of an Eco Sinner: Travels to Find Where My Stuff Comes from (Eden Project Books, 2008)

50
The Economics of Climate Change
Nicholas Stern

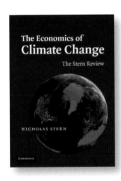

1st and current edn
The Economics of Climate Change: The Stern Review
Cambridge University Press, 2007; 692pp, pbk; 978-0521700801

Key ideas

▶ There is still time to avoid the worst impacts of climate change, if we take strong action now.

▶ The economic costs of doing nothing to combat climate change could be up to 20 times greater than taking action now to avoid catastrophic climate change in the future.

▶ If immediate action is taken, climate change will cost around 1% of global GDP per year on prevention and adaptation.

▶ The shift to a low-carbon economy will also bring huge opportunities: markets for low-carbon technologies will be worth at least $500 billion.

▶ Tackling climate change is the pro-growth strategy; ignoring it will ultimately undermine economic growth.

Synopsis

The Economics of Climate Change is the report from the Stern Review to the UK Prime Minister and Chancellor, commissioned in July 2006. The brief was to assess: the economic, social and environmental consequences of climate change; the implications for energy demand and emissions of the prospects for economic growth; the costs and benefits of actions to reduce the net global balance of greenhouse gas emissions from energy use and other sources; and the impact and effectiveness of national and international policies and arrangements in reducing net emissions.

In addition, the report was asked to provide: an assessment of the economics of moving to a low-carbon global economy; and an assessment of the potential of different approaches for adaptation to changes in the climate. The report concluded that:

- There is still time to avoid the worst impacts of climate change, if we take strong action now;

- Climate change could have very serious impacts on growth and development;

- The costs of stabilising the climate are significant but manageable, but delayed action would be dangerous and much more costly;

- Action on climate change is required across all countries, and it need not cap the aspirations for growth of rich or poor countries;

- A range of options exists to cut emissions, but strong, deliberate policy action is required to motivate their take-up; and

- Climate change demands an international response, based on a shared understanding of long-term goals and agreement on frameworks for action.

Stern calculated that, if we don't act, the overall costs and risks of climate change will be equivalent to losing between 5% and 20% of global GDP each year, now and forever. In contrast, the costs of action can be limited to around 1% of global GDP each year. Hence, our actions now and over the coming decades could create risks of major disruption to economic and social activity, on a scale similar to those associated with the great wars and the economic depression of the first half of the 20th century. And it will be difficult or impossible to reverse these changes.

Emissions can be cut through increased energy efficiency, changes in demand, and through adoption of clean power, heat and transport technologies. However, since the global economy will remain predominantly fossil-fuel-based until 2050, extensive carbon capture and storage will be necessary, as well as cuts in non-energy emissions, such as those resulting from deforestation and agricultural and industrial processes.

Stern concludes that with strong, deliberate policy choices, it is possible to reduce emissions in both developed and developing economies on the scale necessary for stabilisation (more than 80% below current levels) while continuing to grow. Three elements of policy are required for an effective global response: the pricing of carbon, implemented through tax, trading or regulation; support for innovation and the deployment of low-carbon technologies; and action to remove barriers to energy efficiency, and to inform, educate and persuade individuals about what they can do to respond to climate change.

From the book

- Climate change will affect the basic elements of life for people around the world – access to water, food production, health and the environment. Hundreds of millions of people could suffer hunger, water shortages and coastal flooding as the world warms.

- Climate change represents the greatest and widest-ranging market failure ever seen.

- Delay in taking action on climate change would make it necessary to accept both more climate change and, eventually, higher mitigation costs.

- The investments made in the next 10–20 years could lock in very high emissions for the next half-century, or present an opportunity to move the world onto a more sustainable path.

- The next 10–20 years will be a period of transition, from a world where carbon-pricing schemes are in their infancy, to one where carbon pricing is universal and is automatically factored into decision making.

About the author

Sir Nicholas Stern (born 1946) is currently the IG Patel Professor of Economics and Government at the London School of Economics (LSE), heading a new India Observatory within the LSE's Asia Research Centre and also a Visiting Fellow of Nuffield College, Oxford. He is also Special Adviser to the Chairman of HSBC on Economic Development and Climate Change. Sir Nicholas will be responsible for advising HSBC on economic development issues and the implications of climate change on the Group and its clients.

Stern was Advisor to the UK Government on the Economics of Climate Change and Development, reporting to the Prime Minister from 2003 to 2007 and, during that period, headed both the Stern Review on the Economics of Climate Change and the Government Economic Service. From 2003 to 2005, he was Second Permanent Secretary to Her Majesty's Treasury and from 2004 to 2005 Director of Policy and Research for the Prime Minister's Commission for Africa.

From 2000 to 2003, Stern was World Bank Chief Economist and Senior Vice-President, Development Economics. From 1994 until late 1999, he was Chief Economist and Special Counsellor to the President of the European Bank for Reconstruction and Development. Before 1994, his roles were mostly academic: including 1986–1993 at the London School of Economics (LSE), where he became the Sir John Hicks Chair in Economics.

Stern holds a BA (Mathematics) from Cambridge University and a DPhil (Economics) from Oxford University. He has served on committees for Oxfam, ODA and the UN and is a Fellow of the British Academy.

Photo: Nigel Stead/LSE

MORE INFORMATION

The Stern Review (full text):
www.hm-treasury.gov.uk/independent_reviews/
stern_review_economics_climate_change/stern_
review_report.cfm

Conclusion

The tremendous response of the Cambridge Programme for Sustainability Leadership's alumni to our poll for the top 50 sustainability books left us in no doubt that books matter to senior leaders – and that certain titles have helped to shape their thinking, the direction of their careers, and how they go about their work today.

Equally clear, and hardly surprising, is that many sustainability books are more referenced than read. Be that as it may, the ideas contained within them have had an important impact. For example, while few people today – even among those specialising in the sustainability field – have read Rachel Carson's *Silent Spring*, the way they discuss environmental issues and the role of companies in sustainability has been shaped by the book's ideas and the responses it spawned.

How, then, can we understand the legacy of this seminal sustainability literature, much of which has been generated in the last few decades? And how might it shape thought and action over the next 50 years?

Taking the views of the selected authors as a starting point, our research interviews highlight how their ideas have developed in response to the evolving challenges they see today. Collecting the wisdom of the authors in this way, the following paradoxes stand out:

- We face immense, urgent and life-critical problems, yet we have the ability to tackle and overcome them.

- We think we know the problems we face, but opinions differ about priorities and solutions.

- We have much of what we need to solve the problems, yet lack the necessary political (and hence public) will.

- Radical, disruptive change is inevitable, but will be less painful and destructive if we consciously take action now.

- Business may be the most effective way to provide innovative solutions at scale, but this requires long-term progressive government policy to set the rules of the game and create a level playing field.

- Business reformation needs pressure to come from within (through corporate sustainability and leadership initiatives) and from without (through public activism and government policy).

There are lessons for us all here, and certainly for the Cambridge Programme for Sustainability Leadership. It confirms that our ambition to raise awareness about the most significant challenges we face in the world today remains highly relevant, as does the need to support effective responses to these challenges. Hence, we will continue to engage with leaders from business, government and civil society through our flagship executive education programmes and leadership groups.

It also confirms the timeliness of two major new projects that will help to clarify what people mean by sustainability – what really counts – and how different parts of society might respond. The first initiative is the Next Economy Dialogue, which will focus on near-term action and influence for sustainability, and the second is the Cambridge 100 Questions Project, a year-long public debate that will focus on wide engagement and long-term thinking.

The Next Economy Dialogue

In the context of ever-increasing sustainability challenges and shifts in the economic, political and geopolitical landscape, there is an urgent need to unite key influencers behind a shared vision for a low-carbon, sustainable economy. The Next Economy Dialogue is designed to meet this need, through an exploration of the key system shifts that might be achieved through business leadership and influence within the next year.

Through consultation with international sustainability thought leaders, we have generated a shortlist of areas of critical strategic significance – the system-level changes – that we need to achieve if we are to address the fundamental flaws in the current economy and build a sustainable economy. In 2010, we will unite key influencers behind a set of international goals that will be critical to the achievement of a sustainable economy, and support the development of national strategies to achieve these.

The Cambridge 100 Questions Project

What are the most important questions we need to focus on so that we thrive together in the future? The Cambridge 100 Questions Project is a highly participative process which, through uniting great minds, influential people and the collective wisdom of the public, encourages the asking of questions that will help humanity to frame the most critical challenges to address to secure a viable, desirable future.

The project is particularly interested in questions that offer a sense of realistic optimism and collective endeavour – suggesting a compelling vision of how the world is changing and how society could adapt to new circumstances.

In 2010, the questions submitted through a public access website will be grouped and analysed to generate a list of the 100 most important questions on which society needs to focus.

In addition to these two landmark projects, we hope that this book, *The Top 50 Sustainability Books*, will play its part in shaping thinking and action. We also trust that it will encourage many readers to buy or borrow some of these exceptional titles and dig further into the compelling ideas, evidence and solutions that these thought-leaders offer.

Mike Peirce, *Deputy Director, University of Cambridge Programme for Sustainability Leadership*

About the author

Wayne Visser is Founder and CEO of the thinktank CSR International, as well as Senior Associate of the University of Cambridge Programme for Sustainability Leadership. He is the author/editor of eight books, including six on sustainable and responsible business, including *Landmarks for Sustainability* (Greenleaf Publishing, 2009), *Making a Difference* (VDM, 2008) and *The A to Z of Corporate Social Responsibility* (John Wiley, 2007).

Before getting his PhD in Corporate Social Responsibility (Nottingham University, UK), Wayne was Director of Sustainability Services for KPMG and Strategy Analyst for Capgemini in South Africa. He has an MSc in Human Ecology (Edinburgh University, UK) and a Bachelor of Business Science in Marketing (Cape Town University, South Africa).

Wayne lives in Cambridge, UK, and enjoys art, writing poetry, spending time outdoors and travelling in his home continent of Africa. His personal website is www.waynevisser.com.

Research associate

Oliver Dudok van Heel is passionate about finding solutions to the sustainability challenges we face as a society. He believes that, by bringing together human ingenuity with respect for our wonderful planet and its people, we can develop solutions and create a planet worth living for.

He tries to make this vision reality in different ways. Oliver founded Living Values to help integrate sustainability within corporations. He is a tutor on the University of Cambridge's Post-Graduate Certificate on Sustainable Business and a facilitator of the Be The Change Symposium. He helped launch the Lewes Pound, a local currency, to support the local community and reduce its carbon footprint, as part of the Transition Towns movement. He is also a co-founder of Transition Training and Consulting.

Oliver speaks English, French, Dutch, German, Spanish and Portuguese and holds a Master of Law and an Insead MBA. He lives in Sussex with his wife and three children.

About CPSL

The University of Cambridge Programme for Sustainability Leadership (CPSL) works with business, government and civil society to deepen the understanding of those who shape the future and help them respond creatively and positively to sustainability challenges.

Our focus on deepening understanding of sustainability through seminars, leadership groups and practical engagement builds on the university's strengths as one of the world's premier academic institutions. Our programmes provide opportunities for leaders to explore and debate key social and environmental trends and their significance within the global economic and political context. We draw on the intellectual breadth of the university and on leading thinkers and practitioners from around the world to help participants examine the array of strategic risks and opportunities and make decisions on the basis of a real appreciation of cutting-edge science, world-class thinking and best practice in business and government.

Our programmes include flagship initiatives inspired by the vision of our Patron, HRH The Prince of Wales. This unique coalition between the university and His Royal Highness gives the Cambridge Programme for Sustainability Leadership the power to convene thought leaders and top-level decision-makers from across the world in order to advance innovative thinking and transformational change.

www.cpsl.cam.ac.uk

An imaginative repertoire is urgently needed by which the causes and consequences of climate change can be debated, sensed, and communicated . . . Literature has a role to play in inducing this gut feeling, for one of its special abilities is that of allowing us to entertain hypothetical situations – alternative lives, or futures, or landscapes – as though they were real. It has a unique capacity to help us connect present action with future consequence.

**Robert Macfarlane,
University of Cambridge**